Royal Legacy

Royal Legacy

HOW THE ROYAL FAMILY HAVE MADE,
SPENT AND PASSED ON THEIR WEALTH
FROM QUEEN VICTORIA TO QUEEN ELIZABETH II

David McClure

THISTLE
PUBLISHING

All Rights Reserved

Copyright © David McClure 2014

First published in 2014 by:

Thistle Publishing
36 Great Smith Street
London
SW1P 3BU

www.thistlepublishing.co.uk

ISBN-13: 978-1-910198-65-0

Contents

Prologue ... ix

1. The Queen's True Worth – 2014 ... 1
2. Edward The Caresser – 1901-1910 ... 21
3. Mary's Bad Brother – 1910-1922 ... 50
4. The Princes At War – 1936-1945 ... 71
5. The Princesses Of Nothing – 1948-1952 ... 96
6. George And Mary's Legacy – 1952-1953 ... 114
7. The Duchess And The Countess – 1960-1968 ... 140
8. The Burial Of Bad News – 1969-1971 ... 162
9. The Windsors And Their Wealth – 1972-1986 ... 195
10. Diana's Estate Of War – 1997-1998 ... 221
11. Margaret, Mustique And Money – 2002 ... 256
12. From Queen Mother To Daughter – 2002 ... 277
13. A Royal Car Boot Sale – 2006 ... 308
14. The Princess's "Love Child" – 2006-2008 ... 328
15. The Storming Of The Palace – 2008 ... 350
16. The Best-Laid Plans Of Alice And Men – 2008-2010 ... 359
17. Charles's Cash Cow – 2010-2014 ... 395

18. Sovereign Grant Or Sovereign Greed? – 2011-2013	413
19. The Duke's Farewell – 2014	426
20. A Nation Mourns – 2022	438
Acknowledgements	457
Select Bibliography	460
Archival Sources	465
Notes	467

For Jane and William McClure

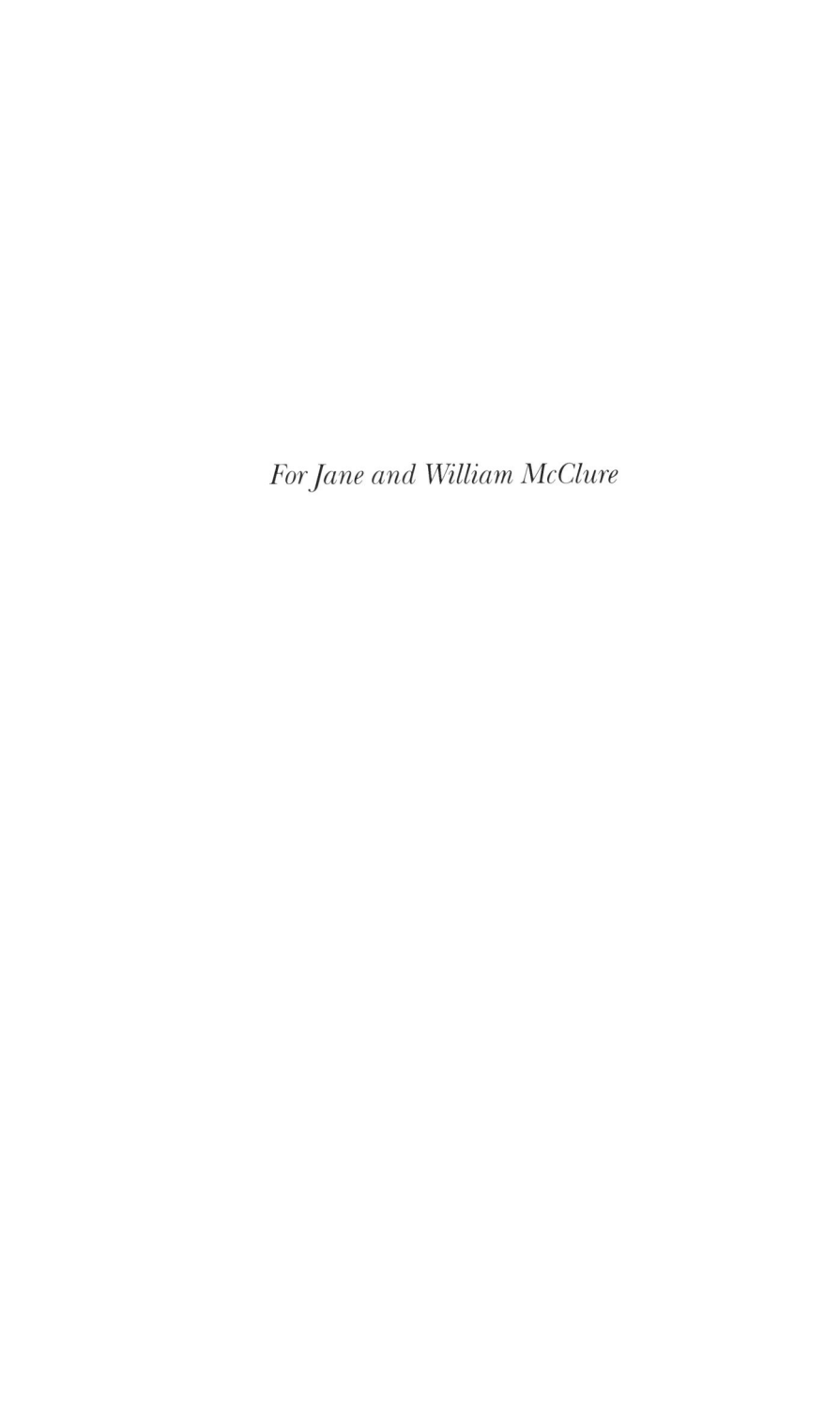

Prologue

"This is yet another example of him [Prince Charles] setting out his stall for his future inheritance"
Royal historian Brian Hoey on the palace's new media operation[1]

It was a symbol of the changing of the guard. When on 6 June 2014 the Queen joined President Obama and twenty other world leaders on Normandy's Sword Beach to commemorate the seventieth anniversary of the D-Day landings, seated immediately behind her on the stage was not just her customary escort the Duke of Edinburgh but also her heir apparent the Prince of Wales. Having already received the same formal reception accorded to the heads of state, Prince Charles was there to shoulder some of the heavy workload for the eighty-eight-year-old sovereign and the ninety-two-year-old consort on their state visit to France which included a punishing schedule of engagements in Bayeux, Ouistreham and Paris crowned by a state banquet at the Élysée Palace with President Hollande.

The presence of the heir apparent could be viewed as the most high profile sign of Charles's gradual succession to the throne. Dressed in the gold-braided black uniform of an admiral of the fleet, complete with a set of naval medals glinting in the afternoon sun, he looked suitably magisterial next to the Queen in her lime-green coat, matching hat and diamond brooch. From now on, Her Majesty would be subcontracting some of her official engagements and doing fewer foreign visits – particularly to long-haul destinations. Earlier in April she had kept her appointment in Rome with Pope Francis but tellingly it was an away-day with no overnight stay, after being rescheduled due to ill health.

In public the palace dismissed any talk of a winding down, let alone a co-regency. Her Majesty was "as busy as she has ever been," at least on the domestic front.[2] At her coronation in 1953 she had vowed to serve her country for her whole life and having as a young girl lived through the trauma of the 1936 abdication crisis, there was certainly no possibility of her taking a lead from the seventy-six-year-old King Juan Carlos of Spain who in the week of the D-Day commemorations suddenly announced his wish to step down in favour of his son, Crown Prince Felipe. The "A" word was not part of the Queen's English.

But in private royal aides admitted to "a gradual lessening of the burden," "a gentle glide" or "passing of the baton" - a handover strategy where official duties would slowly pass to the younger generation.

Less deferential Windsor watchers dubbed it "a royal job-share."[3]

During the three-day state visit to France, it was notable that Prince Charles was assigned as many official engagements as the Queen. On day one, while his mother was being entertained by President Hollande in Paris, he lay a wreath at the Glider Pilot Memorial in Normandy, visited the 70th Power Boat Squadron active in the D-Day landings, lunched with British veterans, witnessed a commemorative parachute drop by representatives of the allied forces and attended a memorial service for the parachute regiments. Day two saw him taking part in a British Legion service of remembrance in Bayeux Cathedral, joining the Queen and Prince Philip at another service at the nearby Commonwealth War Graves Cemetery and then going on to the Juno Beach Centre for a third service honouring Canada's contribution to the greatest amphibious landing in history. Clearly he had been tasked to do the bulk of the heavy lifting.

In truth, the transition process had been going on well before Prince Charles set foot on the Normandy sands. As early as January 2014 had come the major announcement that the press offices of the Queen and the Prince of Wales would merge, ending a media divide that had existed for over twenty years with the sniping particularly vocal at the height of the Diana divorce. With the press office of Prince Harry and the Duke and Duchess of Cambridge also moving to Buckingham Palace, the House of Windsor could now speak with one single voice.

The prince's ten-strong team of PR and media advisors who had been so adept at buffing up his tarnished image before and after the marriage to Camilla would have to move to Buckingham Palace, but crucially the captain of the new ship of spin would be a Charles loyalist, his fifty-four-year-old Director of Communications, Sally Osman, who had earned her stripes running the BBC's media operation. Formally she would report to the Queen's Private Secretary, Sir Christopher Geidt, but her salary would be paid, initially at least, by Charles out of his Duchy of Cornwall income.

Little by little without any royal fanfare, the Prince of Wales had begun over the previous year to take on more duties traditionally associated with the head of state. In May 2013 he sat at the Queen's right as she opened parliament and later in December he stood in for her at the funeral of Nelson Mandela in South Africa where all the globe's heads of state and government gathered in one informal international summit. But the most significant event came a few weeks earlier in mid-November when he opened the Commonwealth Heads of Government Meeting in Sri Lanka. It was both the first time his mother had missed the conference since 1971 and the first time he had represented her as Head of the Commonwealth. Given that Charles was not as popular with some Commonwealth leaders as the Queen on account of their religious objections to his divorce, it was important he made a good impression, particularly since the title of Head of the Commonwealth is conferred by the member nations and not automatically by hereditary right.

With Charles now shouldering some of the Queen's constitutional responsibilities, he would have to do less campaigning. The prince holds strong views on everything from genetically modified foods and homeopathic medicine to modern architecture and climate change. As sovereign or even stand-in sovereign, he could never snub the Chinese head of state in the way he did when he boycotted an embassy banquet for President Zemin in October 1999 to indicate his distaste for China's actions in Tibet.[4] The media storm that was triggered in May 2014 by one unguarded remark to a Holocaust survivor likening President Putin's actions in Crimea to Adolf Hitler's attack on Poland only served to underline the need for a shadow king to keep as mum as his mother on matters of public policy.

But the unprecedented feature of this handover was that with the octogenarian Queen having not just children but also grandchildren and even a great-grandchild there were several generations of royals alive at the same time. This meant that Charles could pass over some of his work to his offspring and it was noticeable that Prince William was assigned a part in the D-Day commemorations: accompanied by the Duchess of Cambridge, he attended a veterans tea party in Arromanches before giving a speech and presiding over an evening parade of ex-servicemen through the streets of the town.

There had already been signs that the Prince of Wales's eldest son was prepared to champion a few of his favourite causes. In February 2014 the Duke of Cambridge flanked by Prince Charles and Prince Harry took the lead at a Conference on the Illegal Wildlife Trade, calling on the world to turn its back on elephant poaching and suggesting that he wanted all the ivory in the Royal Collection at Buckingham Palace to be destroyed.[5] He also helped to lighten his father's workload by taking a college course in agricultural management in preparation for running the Prince of Wales's landed estate, the Duchy of Cornwell. This followed his individual tuition in constitutional affairs from his special advisor and *éminence grise*, the former ambassador to Washington Sir David Manning.[6]

Manning accompanied the prince on his subsequent tour of Australia and New Zealand in April 2014 which attracted unprecedented media coverage from all round the world – aided no doubt by the first overseas appearance of baby George and the willingness of his photogenic mother to perform for the cameras. But even the more jaundiced members of the press pack had to concede that it was one of the most successful royal tours in living memory. Many palace-watchers now regarded "William and Kate" as the royal family's greatest asset.

William had more time to take on these extra responsibilities because in September 2013 after eight years of military service he left his job as a RAF search and rescue helicopter pilot. It was no coincidence that shortly afterwards Prince Harry also hung up his helmet as a helicopter pilot in Afghanistan to take a desk job with the army. He is normally based close to Buckingham Palace's media operation at Horse Guards Parade where he organises commemorative events for the military. Now that he is pursuing a more prominent role in public life (including organizing Trooping the Colour, standing in for the Queen at the 2014 memorial service for Nelson Mandela and going on tours of Brazil and Chile) he has taken the precaution of protecting his image. During the handover process, it was revealed that much like celebrities such as David and Victoria Beckham he had founded a company to safeguard his brand and intellectual property rights. With his private secretary Jamie Lowther-Pinkerton as its director, the firm was called Tsessebe - the name of an African antelope. A palace spokesman explained that "it is a pre-emptive move to give them a vehicle for intellectual property, if they needed to trademark anything in the future, but there are currently no plans to use them."[7] Around the same time the Duke and Duchess of Cambridge set up similar "brand" companies, William's APL Anglesey, and Kate's CE Strathearn.

Having now delivered an heir to the throne, the Duchess of Cambridge was also being groomed to take on a bigger role. In another gesture heavy with symbolism, in January 2014 the Queen offered Kate the services of her personal dresser and jewellery advisor, Angela Kelly, to help her prepare for the tour of Australia and New Zealand, her most high profile foreign engagement to date and one that mirrored Princess Diana's much garlanded trip in 1983. The move was seen as a way of giving her a royal make-over, changing her middle class image from High Street to Highness. The palace would never admit it of course but she was to be made more regal. It was reported that Her Majesty would lend Kate jewellery from the fabulous Delhi Durbar Parure – a suite of gems given to Queen Mary at her Indian coronation in 1911 which was then handed down the generations to the Queen and in part to Diana as well, although many royal jewels were later returned to the sovereign as part of the divorce settlement.[8]

Putting the Queen's priceless collection of jewellery under the eyeglass brings into focus one little discussed aspect of the succession process. While all the headlines concentrated on the handover of constitutional and ceremonial duties, an arguably more important transition slipped under the radar - the transfer of the Windsor wealth. The Queen alone has an extensive portfolio of land, art works and financial investments rumoured to be worth hundreds of millions of pounds. Wouldn't any succession planning involve estate planning too?

It is inconceivable that a sovereign in her ninth decade would not have undertaken the most meticulous planning to safeguard her financial legacy. The best professional advice would have been near at hand. At their elegant offices overlooking Lincoln's Inn Fields the royal family's long-standing lawyers Farrer and Co have a legion of tax consultants and other experts offering guidance on "wealth preservation." The Queen's private solicitor, Sir Mark Bridges, boasts on his web page that "he specialises in tax, trusts and succession issues for clients from all over the world, including some of the world's wealthiest families."

Within her own family the Queen would have witnessed how much time and effort goes into inheritance planning. Her grandmother Queen Mary who was famous for being, in Churchill's words, "practical in all things" spent the last two months of her life cataloguing her priceless jewellery collection so that family heirlooms could be separated from Crown property. Her sister Princess Margaret who was known to intimates as a great planner went one step further by transferring to her son a full decade before she died her most cherished possession – her holiday home on Mustique.

This all goes to show that the House of Windsor dislikes leaving things to chance. Planning is part of the wiring of Buckingham Palace. Courtiers are rewarded for foreseeing potential fire hazards and preventing any sparks from flying. Sir Christopher Geidt – the palace official credited with masterminding the recent handover - was given a second knighthood for his work on what the formal citation called "a new approach to constitutional matters... [and] the preparation for the transition to a change of reign."[9]

The discretion of courtiers is not the only reason why the process of wealth transfer has received little publicity. The royal family benefits from a number of privileges that help to keep their financial affairs away from prying eyes. By statute the sovereign's will is sealed and it is customary for the wills of other royals to be closed to the public and probate details kept under wraps. Over the last century, any embarrassing documentation relating to money and other matters has regularly been destroyed by staff and family members. Senior royals are now exempted from Freedom of Information requests and no comprehensive catalogue of their private jewellery collection is available to the public.

As a result, tracing the inherited wealth of the royal family can at times feel like tracking a pod of whales swimming deep below the ocean waves. You know that that these behemoths are lurking there somewhere under the surface but pinpointing their exact location is a task that would try the patience of Captain Ahab. Sometimes a tell-tale water spout is sighted on the far horizon (say, in the form of a public auction of royal property), but only a small proportion of their true size is revealed before they disappear again leaving a tantalising trail of foam in their wake. At other times one of their number is found lifeless beached on the shore (as in the case of a sudden royal death and the public grant of probate) but you are not permitted to get too close to inspect the entrails for fear of causing damage. Both whales and Windsors enjoy the protection reserved for an endangered species.

My fishing expedition began one spring morning in the unlikely setting of the London probate registry on High Holborn. By chance I hooked two royal wills that the staff initially believed off-limits to the public - the last testaments of Princess Helena Victoria (Queen Victoria's granddaughter) and Princess Alice (the Queen's aunt). Their discovery set me off on the trail of other royal estates over the last century - from Edward VII's to the Queen Mother's - with the hope of dredging up hidden treasures.

Of course there is a world of difference between the probate value of an estate and the true wealth of the deceased. More often than not the former is just the tip of the iceberg. But that small icy ledge serves as a useful jumping off point to plunge deeper into the greater wealth hidden beneath the official figures. If you know, say, that Queen Mary left an estate of under half a million pounds yet possessed the most valuable collection of jewellery of any queen of England, then you are bound to delve further and wonder where are the missing millions.

For any sleuth on the trail of royal wealth, probate value is the dog that did not bark in the night. More useful clues to the true worth of the Windsors' assets are often found in auction records from the sale of their property which not only put a price tag on valuables that are rarely valued but also give details of ownership and how the property has been passed down through the family. In the case of this story, the auction records of the property of Princess Margaret, the Duchess of Gloucester and the Duke of Kent have proved essential in unwinding the chain of inheritance. Court records from the legal action of a Jersey accountant claiming to be Princess Margaret's illegitimate child and the trial of Princess Diana's butler have also produced a wealth of new information about how the Windsors conceal their wealth. Land registry documents can also be revelatory by showing, as in the case of the Gloucesters, how royal property can be safeguarded well before death by being transferred into a trust.

You don't have to be a dyed-in-the-wool republican to be naturally curious about how members of the royal family manage their money. One can be nosy without being nasty. Indeed, asking one prying question about the Windsors' riches can set off an inheritance chain reaction. Where did their private wealth come from in the first place? Was it made, inherited, acquired through marriage or amassed through tax privileges and state subsidy? How much of it came from gift-giving and where do you draw the line between a private and an official gift? How much of it has been saved and how much spent? How is it retained and not salami-sliced by multiple deaths or marrying out? And how is it kept away from the scrutiny of parliament and the general public? Whatever could they be hiding?

This book takes a peek behind the palace curtains.

Chapter One
The Queen's True Worth – 2014

"To Have and To Hold"
The motto for the Queen suggested by her biographer Robert Lacey

Over the past century British monarchs have divided into either spenders or savers. The epicurean Edward VII devoted his life to conspicuous consumption spending a small fortune on women, horses and gambling while his abstemious son George V preferred to save for a rainy day limiting his expenditure to shooting grouse and collecting stamps. Edward VIII loved to shower luxury jewellery on his women friends, his brother George VI was content to stay at home with the family and watch the pennies. Elizabeth II has taken after her father and grandfather. For all the rich pomp and pageantry of her sixty plus years on the throne, the Queen belongs to that breed of monarch who would rather check that the palace lights are switched off at night than burn the midnight oil herself. Famously, she marks the level of bowls of nuts in Buckingham Palace to discourage security police from eating all the nibbles. Her regality is one crowned by frugality.

Although certainly not mean, the Queen is without doubt thrifty - a royal trait inherited from her great-great-grandmother Queen Victoria who wallowed in a reputation for parsimony as alone on her bleak Balmoral estate she mourned the death of Prince Albert. Distaste for waste was nurtured in Elizabeth as a girl by her canny Scottish nursery-maid Bobo MacDonald who encouraged her to save and recycle wrapping paper from her Christmas and birthday presents.[1] When it came to toys, she much preferred inexpensive things they got for themselves, according to her governess Marion Crawford who recalls buying her a set of farmyard animals from Woolworth's.[2] If the young Elizabeth was raised with less than regal tastes, it is hardly surprising since at the time no one expected her to be queen. Up until the age of ten, her uncle David (the future Edward VIII) was heir to the throne and once he had children the line of succession would pass away from father's side of the family. Before the abdication she had as much prospect of being crowned as Princess Beatrice, another daughter of the sovereign's second son, does today. So, it should come as no surprise that the young Lilibet told her governess that when she grew up she would marry a farmer so that there would be no shortage of horses and dogs.[3]

As a teenager growing up in wartime Britain, she learned that a princess had to accept privations like the rest of the nation and she regularly wore hand-me-down versions of her mother's dresses before passing them on to her younger sister. As queen she showed an equal distaste for throwing out clothes or paying too much for anything - on several occasions chastising her dress-maker Sir Hardy Amies over the cost of his designer-ware.[4]

In this respect, she resembles her grandmother Queen Mary who was notorious for dropping strong hints to any purveyor of royal goods of her expectation of a discount. But in sharp contrast to the jewellery-obsessed Mary, Elizabeth has never displayed a passion to add to her fabulous collection of gems and unlike her mother she has shown no penchant to collect paintings or other fine art. While her sister Princess Margaret had a keen eye for fashionable clothes and the smart West End set associated with the performing arts, the Queen's tastes are less metropolitan and more tweedy. Apart from an occasional Launer handbag, her wardrobe is functional rather than flamboyant and she feels most at home not with dancers and directors at Covent Garden or Saddler's Wells but with her dogs and horses at Sandringham and Balmoral. She has been photographed stomping the fields round Sandringham in a simple headscarf and Wellington boots like any farmer's wife. When as a child Prince Charles lost a dog lead in the grounds, she acted in much the same manner as any cost conscious mother would and sent him out the following morning to hunt it down.[5] At heart she is a country person who finds in rural pursuits an escape from the gilded cage existence of being the sovereign.

Yet this frugal, penny-pinching woman of the shires is reputed to be worth over one billion pounds. In truth, no one can agree on the precise contents of her portfolio of assets and as a consequence valuations of her wealth vary enormously. On one end of the spectrum, in 2001 The Mail on Sunday's Royal Rich Report valued her personal fortune of shares, property, jewellery, art and other general assets at £1.15 billion, while in 1989 Fortune magazine estimated her worth at a staggering £7 billion. Both these valuations include some of her inalienable assets - in the case of Fortune the royal palaces (Windsor Castle, Buckingham Palace), the Crown Jewels, the Royal Collection of paintings and art and the Royal Archive, and in the case of The Mail on Sunday, the hereditary revenues from the Duchy of Lancaster. But being inalienable assets, the Queen can never sell them. As palace spokesmen are quick to point out, they are held in trust for the nation by the sovereign and must be passed on to her successor. For all intents and purposes, they are public assets and should not be included in any calculation of her private wealth. But the fact that they are often lumped together leads to confusion and perversely an underestimation of her worth as the palace can use this common error to discredit other higher estimates of her private riches.

On the other end of the spectrum, Elizabeth's former private secretary, Sir John Colville, put her wealth in a letter to The Times in 1971 at no more than £2m. He went on to inform The Daily Telegraph: "it particularly upsets her when she is described as being worth £50-100m...If she has got more than £2m today I will eat my hat."[6] This all took place at the time of intense debate over a pay rise for the Queen in the new Civil List and when the palace was keen to play down any elevated valuations of her personal fortune. Lord Cobbold, the Lord Chancellor and head of the Royal Household, gave assurances to a parliamentary select committee that any suggestions that the Queen's private funds were of the order of £50m-£100m were "widely exaggerated." This was repeated in 1993 by his successor, Lord Airlie, who said that claims that her private investments were worth £100m were "grossly overestimated". So, from the viewpoint of the palace at least, her private riches stood at anywhere between £2m and £50m.

The truth probably lies closer to the middle of the spectrum of valuations. In 2013 the US magazine Forbes estimated her fortune at £330m ($500), which with the exclusion of her inalienable property made her the 40th most powerful woman in the world. In 2014 The Sunday Times Rich List ranked her 285th in Britain as a whole and put her income at £330m. It was estimated that her landed property was worth

£140m and her share portfolio £105m but apart from the £2m art collection it gave no detailed breakdown of her personal possessions.

Some of her more valuable assets come from less obvious sources. She inherited from her father George VI a set of stamp albums that today is acknowledged as the world's most comprehensive collection of postage stamps of Britain and the Commonwealth. It was started by Queen Victoria's second son, Prince Alfred, in the mid 19th century after Sir Rowland Hill introduced the uniform Penny Post throughout the country. But when his personal finances took a nosedive, Alfred was later obliged to sell the collection to his brother, the future Edward VII who in turn passed it on to his son, George V. He soon became as obsessed with stamps as his wife was with jewels, telling one fellow philatelist that he wished to have the best collection in England, and true to his word he went on to collect almost every issue of stamps of Great Britain, the Dominions and the colonial territories in his reign up to 1936. In 1904 he bought the first stamp produced for a colony - the Two Pence Post Office Mauritius - for £1,450, the highest price ever paid for a single stamp. Even at the height of the First World War he was with the aid of Foreign Office staff scouring the globe for new colonial stamps, on one occasion dragooning the diplomat Harold Nicolson into hunting down a rare batch of British military stamps with the word "Levant" misprinted on the face (later as a diarist he got his own back by writing of George V - "for 17 years he did nothing at all but kill animals and stick in stamps").[7] On his death the king left all his stamps to George VI who added more albums to the collection before passing it on to the present queen.

Today the Royal Philatelic Collection, as it is now known, runs to around 400 albums and some 200 boxes which are all housed in the strong room of St James's Palace. The bulk of the collection is George V's 328 albums of about 17,500 pages bound in colour-coded red leather volumes. Next biggest is George VI's "Blue Collection" of 78 boxes and 10 albums bound in dark blue and then comes the Queen's own "Green Collection" stored in distinctive green boxes. It is impossible to say how many stamps there are in the Collection, which also includes drawings and proofs, as no comprehensive inventory has so far been made.

Originally some of Elizabeth's biographers presumed the stamps were part of the Royal Collection and as such inalienable state property but recently the official royal website has confirmed that they are in fact the Queen's *private* property. Charles Goodwyn, the Keeper of the Royal Philatelic Collection between 1995 and 2003, has declined to put a value on the collection saying only that it is "priceless" and claiming that they did not know the full extent of the collection.[8] According to the current official website, "it is impossible to say how many stamps there are in the Collection, or to put a value on it. The Royal Philatelic

Collection has never been counted in terms of total stamp numbers."

This reluctance to undertake a detailed, transparent inventory - which also extends to parts of the Royal Collection and the Queen's personal collection of jewellery - conveniently prevents any independent valuer from placing a precise price tag on their worth. In fairness, stamps of this scarcity are rarely put up for auction and their real commercial value is determined not by any intrinsic worth but by the volume of stamps that are released into the market place. Nevertheless, a few shafts of light have recently fallen on the albums that allows one a clearer idea of their worth. Just before the Millennium the Queen agreed to pay £250,000 for a unique first day cover of ten penny blacks posted on 6 May 1840 – known as the Kirkcudbright Cover. Since she did not have sufficient cash from the Privy Purse or her personal savings to fund the purchase, it was decided to self-finance the deal by selling off some less important stamps, many of which were duplicates or surplus to requirements in the collection. The auction at Spink's in May 2001 of this batch of 200 stamps brought in £645,000[9] - more than double the estimated price – and offered a glimpse of the market value of the wider collection. One stamp that was not put up for sale, however, was the jewel in the collection - the two pence "Mauritius Blue" whose 1904 record price proved a good investment since it is now valued at £2m. Another Mauritian stamp is thought to be worth

£1.5m. With the Kirkcudbright Cover having already doubled in value and other stamps now commanding six and seven figures, the Queen's total collection must be worth well over £10m and some estimates put the figure as high as £100m.[10]

Another surprise windfall to the Queen's wealth was also housed in St James's Palace but this time it came through marriage rather than inheritance. When she wed Prince Philip in November 1947 in a ceremony at Westminster Abbey attended by kings, queens and other heads of state from round the world, she received an exotic waterfall of wedding presents. The volume was so great that a souvenir book had to be published listing all 2,428 items and the gifts put on display at St James's Palace. They ranged from the perverse (Mahatma Gandhi sent a lace tray cover made from a spinning wheel which a horrified Queen Mary mistook for the Indian leader's loin cloth) to the practical (many subjects sent in nylon stockings and knitted sweater, while her government gave her the standard extra 200 clothing coupons allowed to all brides). But others gifts - especially those involving jewellery - were exceedingly valuable. The emperor of Ethiopia sent a gold tiara, the Nizam of Hyderabad a floral diamond tiara, the Maharajah of Bundi a headdress of pearls and rubies and the Dominion of India a diamond necklace fashioned from jewelled anklets. In addition to the other fabulous jewellery she received from her grandmother and her parents (which we explore in later chapters), the French government gave a Sevres dinner service, to complement the 175 piece porcelain dinner service from Taiwan's leader Chiang Kai Shek, and the Kenyan nation a hunting lodge in the Aberdares. Normally, gifts given during an official engagement - typically, from one head of state to another – are not regarded as private property, but more personal wedding gifts may be accepted as private property - as was shown after the death of Princess Margaret when her heirs auctioned her wedding gifts for five figure sums. Some of the family jewellery – particularly the many items given by the dowager Queen Mary - may have been a mixture of both inalienable and private property. Again it is difficult to put a precise price figure on the wedding gifts, but in 1947 their total worth was estimated at £2 million - close to £50 million at today's prices.

One wedding gift from the Aga Khan was of special value to Princess Elizabeth - a chestnut filly called Astrakhan which went on to win a number of prestigious races. She inherited a passion for the sport of kings from her mother with whom she bought in 1947 her first race horse, a bay gelding called Monaveen. Within months, its purchase price had been recouped many times over in prize money and with the bit now firmly between the teeth, the Queen felt emboldened to build up a significant racing enterprise and develop a specialist knowledge of breeding and bloodstock. For the first ten years of her reign, she was one of the largest owners in the country, becoming champion owner in 1953 with winnings of more than £40,000 (the equivalent of more than £750,000 today), although later she scaled down her activity as it became impossible to continue to train her horses in Ireland due to the Troubles and she found she could not compete with the new breed of mega-rich Arab owners - or as some more cynical voices have suggested - *be seen* to compete in such multi-million purchases when claiming to the government to be financially stretched.

In 2001 her 30 race horses and 26 broodmares were valued at £3.6m with an annual maintenance outlay of about £500,000[11] although by 2011 she had reduced her stable to about 25 horses in training. Around this time she reportedly paid £500,000 for a three-year-old filly called Memory which was used only for breeding at the royal stud since it failed to perform on the racetrack.[12] The Queen's distinctive colours of purple, scarlet and gold had not graced a Classic winner since Dunfermline won the St Leger in 1977 when in 2013 Estimate ran off with the Gold Cup at Royal Ascot. But despite many near misses including the favourite Carlton House coming third in 2011, the big prize of winning the Derby has eluded her, with her great grandfather Edward VII remaining the only British sovereign to hold that honour.

Whether or not the stable of horses ever really made a profit or even broke even is debatable but what is certain is that the physical stables in terms of bricks and mortar have proved a good long-term investment. In 1952 she inherited from her father the royal studs at Sandringham and nearby Wolverton in Norfolk and in the sixties she began leasing the Polhampton Lodge Stud in Hampshire which she bought in 1971. A decade later in 1982 she completed her property portfolio by purchasing the West Isley Stable in Berkshire for around £750,000. These acquisitions would have boosted the value of her overall horse racing venture to well over £30m.[13]

Another valuable possession often forgotten when assessing her wealth is her wine cellar. Again the waters are muddied by the fact that public assets such as wine and spirits bought for official receptions like a state dinner for a visiting dignitary are hard for an outsider to separate from alcoholic wares bought for private use. In his memoirs Tony Blair remarked on the availability of alcohol at Balmoral during an early visit there as Prime Minister noting that some of the hard stuff kicked as much a punch as rocket fuel.[14] Her Majesty's favourite tipple has long been gin and Dubonnet, although she is not averse to sharing a whisky with the prime minister of the day after their weekly royal audience.

According to the official expenditure report, on average about £400,000 is spent each year on wine and spirits. The cave is administered by a part-time Clerk of the Royal Cellars who is normally an experienced wine merchant who advises on maintenance and investment and by a full-time Yeoman of the Royal Cellars who keeps an inventory of the stock and handles the day to day buying. Most of the wine is laid down in the stone chambers of the Buckingham Palace's basement, but there is also a sizable stock at Windsor, Sandringham and Balmoral - as well as in storage at wine warehouses. With the Queen known to be partial to champagne, it has been reported that there is £100,000 worth of Krug stored in the vaults and that the wine collection as a whole may be worth as much as £2m.[15]

The Queen also possesses a little known but valuable car collection which has been valued at over £7m. She first took an interest in cars at the end of World War Two when she joined the Auxiliary Territorial Service as an 18-year-old army cadre and was taught how to repair motor engines and drive to a professional standard. The vintage cars are spread amongst the royal residences. In addition to the two modern Bentleys, three Rolls-Royces and three Daimlers, the Royal Mews at Buckingham Palace houses a 1950 Rolls-Royce Phantom IV known as the "Old Beast". But the main motor museum is at Sandringham where over a dozen historic vehicles are garaged. The most valuable is a 1900 Daimler Mail Phaeton – the first ever royal car thought to be worth well over £3m and bought by Edward VII although there is no proof that he could actually drive. The same is true of George V but this did not stop him buying a 1924 Daimler shooting brake - designed especially to accommodate his guns and shooting requirements – which has been valued at £600,000.

As we saw with her wedding presents, foreign gifts of jewellery have also proved a lucrative wealth stream. Just before her marriage, during an official tour of South Africa the government gave her for her 21st birthday a necklace of 21 diamonds which she regarded as her "best" diamonds[16] and which were soon complemented after a visit to the Kimberley mines by a gift from De Beers of a stunning six carat blue white diamond. With a regular flow of gifts such as these to go alongside her inherited gems, it is not surprising that her total jewellery collection has been valued as high as £70m - although recent auctions of royal jewellery have shown that the added cachet of the royal name can raise their value by a factor of five or more.

The value of her portfolio of shares (rumoured to be in blue chip British companies) is much harder to pin down since its secrecy is guaranteed under a mechanism granted only to the world's heads of state known as the Bank of England Nominees whereby any share dealing is conducted through an anonymous nominee company. In 2014 the Sunday Times Rich List put their value at £105m but the figure is highly speculative due to our near complete ignorance of her equity investments.

On the other side of the ledger, the Queen has considerable outlays and like many a parent, she has been obliged to give financial support to her children. Often this has occurred at significant rites of passage such as marriage. When Princess Anne married Mark

Philips in 1976, she bought the couple Gatcombe park - the 730-acre Gloucestershire estate of the former cabinet minister R.A. Butler - for £500,000 and a year later lent them the money to buy the neighbouring 600-acre Aston Farm.[17] Similarly a decade later in 1986 when Prince Andrew married Sarah Ferguson, the Queen bought them their first home - Sunninghill Park (or as it was soon dubbed "South York") in Berkshire for £3m. Prince Edward's wedding present from his mother in 1998 was the 50-year lease on the 88-acre Bageshot Park near Windsor with its 57-room house which is today worth over £30m. At the time the purchase prompted raised eyebrows at the palace with one courtier wondering why they wanted to live in such a costly Victorian pile.[18] In 2013 the Queen also gave Prince William Anmer Hall on her Sandringham estate as a thirtieth birthday present and after a £1.5m refurbishment it will become the country home of the Cambridges.

Ironically it has been the end and not the start of the marriages that have proved the biggest drain on the Queen's bank balance, with her sister and three of her children all getting divorced. As one royal insider put it, "divorce has cost her a fortune". The largest outlay came with the separation of Prince Charles from Diana which reportedly cost her up to £17m as Charles did not immediately have the cash to settle the huge divorce bill (according to his financial advisor he had to "liquidate everything, all his investments.")[19] The divorce of Prince Andrew was less costly since his assets were smaller being a modestly-paid naval officer and the Queen retained ownership of Sunninghill Park before it passed into a trust but she was still required to contribute £400,000 towards the purchase of Birch Hall in Surrey for the duchess and the children. Going further back to the divorce of her sister Princess Margaret in 1976, it was reported that the Queen as part of the settlement had to buy a house in South Kensington for Lord Snowdon which is now worth around £4m and owned by his son and daughter.

The Queen also has to pay allowances to her close family. This arrangement dates from 1992 when it was agreed that parliamentary annuities from the Civil List would be limited to the Duke of Edinburgh and the Queen Mother and that the Queen would refund to the Treasury parliamentary payments to other close relatives. As a result, in the following decade the Queen had to find over £1.5m a year to bankroll her family, although the bill was reduced by the deaths of Princess Margaret in 2002 and the Duchess of Gloucester in 2004 and by the fact that the repayments are tax deductable.[20] In 2010, the last year in which full details were provided, she paid Prince Andrew £249,000, Prince Edward £141,000, Princess Anne £228,000, Princess Alexandra £225,000 and the Duke and Duchess of Kent £236,000.

These annuities are paid out of the Privy Purse, the Queen's private income which is derived from the revenues of the Duchy of Lancaster. The duchy is a hereditary landed estate of nearly 20,000 hectares that has been held in trust for the sovereign since 1399. Today it includes some valuable real estate, the jewel of crown being the Savoy estate stretching along the Strand from the Savoy Hotel to Somerset House. The Queen is not allowed to dip into its capital but she is entitled to its net revenues - an income stream that has grown considerably since the start of her reign. In the last two decades as commercial rents have mushroomed her revenue has grown by almost £10m rising from £3.75m in 1992 to £13.6m in 2014. Between 2013 and 2014 alone the net surplus jumped by a more than healthy 8.5%.

So after paying her relatives around £1.5m in allowances (as well as picking up the bill for Prince William's constitutional advisor and of course paying her taxes at the top rate of 45%) how does the Queen spend the remaining £5-6m? Much of the duchy money must be consumed in the upkeep of the private residences. Balmoral alone costs over £3m gross a year to run.[21] The Queen decamps there for two months every summer and when Tony Blair made his first prime ministerial visit in 1997 he was struck by the number of servants (he was even given his own valet) and the lavishness of the hospitality (all the meals were so large he feared he could put on a stone in weight).[22]

Despite the rental of lodges on the estate (Connachat cottage is available at £696 a week) and the opening of the house to the paying public (you can pick up a bottle of branded malt whisky for £40 or tea towels for £14.99 a pair) Balmoral has never been a going concern. Its rocky Highland location means there is little arable land. As a result it haemorrhages more money than the Sandringham estate which can offset its high running costs from the rental of farmlands as well as the leasing of game shooting rights.

Notwithstanding their huge maintenance costs, the two royal residences remain extremely valuable land. In 2001 Balmoral house was valued by a *Mail on Sunday* report at £2.15m and the estate as a whole £14m. Her Majesty's Scottish holdings also include the nearby Bachnagairn Deer Forest which she originally inherited from George VI in 1952 and then in 1997 paid the Earl of Airlie £300,000 to double the acreage raising its total value over £2.5m. Much more valuable is the 20,500 acre Sandringham estate that was valued in 2001 at £30m - although this figure like all the others for landed assets does not take into account the premium of the royal name which could easily double or treble their value.

This all underlines the fact that the Queen like much of the landed gentry is asset rich and comparatively income poor - although it is difficult to assess her more liquid assets without access to information about the investment interest and dividends which might accrue from her hidden stocks and shares portfolio. More than likely her cash assets have been eaten into by inflation – particularly in the sixties and seventies and again in the 2000's. It is worth stressing that an important factor in the wealth of a sovereign with a fixed Civil List allowance is whether or not they reign through a period of price stability. George V was lucky enough to live through a period of relatively low inflation (and indeed at times recession) and as such was able to make considerable savings. His granddaughter has been less fortunate.

When it comes to assessing the relative cash and fixed assets of the sovereign, it is also worth remembering that the Queen Mother found herself so short of cash in her long dotage that she had to rely on the Queen to pay for her day-to-day expenditure despite having an estate of assets reportedly worth over £50m. Although the Queen as she approaches her own centenary is not so strapped for cash, there is clearly an imbalance between liquid and fixed assets which has been acknowledged by others members of the family. In 1971 Lord Mountbatten referred to Her Majesty as having a large fortune but then added that the vast bulk of it was in art treasures which brought in no income and which she could never sell.[23]

It is clear from this stocktaking of the Queen's assets that her wealth - like that of many rich Britons - is largely inherited. But unlike her fellow multi-millionaires, the exact nature of her inherited wealth is complicated by the confusion over whether the assets are purely private or partly public - particularly when it comes to some of her jewellery and artworks. The picture is further blurred by a special privilege granted to the sovereign and senior royals that prevents the public from inspecting their wills and finding out precisely who inherited what. The only way to lift the fog surrounding her inherited wealth is to unwind the chain of inheritance three generations and investigate how a hundred years ago her great-grandfather Edward VII modernised the monarchy and fixed its finances.

CHAPTER TWO
EDWARD THE CARESSER – 1901-1910

"A typical Englishman – with the lid off"
J.B. Priestley on Edward VII

In death just as in life Edward VII helped drag the British monarchy into the 20th century by turning the succession process into grand spectacle. He was the first sovereign whose body was laid in state in Westminster, establishing a tradition that would be followed by George V in 1936, George VI in 1952 and most memorably the Queen Mother in 2002. His body was put on public display in Westminster Hall on 17-19 May 1910 and an estimated 400,000 people solemnly filed by the catafalque underneath the oak beams of the mother of all parliaments. The queue meandered back four miles as far as Chelsea Bridge and so great was the demand from ordinary citizens to pay their respects that the hall had to be opened at six every morning. Vast crowds also lined the London streets on May 20 to watch in silent tribute the funeral procession. It was one of the grandest gatherings of royalty of all time - as the gun carriage bearing the coffin was escorted on horseback by George V, the German Kaiser and eight kings on its last journey from Buckingham Palace to Paddington Station prior to the burial in a vault in St George's Chapel at Windsor. Newsreel footage of crowds one hundred yards deep straining to get a last glimpse of the cortege took the spectacle to a wider audience throughout the truly United Kingdom.

Dismissed as Bertie the playboy prince for much of his life he had finally won the respect of the people and been accepted as a serious sovereign. He was now regaled as the father of the nation. A natural showman with his love of uniforms and decorations, he managed to catch the public mood with his embrace of ceremonials and pageantry. His decade on the throne had seen the introduction of many new royal rituals - including a more meritocratic honours system based on the Order of Merit and a revamped state opening of parliament – which were designed to reconnect the monarchy with the people after the austerity of Queen Victoria's era and the awakening of dangerous republican sentiments. He also established the custom of sending congratulatory telegrams to anyone reaching the age of one hundred.

But before *he* could even reach the age of seventy, his austerity-averse lifestyle had begun to take its toll on his health. Although no more than five foot seven inches in height, he weighed sixteen stone and had a forty-eight inch girth – a perfect build for his favourite position of goalkeeper in ice-hockey matches at Sandringham. Following a long struggle against emphysema and a host of other lung complaints brought on by his prodigious smoking he collapsed while on holiday in Biarritz in March 1910 and on his return home after a short convalescence he suffered a fatal heart attack at Buckingham Palace on 6 May. It was typical of the man that his last words were about horseracing. On being told by the Prince of Wales that his horse Witch of The Air had won the 4.15 at Kempton Park by half a length, the turf-loving king replied: "yes, I have heard of it. I am very glad."

As sovereign Edward VII's will was sealed by right. An 1862 statute stipulated that neither the will nor the size of the estate of a monarch could be made public, although it is now reliably thought that Edward's estate was worth £2 million (over £100 million at today's prices). This was the figure given in a newspaper interview in June 1971 by Sir John Colville, the Queen's former private secretary, based on information supplied to him by an unnamed member of the royal family.[1] It is believed, though, that this sum did not include the private residences of Balmoral and Sandringham which were officially valued at £300,000 in 1936 and which if converted into 1910 prices would have pushed up the size of the estate by about £100,000.

But the real mystery of Edward's £2 million plus estate is not so much *what* was its precise size or indeed *who* received it under the will but rather *how* he amassed it in the first place. His lavish lifestyle had drained his bank balance as rapidly as pouring champagne, his favourite tipple, down the sink. So conspicuous was his consumption that the man nicknamed "Tum Tum" often ate a twelve course dinner before tucking into supper. The next morning a brisk breakfast might mean just buttered toast, bacon and eggs, haddock and chicken. It came as no surprise that the epicurean King Edward took great delight in having a potato named in his honour. When not cramming his mouth with food and drink, he found time to smoke twelve large cigars and twenty Egyptian cigarettes a day.

His official biographer revealed that he only just got of debt in 1907, yet we now know that by 1910 he had somehow accumulated a fortune of over £2 million. This would have made him one of the richest men in England. To give some yardstick of his wealth, his friend Leopold de Rothschild - another man close to the top of nation's rich list thanks to his part ownership of the family bank and his extensive portfolio of landed and equine property - left an estate valued at £1.5 million in 1917, while Leopold's brother Alfred, another bank director who died the following year, left a sum of £2.5 million.

Bertie's extravagant behaviour was in part an act of rebellion against the puritan strictures of his father who wanted him to be educated to the highest academic standards and to eschew the raffish lifestyle of his Hanoverian uncles (at Oxford University he was not even permitted to live in college). The straitlaced Prince Albert (known as "the German professor") famously gave him a severe dressing down when it became common gossip that a woman of easy virtue had been discovered in Bertie's bed while he was serving as a young officer in the Grenadier Guards camp at the Curragh outside Dublin. The "lady" in question, an actress called Nellie Clifden, would be the first of a legion of female conquests, with the number of royal mistresses alone running to well over fifty.

But the root cause of Bertie's financial woes – and perhaps his overall extravagance - was the fact that he had too much time on his hands. He reigned for less than ten years after coming to the throne in 1901 aged fifty-nine after decades living in the shadow of his indomitable and seemingly indestructible mother ("Queen Victoria," as one wit joked, "keeps reigning and will not let the son shine"). In contrast to the well-rounded apprenticeship that Queen Elizabeth provided Prince Charles and the latitude he was accorded to liaise with all government departments (sometimes to the frustration of the prime minister of the day)[2] Queen Victoria refused to give her son any meaningful training for his future role as sovereign and even denied him access to state papers. As an incorrigible gossip, he could never be trusted with state secrets. The Widow of Windsor's obsessive mourning for Prince Albert may also have made her reluctant to put her faith in any substitute royal consort, particularly one she blamed for the premature death of her husband. In retrospect this was both short-sighted and unfair to Bertie who, while no intellectual had a lively mind, spoke French and German fluently and had a genuine interest in diplomacy and international affairs which would be put to good use much later as sovereign with his skilful handling of the Entente Cordiale between Britain and France.

Denied access to the levers of political power, the prince found solace in mixing with those who held financial power. His friends and acquaintances were all immensely wealthy – not just the old money of landed aristocrats like Lord Cadogan and the Dukes of Bedford and Westminster with their steady income stream from metropolitan rents, but also the new wealth from financiers and speculators like Horace Farquhar and Cecil Rhodes who had made fortunes in southern Africa and other colonial territories. When Rhodes was blackballed by the Travellers Club on account of some dubious overseas venture, the king registered his protest by automatically taking his own name off the members' list. He saw money, according to his official biographer, as a convenient social indicator[3] and he also saw how those who had money used it to pursue pleasure beyond their wildest dreams.

When the lustre of his marriage in 1863 to the beautiful Princess Alexandra began to pale Bertie's eye soon wandered. Although it had grown into a genuine loving relationship following the arranged union between the Danish and British royal families, the Prince of Wales's gargantuan appetite could never be satiated by one woman alone and Alexandra's sparkle may have been dimmed by the effect of childbirth and an attack of rheumatic fever (even official photographs had to be retouched to enhance her fading beauty). After a major refurbishment to his spacious Pall Mall mansion - which cost him a rumoured £100,000[4] and the government a further £60,000 – it soon became the society venue for the raffish Marlborough House set where royalty and peers of the realm brushed shoulders with the parvenu rich and the world of entertainment. Bertie is known to have had adventures with the actresses Nellie Clifden and Sarah Bernhardt, as well as a series of longer affairs with married women including Mrs Lillie Langtry, Mrs Daisy Brook, Mrs Wally Paget and Mrs Alice Keppel – and possibly Mrs Jennie Churchill, mother of Winston. Not for nothing was he known as Edward the caresser.

His pursuit of pleasure, however, did not come cheap. On top of the cost of keeping a string of well-heeled women in the style to which they were accustomed (Alice Keppel among others was showered with jewellery), he liked to go to the races and gamble with rich friends such as Leopold de Rothschild who became almost as well-known as a horse breeder than as a merchant banker on account of his highly successful stud at Ascott. In the 1890s it was *de rigueur* for the wealthy to breed horses and bloodstock sales became an unlikely venue for high society. The Foreign Secretary Lord Rosebery purchased a future Derby winner (to add to the stud he acquired on marrying the heiress Hannah de Rothschild, a cousin of Leopold's) and several of his cabinet colleagues were like Bertie members of the Jockey Club in Newmarket. It was not lost on politicians and plutocrats (nor indeed royalty) that the turf provided a useful place to connect with the mass of the population. At the time, the Epson Derby was the most sacred event in the sporting calendar - on a par with today's FA Cup Final at Wembley or a Lords test against Australia - and one of the rare occasions when the whole country came together. The Derby-winner was the toast of the nation.

Following in the Rothschilds' footsteps, in 1885 the Prince of Wales opened his own stud at Sandringham and soon after bought the prized mare Perdita II. His horses went on to win the Ascot Gold Cup, the St Leger and in 1896 the Derby, when much to his delight Persimmon beat by a neck St. Frusquin owned by Leopold de Rothschild. In his most successful year, 1900, he earned £29,586 in prize money but prior to that his annual average was as little as £250.[5]

Such earnings hardly offset the considerable outlay of running a large stable of horses that ran both on the flat and over fences. Some of his closest advisors - including his private secretary, Sir Francis Knollys and the soon-to-be auditor of the Civil List, Sir Edward Hamilton - had come to the conclusion in

1896 that HRH ought give up racing.[6] The only way to balance the equine books would be to put out to stud his two prize stallions Persimmon and Diamond Jubilee whose sires according to Hamilton's later estimate might bring in £20,000 a year. Bertie was highly sensitive to any criticism that his horse racing hobby might be extravagant and in any way a drain on his finances telling dinner guests as late as December 1902 that "his racing paid [for] itself owing to his valuable sires" - although given his poor head for figures one suspects he was overstating their true value.[7]

He also loved ocean racing at Cowes, a fashionable playground for the rich akin to today's Monte Carlo or Porto Cervo, where in 1863 he succeeded his father as commodore of the Royal Yacht Squadron. At considerable expense he then developed his yacht "Britannia" into a three hundred ton racing cutter with a crew of twenty-eight. It won a number of prestigious races in 1892-3 and was later used as a base during his tours of the Mediterranean. In the early 1890s he was spending each year tens of thousands of pounds on yachting alone. One courtier who had the thankless task of managing the Privy Purse after Bertie acceded to the throne wrote "the king has no idea of the value of money and consequently gives orders wholly irrespective of expense which it is difficult to avoid executing".

No wonder the new king soon found himself heavily in debt. According to a 1904 letter to the Treasury from Sir Edward Hamilton, now the auditor of the

Civil List, "The King does not think that the present state of things ought to be allowed to carry on...For he has absolutely no private fortune on which to fall back."[8] One other reason for his financial woes were the high overheads of maintaining the Sandringham estate, although his own extravagance - particularly when it came to fitting the latest household installations in the Big House - was in large part to blame for this. Even Sir Edward Hamilton, who customarily took the king's side on financial matters, blanched in April 1904 when he discovered that the cost of Sandringham in the previous year was - "no less than £52,000. The Civil List was fixed on the belief that the cost was about £30,000 a year. Last year there were some special items in connection with the installation [of electric light] but notwithstanding them the total is appalling."[9]

When the new Civil List first came up for discussion in 1901 the king dropped thinly veiled hints that he wished to be exempted from income tax. Hamilton records in his diary on February 2, 1901 that "he liked the idea of being relieved (if it were possible) of such charges as the payment of income tax." Such discreet lobbying went on for a number of years until he grudgingly ceded to the inevitable with Hamilton writing in a Treasury memo in June 1904 "the present king only agreed to continue the arrangement under protest."[10]

He was left with no option but to turn to his banker friends to bail him out. The most influential of these was Sir Ernest Cassel whom he had first got to know when Prince of Wales through their shared interest in horseracing and who was a close friend (and later executor of the estate) of his previous main advisor Baron Hirsch who died in 1896. On top of his lucrative investments in bloodstock, Cassel had amassed with the help of his network of associates in every European financial centre a multi-million pound fortune, mainly through investments in booming overseas ventures like North American and Mexican railways. He also financed the building of the Central Line on the London Underground and Egypt's Aswan dam. A dour, humourless widower devoid of social graces, Cassel at first sight seemed an unlikely friend to the sybaritic Bertie but through a long and frequent correspondence with "*Ec*" (sixty-three letters in 1901, forty-five in both 1904 and 1905 and fifty in 1906, the majority on financial matters) he became the king's most intimate male friend.[11] Almost inevitably, censorious courtiers dubbed him "Windsor Cassel."

The king's other financial advisors included Nathan Rothschild, chairman of the London bank NM Rothschild and Sons (on the board of which also sat his brothers Leopold and Alfred) and the two Sassoon brothers, Arthur and Reuben ("the Rothschilds of the East"). The fact that they were all Jewish (although Cassel later converted to Catholicism) caused muttering among an establishment that was openly anti-semitic. His mistress

Lady Paget voiced her regret that he was always surrounded by "a bevy of Jews" and racing people and that he shared their "love of pleasure and comfort."[12] This view was reinforced in January 1881 by his attendance at the Central London Synagogue for the marriage of Leopold de Rothschild to Marie Perugia which received wide press coverage and elicited many a raised eyebrow in polite society.

In 1885 he also helped elevate to the peerage his friend Nathan ("Natty") Rothschild who as Baron Rothschild of Tring became the first professing Jew to take a seat in the House of Lords. For all his failings, the king was not prejudiced (at least not towards Jews) and he went out of his way to be friendly towards society newcomers - particularly if they were rich and smart. But the more traditionalist Prince George (known as "HRH") took a dim view of some of his father's financial friends and was not afraid to voice his dismay in public: "HRH (Lady Londonderry says) was a good deal down on Mrs G Keppel and spoke, as I have heard him speak, strongly against the *moneyed associates* around the king," Hamilton recorded in his dairy. "The crown will certainly not fall off Prince George's head. It might be a dull Court, but it will certainly be a respectable one."[13]

Bertie gave his rich Jewish friends the easy entrée into high society that their background often denied them; in return they gave him the financial guidance that his background never provided. The exact details of how his portfolio of shares and bonds was reorganised remain to this day a closed book but his official biographer records that his banker friends helped him "make handsome profits out of judicious investments" and that by 1907 he was out of debt. His advisors took out life insurance policies and established an amortisation scheme that proved a big money-spinner.[14]

It has sometimes been unfairly rumoured that the king may also have sold titles to boost his bank balance. It is certainly true that he conferred on Ernest Cassel the Grand Cross of the Royal Victorian Order, the highest rank in the sovereign's personal order of chivalry, and also honoured him with a knighthood, the title of Privy Councillor and the Grand Cross of the Order of the Bath (his attempt to make him a peer was vetoed by the Salisbury government) but there is no suggestion that any cash payment was part of the deal. Some evidence, though, has been unearthed that he may have helped Alfred Harmsworth, the wealthy proprietor of the Daily Mail and the Times, get a baronetcy in 1904 ("the father of modern journalism" was later created baron and then viscount), but again there is no definite proof that the king acted in a corrupt manner or personally benefited from any financial transaction. One writer, however, has suggested that if money did indeed change hands, it might have gone not to the king but his long-term mistress, Alice Keppel, who was experiencing difficulties financing her new elevated lifestyle and had sought financial advice from Sir Ernest Cassel.

What is beyond dispute is that he had long used his royal status to request, push or garner honours for his friends and favourites. This had begun in the 1880s when as Prince of Wales he yearned to be allowed a say in public affairs and was not averse to doing political favours to business associates like Nathan Rothschild, who was once a Liberal MP and now took a shine to Disraeli's One Nation Toryism. In the light of Bertie's affair with Lady Kilmorey who as we shall see in the next chapter had a penchant for lovers who were members of the royal family, it is interesting to note that in 1888 he made representations to the Conservative government to grant her husband, the third Earl of Kilmorey, the Order of St Patrick, the highest Irish honour. Bertie wrote a letter to the Prime Minister Lord Salisbury saying that Kilmorey was a longstanding friend from his days at Oxford and would be pleased if his name were given proper consideration.[15] Lord Kilmorey was made a Knight of St Patrick in 1891 and in 1902 selected as one of the king's aides-de-camp. It is not known exactly when Lady Kilmorey was having an affair with the king (although it must have been before the coronation of 1901 when she was included in the entourage for royal mistresses) but whatever the precise chronology of events, the favour to the earl would be repaid in kind.

In July 1901 he conferred another of his personal honours for services to the royal family, the Knight Commandership of the Victorian Order, on Sir

Edward Hamilton, who had advised him while Prince of Wales. A frequent guest at Balmoral, Windsor and other royal residences the Eton-educated Hamilton was a trusted member of Bertie's social set. He was also a firm friend of Sir Ernest Cassel whom he regarded as "the ablest man in the city" and was often invited to his country estate in Newmarket and even stayed at Villa Cassel in Switzerland. They shared a friendship with the Rothschild brothers and attended luncheons at their Ascott and Tring family seats. It is worth recording that fourteen months after awarding him the KCVO, the king asked him in September 1902 to be auditor of the Civil List. Despite the occasional grumble, the king's old advisor who had also counselled his son Prince George on constitutional matters backed the king in most disputes over the Civil List. Although in the official Treasury papers he gives the impression of neutrality on questions of whether the king should be exempted from tax, in his private diaries in 1901 he reveals that he thought the paying of income tax was "on the whole wrong and unnecessary"[16] and then a few years later writes: "we came to the conclusion that no (1) ['he might be released from his undertaking to pay income tax'] is the best alternative."[17]

It is impossible to give a definitive answer to the question of how Edward was able to get out of debt and leave behind such a large legacy as his private secretary Sir Francis Knollys assiduously followed his instructions and burnt all his personal and financial papers, but the most likely explanation lies in the generosity of Ernest Cassel. When Bertie first got into serious debt in the late 1870s, his then financial advisor Baron Hirsh lent him money (rumoured to be of the order of £250,000-£300,000) but when Hirsch died in 1896 he left instructions to his executor Cassel that the whole debt should be written off. But according to the king's latest biographer Cassel went one step further and took over the administration of Bertie's financial portfolio, fully understanding that he himself would absorb any losses.[18]

In 1901 Edward gave Cassel £20,865 to invest and not long after the king's anxiety over money seemed to alleviate. It was only on his deathbed that the true extent of his benefactor's largesse became apparent. On hearing that the king was slipping away, Cassel rushed to Buckingham Palace and deposited a thick envelope by his bedside. It contained £10,000 in bank notes, the equivalent of £250,000 today. When the money was returned to Cassel after the king's death, he refused to accept it saying that "it represented interest I gave to the King in financial matters I am undertaking."[19] If it had indeed been interest then the initial investment would have had to have been much larger than the £20,865 invested in 1901. Many biographers now believe that the money was a gift intended for the king's mistress Mrs Alice Keppel whose husband's modest salary was insufficient to keep her in the style to which she was accustomed.

Soon after Bertie's death, she moved into a sumptuous Mayfair mansion in Grosvenor Street.

⚜ ⚜ ⚜

Any attempt to put a monetary value on the estate of Edward VII must take into account that most of his inherited fortune came from landed rather than liquid assets. When Queen Victoria died in 1901 she left him little if any cash - as is the convention with the Prince of Wales who benefits from generous revenues from the hereditary estates of the Duchy of Cornwall. Instead, she bequeathed him her private residences: Osborne House and Balmoral Castle.

During her long reign Queen Victoria had been able to build up a highly valuable portfolio of private property thanks in large part to the financial astuteness of Prince Albert and the passing of one important piece of legislation in 1800. Prior to that date, the monarch had only a public legal identity - and no private one. This meant that his or her private possessions were inextricably linked to the public possessions of the crown. In effect, the sovereign was the state - and vice versa. It also meant that his will was probably not legally binding. Since he owned property only in his capacity as king and not as a private person, then on his death it should automatically pass to his rightful successor rather than to any private individual named in his will. The Crown Private Estate Act (1800) changed all that. It gave the monarch a private financial status: he could own land privately and make a will.

After his marriage to Victoria in 1840, Prince Albert with no constitutional duties to perform devoted his considerable energies and Germanic zest for order to the reform of the royal finances, conducting a cost-cutting drive in the royal household and ensuring that the queen had an independent source of wealth. She had succeeded to the throne, according to one royal biographer, penniless: "her father had been so poor he had driven the family in his own carriage because he could not afford servants."[20] Her husband went so far as to complain to the Prime Minister Lord John Russell that the nation takes from the monarch his hereditary monies but does not allow him to amass a private income.[21] When prior to 1800 the sovereign was unable to have a private income, there was little incentive to boost revenue from the crown estates or landed property since it all went into the public pot, but now Queen Victoria enjoyed an independent financial status it was in her interests to manage and maximise her wealth. One way to achieve this was through capital accumulation. She is now known from Treasury papers to have saved £824,000 in the first fifty years as queen from her Civil List revenue[22] and gained an estimated £1.5m more from her Duchy of Lancaster revenues.[23] She also received a £250,000 windfall when in 1852 the eccentric property developer John Nield left her almost all his landed fortune.

Wisely Prince Albert converted much of this cash into the more solid long-term investment of bricks and mortar. The royal couple's first private purchase was Osborne House, a large estate near Cowes on the Isle of Wight which was to be their summer palace. In 1845 they paid £45,000 for the property but the total cost rose to £200,000 (over £10 million in today's values) after all the interiors were rebuilt in an Italianate style complete with marble columns and palazzo-type fittings. This was not to the taste of Edward, Prince of Wales, and Alexandra who detested the mausoleum-like atmosphere (their grandson George VI called it the family necropolis). This posed a problem when after the death of Victoria at Osborne in January 1901, Edward VII inherited a part share of the house along with his siblings. We now know from a 1901 Treasury document that the property cost a hefty £17,000 a year to run.[24] His immediate response was to hand it over to the nation for conversion into a naval college and nursing home but after it was pointed out that his mother's wish as clearly stated in her will was for the property to remain in the hands of the family, he felt obliged to consult with his three sisters about the matter. Following considerable arm-twisting, it was decided after all to give it to the nation but to achieve this a special act of parliament had to be passed in order to overturn Queen Victoria's testamentary wishes.

Victoria's most important property investment by far was Balmoral castle in the Scottish Highlands - but she did not acquire it in her name. The freehold was formally bought in June 1852 by Prince Albert from the Earl of Fife after it was discovered that the 1800 Crown Estates Act did not apply to Scotland and as such the property would belong to the state if the queen signed the contract (this loophole was closed in 1864 to allow Victoria to inherit the property after Albert's death). Albert had been able to knock the price down to £31,500 since he had cleverly leased the property for the previous four years which meant that the vendor could hardly sell the land to anyone other than the royal couple and had to settle for a below market rate. The rugged setting on Deeside reminded Albert of his German homeland and with the assistance of the architect William Smith he spent the next three years building on the 23,000-acre estate a new castle in a Teutonic style. He turned it into a romantic time capsule, a world away from metropolitan life where one could hunt, shoot and fish to ones heart's content. Once again it was not to everyone's taste - the Prime Minister Lord Rosebery observed that he had thought the drawing room at Osborne was the ugliest room in the world until he witnessed the drawing room at Balmoral. When Edward VII inherited the property, the only thing he liked about it was the shooting; his wife reputedly loathed the place. As with Osborne, the running costs also put a significant strain on his finances representing in 1901 £20,000 a year and as with Osborne he even tried to transform its status into an official rather than private residence, presumably to make it eligible for more public funding.

Prince Albert also turned his business brain to the reform of the hereditary revenues from the Duchy of Cornwall. Consisting of 135,000 acres mainly in the south west of England, the duchy was created in 1337 by Edward III for his son and heir, Edward, the Black Prince, and thereafter it became the main source of private income for all Princes of Wales. Under the 1337 charter the Duke of Cornwall was not entitled to the proceeds from the sale of land but only from their rental income. Since much of the land was only semi-arable and the urban properties were in poorer areas of south London it never produced great profits and this may in part explain why it was unaccountably excluded from the 1760 financial settlement that transferred the Crown lands to the state in return for the Civil List. But by the mid 19th century with the rise in city rents and the expansion of the railways requiring the acquisition of rural land this seemingly worthless anomaly became potentially profitable. Under Prince Albert's guidance, city dwellings were modernised, arable land improved and tenancy agreements renegotiated. Over the next quarter of a century net revenue from the duchy almost doubled rising from £25,000 to £46,000 a year.[25] Although Bertie complained bitterly about having nothing to do during his long apprenticeship to be sovereign, the wait did have a considerable financial advantage in so far as it meant that for forty years he was Duke of Cornwall and in receipt of on average £35,000 a year. He even benefited from the accumulated revenues built up as a minor before he became duke. According to a confidential 1937 Select Committee Report which examined the Duchy of Cornwall revenues he "possessed the revenues which were then somewhat fewer during his whole minority. It appears that the accumulated sum which he received on majority was about £600,000 in stock, bringing in £18,000 a year."[26]

The longer the wait, the greater the cumulative income - providing of course he did not spend it all. This financial calculus applied equally to his son, the future George V who enjoyed almost a decade of Duchy of Cornwall revenues and also to his grandson, the future Edward VIII, who had more than twenty years of income. Indeed, it is often forgotten that today's Prince of Wales like Bertie has had forty plus years of revenue from the Duchy of Cornwall, although in his case the revenues have been much greater since the duchy is today much more profitable than it was in the 19th century.

Prince Albert also overhauled the revenues of the Duchy of Lancaster, another anomalous portfolio of hereditary land that somehow escaped the 1760 settlement and in this case became the personal source of revenue for the sovereign.[27] In the early years of Victoria's reign revenue was as low as £5,000 per annum but by the end it was closer to £60,000,[28] although it never reached the level of the Duchy of

Cornwell. One possible reason why Bertie may have got into debt as a sovereign was that on his accession his personal source of income switched from the Duchy of Cornwall (which produced £92,085 in 1910) to Duchy of Lancaster revenue (which produced just £64,000), although of course he did get a uplift in Civil List payments as sovereign.

Albert also had his eye on a property in Norfolk for Bertie - Sandringham Hall set in 7,000 acres of prime game country on the southern shore of the Wash. But when he died suddenly from stomach cancer (and possibly undiagnosed Crohn's disease) in December 1861 it was left to Bertie (with perhaps some aid from Queen Victoria) to pay the hefty £225,000 asking price, although at least one tenth of the sum came from Duchy of Cornwall revenues.[29] It had been the hope of Bertie's parents that he would be distracted from the fleshpots of London by the estate's bucolic charms but in the event their plans backfired spectacularly. He took such an immediate shine to the place that he invited all his lady friends and fun-loving financiers down for bacchanalian weekends in the country. Shooting, hunting and eating were favourite pursuits.

Finding the original house too cramped for his needs, he soon demolished it and built at considerable expense a new Jacobean-style redbrick mansion known as "The Big House". With an entrance hall that doubled as a ballroom which was dominated by a stuffed baboon, the interior decoration was on a par with Balmoral and Osborne. One royal biographer thought the house had all the majesty of a Scottish golf hotel.

In time Bertie made extensive changes to the estate. New roads were constructed, a spectacular ironwork gate was installed and extra stables and cottages were built - including York Cottage which was to be the much-loved home of his son, the future George V. In addition to spending £200,000 on new buildings, repairs and landscaping, he purchased more land in nearby Anmer and Flitcham almost doubling the total holding to 15,000 acres.

When Edward finally died in 1910, he left George V not just Sandringham but also Balmoral. He also bequeathed him many priceless family art treasures but according to the testimony of George's private secretary no cash. This was because as Prince of Wales George would have been able to accumulate a considerable fortune from the revenues of the Duchy of Cornwall. He also received a generous annuity from the Civil List from which he saved money.

Although Edward's will left ownership of the Sandringham estate to his eldest son, it also granted his wife Alexandra the use of Sandringham House for her lifetime. Even though it would have made more sense for her to swap places with George V and allow him to use the spacious Big House instead of the cramped York Cottage where he lived with the queen and their six children, she preferred to stay put. Since Bertie had bought and built up the place as his private country house, she regarded it as totally different to the palaces which belonged to the crown. One royal biographer detected a streak of "spoiled selfishness" in her character and this came to the fore when she became a widow. She led a life of profligacy which might have been a reaction to decades of playing second fiddle to her philandering husband and enduring the sniping of other members of the royal family. Princess Alice was of the opinion that "Alix" could never be a good companion for someone as intelligent as "Uncle Bertie" because she was heavily deaf and not very bright. In fact, her life had been transformed back in 1867 when an attack of rheumatic fever left her with progressive deafness, tinnitus and a permanent limp. While her husband pursued the pleasures of the flesh in London, she had to endure a life of exile in Sandringham, only consoled by the fact that the flat Norfolk countryside reminded her of Denmark.

Alexandra was also left £200,000 in her husband's sealed will. We know this thanks to an entry dated June 30, 1910 in the diary of Charles Hobhouse, the Financial Secretary to the Treasury in Herbert Asquith's cabinet: "the king I find left a fortune of £200,000 to the queen for her life. She is now trying to evade payment of super tax, income tax and death duties."[30]

Balmoral and Sandringham were liable to a relatively new and highly unpopular tax known as Estate Duty which was introduced in 1894 by the Liberal

Chancellor of the Exchequer Sir William Harcourt - partly "to woo the masses" and partly to finance naval expenditure by Lord Rosebery's government. Levied at 8% on estates over £1 million, this "punitive taxation" was regarded as the first deliberate assault on landed wealth – Sir Edward Hamilton, then an assistant Financial Secretary in the Treasury, described the tax scale as "frightening"[31] and even Queen Victoria wailed that it could not fail to cripple all landowners.[32] In 1910, when the rate was up to 15%, the Attorney General, Sir Rufus Isaacs, drew up a confidential memorandum which he submitted to his Prime Minister Asquith stating that unlike crown property, the monarch's landed property was not exempt from estate duty.

This was not the first time that Alexandra had locked horns with the Treasury. At the beginning of Edward VII's reign when the Civil List payments were being negotiated, she rejected out of hand the generous offer of a pension of £60,000 a year in the event of her husband predeceasing her and instead persuaded the Exchequer to grant her £70,000 a year (close to £4 million at today's prices). This proved a considerable income for someone who grew up a member of the cash-strapped Danish royal family. As the Prime Minister Arthur Balfour observed waspishly at the meeting of the Civil List committee: "it would be interesting to know what are the revenues of the court of Denmark."[33] In fact, we now know that her parents, Prince and

Princess Christian, had only a paltry £800 a year to live on.[34]

Alexandra also held out for as much jewellery as possible from her husband's estate. She wanted to keep Bertie's diamond garter insignia and the diamond crown she wore at the opening of parliament. But his will was unclear whether they belonged to the crown or Alexandra personally. Matters were not helped by the fact that Alexandra never made any attempt to differentiate public from personal jewellery in sharp contrast to Queen Victoria who carefully catalogued all her jewels and specifically listed in her will which pieces should be worn by future queens.

In the end, it is believed that she kept the disputed items thanks in part to the intervention of her beautiful sister "Minnie", Dowager Empress Dagmar, the widow of Tsar Alexander III, who had a soft spot for priceless gems and took great delight in upsetting British royal protocol (one exacerbated junior royal called her a "pernicious influence").

Edward would probably have left some of his other private jewels to his three daughters - and his long time mistress Mrs Keppel. It is remotely possible that other paramours were remembered in his will but we have no documentary evidence for this as following the instructions in his will, Alexandra destroyed all his private and public papers, including letters to her and Queen Victoria.

The old queen spent the rest of her life in declining health dividing her time between Sandringham and her London home at Marlborough House. Despite the £200,000 inheritance from Bertie and the Civil List pension of £70,000, she still managed to have money problems. Sometimes she ran up large bills on new furniture, on other occasions she would shower a big sum on a favourite charity or an acquaintance down on his luck. The word "cost" was not part of her lexicon and she was reported as saying that if she got into debt then the government could pay. George V was forced to give her a personal allowance of £10,000 and pay for much of the upkeep of Sandringham and Marlborough House. Even the Treasury agreed to exempt almost all of her annuity from taxation.

But as her health deteriorated, she was able to take less and less pleasure from her vast wealth. On one memorable visit, the Arabist adventurer TE Lawrence found her "a mummified thing" with "red-rimmed eyes" in an "enamelled face" - an image reminiscent of another faded beauty, the stroke-stricken Princess Margaret with her bandaged arm and face hidden behind dark glasses. In her final years, Alexandra was half blind, mentally confused and almost totally deaf. She eventually died at Sandringham of a heart attack on 20 November 1925 aged 80.

Her will did not need to be sealed because she never made one. Unlike her mother-in-law Queen Victoria or her daughter-in-law Queen Mary, succession planning was never her strong suit. Dying intestate meant that her estate was divided according to family closeness as defined in law rather than any personal testamentary wishes. Whether you are a royal or a commoner, this is a traditional recipe for domestic strife.

For Alexandra's estate the difficulty lay in how the jewellery and personal effects were to be split up. On Saturday January 9, 1926 the main beneficiaries gathered at Sandringham House. Present were King George V, Queen Mary and Alexandra's two daughters, Queen Maud of Norway and Princess Victoria (Princess Louise, the eldest daughter, was at home in Scotland). Queen Mary later described how she was faced with a vast collection of good and bad personal possessions that showed what happened when nothing was thrown out for six decades.[35]

Mary quickly assumed the lead role in the distribution of chattels, with the jewellery collection being split into four equal shares.[36] When it came to choosing their joint share, George and Mary were particularly interested in any personal items given to Alexandra by the royal family on her marriage in 1863 and any personal bequests from Queen Victoria in 1901. They also retrieved all the crown jewels that Alexandra had kept for her own use after the death of Edward VII.

By not making a will that could be sealed, Alexandra broke with royal convention and unwittingly allowed some daylight to be shed on her estate. But she could not totally shake off the royal family's atavistic attachment to posthumous privacy. She left instructions that on her death all her private papers be burned.

Chapter Three
Mary's Bad Brother – 1910-1922

"Nunc aut Nunquam" (Now or never)
The family motto of Lady Kilmorey, mistress of Prince Francis of Teck, King Edward VII *et al*

On 22 October 1910 - just four months after the death of Edward VII - The Times reported on its front page: "His Serene Highness Prince Francis of Teck passed away at eleven o'clock." A longer article followed on page ten which gave details of his more famous sister:

"Universal sympathy will be felt by the whole nation and empire with Her Majesty the Queen in the death of her brother his Serene Highness Prince Francis of Teck which occurred at eleven o'clock on Saturday morning at the nursing home in Welbeck Street."

Although referred to as "the Queen," his sister Mary had yet to be crowned - as the joint coronation with George V was not scheduled until June 1911.

Not unrelated to that event was a further report that appeared in The Times on 22 February 1911:

> "He [Prince Francis] left an estate of gross value of £23,154...His will and codicil are both dated January 29, 1902 and probate has been granted to his brothers...By order of the probate division of the High Court dated February 17 probate was granted without annexing a copy of the will and codicil."

In other words, Prince Francis's will was sealed. This would set an important precedent in the sealing of royal wills that almost a century later would have a serious impact on the legal challenge to the estates of Princess Margaret and the Queen Mother. But why was it necessary to keep under lock and key the last wishes of a relatively obscure member of the royal family who died without a wife, any children or indeed an estate of any great value? What was special about Francis? What dark secrets could he be hiding?

Apart from dying in the same year as the king and being his distant cousin, the prince shared one significant thing with Edward VII: a mistress, Ellen Constance, the Countess of Kilmorey. At the king's coronation in 1902 she was seated next to Alice Keppel and Sarah Bernhardt in the special "loose box" reserved for royal mistresses. But to unravel the mystery of the sealed will we first need to rewind Prince Francis's royal lineage.

He was born in Kensington Palace on 9 January 1870. His mother was Princess Mary Adelaide of Cambridge, the Duchess of Teck and the granddaughter of George III, and his father was Prince Francis, Duke of Teck and son of the Duke Alexander of Wuerttemberg. Educated at Wellington College, he had the distinction of being along with his brother the first royal prince to go to a public school. But being something of a rebel he soon got into an argument with his housemaster whereupon he threw him over a hedge for a bet and was promptly expelled. Now judged more suited to a military career, he trained at Sandhurst before joining the Royal Dragoons and serving in India, South Africa and Egypt. For his bravery in the Nile expedition he was awarded the DSO.

The discipline of army life did little to dampen his longstanding passion for gambling. Like his profligate mother ("fat Mary"), he was a spendthrift and lived in a permanent state of debt; like his distant cousin Bertie ("Tum Tum"), he had a love of racing which drained his finances. In one famous bet at Punchestown race course in Ireland, he lost £10,000 - a small fortune in 1895 and more to the point, one he did not possess. His sister, the newly married Duchess of York, came to his rescue and settled the debt. But the family forced him to go into exile in India and before he departed, Queen Victoria counselled him to mend his ways. Even her advice fell on deaf ears. Unrepentant he later wrote from Mahabaleshwar offering to send his sister a betting book as a Christmas present. On his return to England, he ran up another debt of around £10,000 with a professional gambler who threatened to go public with the matter unless it was settled immediately. Once more his sister paid up and fearful of a scandal went to the new sovereign for advice on how to protect the family honour. Edward VII decreed that Francis be sent back to his regiment in India, but this time the feckless Teck insisted on staying in England.

Prince Francis's other great passion was women. Photographs from the period show a dark-haired handsome man with a strong jaw and a melodramatic moustache waxed in the style of an Edwardian rake. His true personality is probably best captured in a 1902 lithograph by the caricaturist Sir Leslie Ward which portrays him as a debonair man about town wearing a top hat, long overcoat and provocatively pointed shoes. Behind his back he carries a sinister walking stick which at any minute might be swung round to ward off a rival suitor or cuckolded husband.

Princess Maud, the pretty daughter of the future Edward VII, was one of his many female admirers. He encouraged her advances through an exchange of amorous letters and then, to the dismay of his scheming mother, dropped her when talk turned to marriage. His sister's nanny denounced his behaviour as "cruel." Broken-hearted, Maud married on the rebound Prince Charles of Denmark, the future king of Norway.

The lady who succeeded in winning Francis's heart was not only ten years older than him but also married. A statuesque woman with an ample bust,

Ellen Constance had something of the physical bearing of his sister Mary. But portraits of her hint at a strong sensuality with one oil painting showing her dressed in a low-cut dress with a come-hither look in her eye. A photograph of her taken in 1897 by the fashionable portraitist John Thomson captures her dressed in 18th century French court costume as the Countess du Barri, the mistress of Louis XV. Ellen was the daughter of Edward Baldock MP who died in 1875 leaving her much of the family fortune derived from the antiques and porcelain trade. In 1881 she married Francis Needham, the third Earl of Kilmorey, who in addition to possessing a sprawling country estate in Ulster and a town house on Park Lane owned two major London theatres - the Globe and St. James's. For a time, he dallied as a theatrical entrepreneur and Gilbert and Sullivan once tried to hire the Globe for one of their new operettas. Socially, the earl was part of the Prince of Wales's set having first become his friend at Oxford three decades earlier.[1] After the coronation in 1902, he was made aide-de-camp to the new king. By this time, his wife had also become a close friend of royalty.

So, around the turn of the century Lady Kilmorey (better known to her friends as "Nellie") was at different times having an affair with both the future Edward VII ("Bertie") and the great grandson of George III ("Frank"). No wonder her family motto read *Nunc aut Nunquam* (now or never). As was clear from her portraits, she also had a hunger for jewellery - one which was inadvertently fuelled by the death of Prince Francis's mother.

In October 1897 the Duchess of Teck passed away without leaving a will, although she left verbal instructions to be buried in the royal vault at Windsor where she was soon joined by her husband whose senility was aggravated by her death. Under the intestacy rules the bulk of her estate passed to her one daughter and three sons. Francis inherited the famous Cambridge emeralds which were valued at several thousand pounds. The collection of matching jewellery included a tiara, stomacher, earrings, ring and eight large cabochon gems set as a necklace, as well as some loose emeralds. Originally they had been won in a Frankfurt lottery around 1800 by Princess Augusta of Cambridge who left them to her daughter, Princess Mary Adelaide. Francis in turn gave them to his mistress as a token of his love and apparently sealed the arrangement in his will.

By 1910 Francis was approaching his fortieth birthday. He had now left the army, put on weight and was beginning to lose his rakish good looks. Although he refused to settle down and was famous for racing around London in a motorised carriage, he had at least made a nod to maturity by working as a fundraiser for the Middlesex Hospital where he was also chairman. In the autumn of 1910 he was himself admitted to hospital for a minor nasal operation. Released prematurely, he went up to Balmoral to enjoy the healthy Highland air with his sister in her newly acquired royal estate. Unfortunately he suffered a bad bout of pleurisy and despite a dash to London for emergency surgery, died of pneumonia on October 22.

Queen Mary, who had only just been reconciled with her brother after the long rift caused by his gambling and his gifts to his mistress, was overwhelmed with grief. At the funeral at Windsor where his coffin was placed next to his mother's in the royal vault, she broke down and wept freely - her first (and, some say, her last) show of emotion in public. Her sadness turned to horror a few days later when she learnt what her brother had done with the Cambridge emeralds. Her first reaction was to contact Lady Kilmorey directly and demand the return of what she regarded as a family heirloom, but when she discussed this with her two brothers they feared that the countess might refuse and cause a public scene. In the end, Mary sent "one of the gentlemen of her household" to Ireland to negotiate a deal by which the jewels were released in return for the payment of £10,000 (the equivalent of £600,000 today). It is rumoured that Lady Kilmorey's co-operation may have been bought by letting her keep an emerald brooch from the collection which she gave to her daughter-in-law as a marriage present and which, to add to the mystery, was later stolen. [2]

This still left the problem of Prince Francis's will and the danger of a publicity disaster in coronation year. Not only were there the gambling debts and a mistress shared with the king of England but there was also talk of a love child. If any of this were made public in the run up to the coronation on June 22, it would bring discredit on the reputation of both the Teck and the royal families. With her customary foresight, Mary duly applied to the President of the Probate, Divorce and Admiralty Division for an order sealing the will. When the court agreed in early 1911, it set a precedent that has been faithfully followed by the Family Division for over one hundred years.

It was not until 1993 that the first shaft of light was thrown on the contents of the will. In that year the Kilmorey family deposited around 4,000 documents in the Public Record Office of Northern Ireland in Belfast. They included, according to the official record, a bundle of letters and papers from 1902-27 relating to "Lady Kilmorey's unspoken but widely recognised role as *chere amie* of Queen Mary's younger brother, Prince Francis of Teck...who made embarrassingly generous provision for her in his will." It was not until a BBC reporter from the Radio 4 programme "Document" dug further into the archive that a draft copy of Prince Francis's will was finally unearthed.

The typewritten document is dated January 15, 1902 - just six weeks after he retired from the army and two weeks before he signed the actual will. It begins by stating that it is the last will of Prince Francis of Teck [PF of T]. Being a draft document it freely uses initials and acronyms rather than full names. Lady Kilmorey is not mentioned by name but referred to as COX - perhaps a contraction of her maiden name Constance or a pet name. Clause four refers to his emeralds - that is, the Cambridge emeralds. All the jewels inherited from his mother he intended to leave to COX. The next clause concerns the jewellery inherited from his father which he also decided to leave to COX.

There are also many references to his two brothers - DT (the Duke of Teck, Aldolphus or "Dolly") and AG (Prince Alexander George of Wuerttemberg or "Alge") who in addition to being beneficiaries of the estate were later named as his executors. In clause nine he leaves his furniture to Adolphus, while in the next he bequeaths his horses and equine equipment to Alexander.

Not all of Francis's chattels went to the Teck family. After the discovery of the draft will, the present Earl of Kilmorey, Sir Richard Needham, revealed to the BBC that he possessed a pair of cufflinks inscribed "FT" - which he assumed was a love token from Francis to his grandmother. "To get someone's cufflinks", he told Radio 4, "you have got to get close to their shirt". As for the Cambridge jewels, Queen Mary wore one of the reclaimed gems at the coronation of George V at Westminster Abbey on 22 June 1911. However, as we shall see in the coming chapters, this would only be the start in the jewels' long chain of ownership as they were passed down from generation to generation. Mary's success in sealing her brother's will would also have long term consequences for the secrecy surrounding royal estates. Not for the first time in royal protocol in the Edwardian era, a tradition had been invented.

⚜ ⚜ ⚜

In the administrative files of the probate registry in London a yellowed A4 sheet was recently discovered by the author revealing that since 1911 a total of 31 royal wills have been sealed (i.e. closed to public inspection) by order of the President of the Family Division. The next entry after 1911 - H.S.H Prince Francis of Teck (probate - £23,154 3s 1d) is dated 1912 and refers to the Duke of Fife, Alexander William George (probate - £1,000,000). The two junior royals were distantly related by the tenuous association of them both sharing George V as a brother-in-law. In 1889 Sir Alexander Duff, the first Duke of Fife, married Princess Louise, the first daughter of the future Edward VII. With one estate in Banff and another near Braemar, the duke came from a long line of wealthy Scottish landowners (including an uncle who sold Balmoral to Prince Albert) but his fortune was greatly augmented by his directorship of the Chartered Company of South Africa - which he helped found with Cecil Rhodes and which went on to acquire lucrative mining and political rights over large swathes of southern Africa. As a privy councillor and a former Liberal MP, he also undertook several diplomatic missions for the government. But in January 1912 just one month after narrowly surviving with his family a shipwreck off the coast of Morocco, he contracted pleurisy - the illness that also finished off Prince Francis - and died in Aswan, Egypt. He was sixty-two and exceedingly wealthy.

Even if one makes no allowance for inflation his 1912 estate is still in nominal terms the third largest on the list of 20th century royal wills. With one million pounds to be divided between the families, it is understandable why for reasons of privacy his executors - his business partner Horace Townsend (Baron Farquhar) and his widow Louise (recently elevated to the august rank of Princess Royal) - applied to the courts to seal his will. Given that the princess's own estate was later worth only £46,000 it seems likely that he left the bulk of his estate to his two surviving children and with no male heir the lion's share would have gone to his eldest daughter, Princess Alexandra who inherited the title Duchess of Fife, married her cousin Prince Arthur of Connaught and then retired to a reclusive existence on her Scottish estate. Another reason why Louise's estate was so modest is that late in life she found herself saddled with an unforeseen new debt. After the death of Baron Farquhar in 1923, it emerged that her husband's business associate (and erstwhile financial advisor to Edward VII) had engaged in some dubious financial practices that left him almost bankrupt and her liable to some of the debts of their business partnership. To balance the books, she was obliged to auction her collection of old master paintings that realised £13,577 at Christie's in July 1924.³

The next names on the list are those of Prince Maurice of Battenberg who died in 1914 and his brother Lord Leopold Mountbatten who died in 1922. What is curiously missing from the roll call of sealed wills is an entry for their uncle - Lord Louis Mountbatten, the Marquess of Milford Haven, who died between the two in 1921. After further inquiries at the Principal Registry in London, it was discovered that his will was in fact open to public inspection. This seemed a remarkable act of full disclosure for a well-connected royal, close to both Edward VII and George V, whose daughter Alice became the mother of the Duke of Edinburgh and whose son Louis, Earl of Mountbatten, became the cousin of the Queen.

At first sight he had every reason to want his will kept secret as he was rumoured to be the father of an illegitimate child. Like Prince Francis of Teck Lord Louis shared a mistress with the future Edward VII. She was Lillie Langtry, the Jersey-born actress, London society beauty and estranged wife of the Irish landowner Edward Langtry. Between 1877 and 1880 she had a passionate affair with the Prince of Wales becoming his semi-official mistress and attaining such an elevated status that she was even allowed to accompany him to the races at Ascot. But true to his sociable nature Bertie was happy to pass on his favourite to Louis, one of his best friends in the Royal Navy, a prominent member of the Marlborough House set and a close relative of the German and Russian royal families (his father was Prince Alexander of Hesse). The tall and handsome sailor who loved dancing and partying and had already gained a reputation for having a girl in every port was immediately smitten with "the Jersey Lily", who for her part was beguiled by his good looks and royal status. With her famed common sense and discretion she managed to keep the affair out of the public eye – until, that is, she fell pregnant in June 1880.

She soon informed Prince Louis that he was the most likely father. To his credit, he did the honourable thing, standing by her and according to some accounts even offering to marry her - but neither her husband nor his own family would agree to the match which would have destroyed his naval career. His German parents dispatched an aide-de-camp from their royal residence in Darmstadt to arrange a financial settlement with Lillie. Now lying low in her old home at Portelet in Jersey, she may have used some of the money to escape to Paris accompanied by a male friend. It was made clear that there could be no question of marriage and in August 1880 the Admiralty who had been alerted to the risk of a royal scandal posted Prince Louis on a long, slow voyage round the world aboard a ship powered only by sail. It was appropriately named "HMS Inconstant".

The baby, Jeanne Marie, was born on 18 March 1881 in the Hotel Gibraltar in Paris, so averting any embarrassing publicity in the London press. Lillie later returned quietly to England, brought up the child as her niece and waited until her 17th birthday before revealing who her real mother was but keeping the father a secret. After completing his naval voyage, Prince Louis went on in April 1884 to marry his cousin, Princess Victoria of Hesse, the granddaughter of Queen Victoria, and they had two sons, Louis and George, and two daughters, Alice and Louise. Meanwhile, his naval career went from strength to strength as he climbed the Admiralty rigging from captain in 1891 to the top of the masthead as First Sea Lord in 1912. But at the start of World War One he was forced to resign his position due to anti-German prejudice. Although a naturalised Englishman he had been born in Austria, christened Ludwig and still spoke with a German accent. The fact that he retained German staff in his household and did little to hide his admiration for German naval efficiency led to whispers that he might be spying for the enemy. On hearing of his resignation, George V expressed his sympathy for someone he considered one of the most loyal men in the country.[4]

Later in the war as the anti-German paranoia deepened, the king instructed his cousin - along with many other German royals - to anglicise his title. Prince Louis then became the Marquess of Milford Haven as the Battenbergs were turned into more English-sounding Mountbattens. Not impressed by this blatant act of window-dressing by the new House of Windsor, Kaiser Wilhelm II remarked in a rare display of wit: "I am looking forward to attending a production of the Merry Wives of Saxe-Coburg-Gotha."

In August 1921 the king elevated Lord Louis to the rank of Admiral of the Fleet on the retired list, an honour bestowed on only the very few. But he did not live long enough to become fully rehabilitated as a fortnight later he caught a chill in Scotland where he was inspecting the battle cruiser "Repulse" on which his youngest son, Louis, was serving. He was sent to bed on his return to London but died of heart failure aged sixty-eight, a somewhat bitter and broken man. Young Louis (known to intimates as "Dickie") vowed that one day he would restore the family name by becoming First Lord of the Admiralty.

With skeletons in the closet in the shape of an illegitimate child and an erstwhile mistress who was now a famous actress, one would have expected Lord Louis's will to have been sealed as a matter of course. This is what happened to the will of Prince Francis of Teck who found himself in a similar predicament with a former mistress of the Prince of Wales and - as mentioned earlier - what happened to the wills of both his nephews, Prince Maurice of Battenberg who died in October 1914 at Ypres serving with the British Expeditionary Force but whose £3,146 estate was not sealed until1917, and Lord Leopold Mountbatten, who passed away within seven months of Lord Louis's death and had an estate of a similar value although no illegitimate issue. But for some reason no application for privacy was made to the Family Court and the will and grant of probate are today freely available from the Principal Registry.

As befits a neat and practical naval officer, the will is short, to the point and altogether ship shape. In one of the first clauses he expressed a wish for a simple funeral with only the most modest of tombstones erected over his remains. Should his wife predecease him and his children were amenable he wanted to be cremated - an almost unprecedented form of burial for a member of the royal family and one that would not be adopted by a senior royal until the funeral of Princess Margaret in 2002.

The accompanying probate document records that he left a gross estate of £6,533 17s 1d (net £4,101 3s 2d). In the will dated 9 July 1921 (just two months before his death) he left almost all his personal property to his wife and sole trustee, Princess Victoria, but in the event of her predeceasing him (or for that matter dying after his passing), certain assets were to be divided between their four children. Under a complex arrangement, all four would get equal shares of the jewellery, books and art works, but the china, silver and glass-ware were to be split equally only between the two sons and the younger daughter. As for the cash and securities, the eldest son, Lord George, would receive half, Lord Louis three tenths, while Princess Alice and Lady Louise would have to be content with one tenth each. Clearly, in the first quarter of the 20th century the aristocratic practice of passing on the bulk of family wealth to a male heir was still very much alive - although Louise would later have the financial compensation of marrying King Gustaf of Sweden, while Alice would wed Prince Andrea of Greece.

Unsurprisingly no illegitimate children nor indeed Lillie Langtry are mentioned in the two-page document although there is one hint that old friends (and perhaps even old flames) might be remembered in the will's last paragraph where he instructs his executors to distribute appropriate mementos to his closest friends. It could be argued, though, that the possibility that his widow who was named as executor would hand out some of his personal possessions to his erstwhile lover seems remote. The other two named executors - Sir Arthur Davidson, a Rhine colonel with the British army, and Vice Admiral Mark Kerr of the royal navy - were rewarded for their services with a small remembrance souvenir. Kerr later wrote a hagiographic biography of him that made no reference to any mistress or lover or indeed his own management of the estate.

An additional reason why he might not have provided for any wider family is more prosaic: he was short of cash. This too might explain why he felt no need to keep his will secret. Even by the standards of a junior royal in 1921, his net estate of just over £4,000 was relatively modest. His nephew, Lord Leopold, who was only thirty-two at the time of his death left an estate of £4,049 5s 8d. The reason why Lord Louis was so financially stretched is that his Russian estate of half a million roubles had been decimated by the revolution with the Bolsheviks seizing £50,000 worth of investments (more tragically, he also lost his two Romanov sisters-in-law to the Bolshevik gunmen). To add to his money worries, his German estate of 734,613 marks was drained by the post war financial crash when after the collapse in the value of the mark he only received a pittance from the sale of his ancestral home - Heiligenberg Castle - in 1920. Now in dire financial straits, he had to move out of his English home - Kent House - and sell his beloved collection of naval medals which he had amassed in the course of compiling an encyclopaedia of numismatics. The absence of any landed property to pass on to heirs - whether directly or through the more common device of a family trust - might provide a further explanation why his executors felt no need to seal his will.

The fact that Lord Louis's will was open and his two nephew's wills were sealed suggests that any decision on testamentary transparency is totally arbitrary. It seems to have nothing to do with a general desire for privacy and everything to do with hiding the scale and ultimate destination of one's wealth. The bottom line was that Lord Louis's open estate was worth almost one million pounds less than the Duke of Fife's closed one.

The only mystery surrounding his estate was the fate of his secret "love child". Shortly before he died in 1979, Dickie - now Lord Mountbatten of Burma having achieved his ambition of becoming First Lord of the Admiralty - decided to come clean about his father's affair with Lillie Langtry. There had long been whispers in high society about a possible illegitimate daughter. In his diary Sir Henry "Chips" Channon tells the story of how the socialite Lady Asquith mischievously broke the news to the twenty-year-old Jeanne Marie who her real father was. In the entry for 15 April 1941 he records a visit to the Gate Theatre to see "The Jersey Lily" by Basil Bartlett: "a pleasant trivial little play, interesting because it actually portrays King Edward VII on the stage; the theme is the love affair between Prince Louis of Battenberg and Mrs Langtry (the offspring of this romance is Lady - - who was only told who her father was, when she was 20, by the then Mrs Asquith").[5]

In October 1978 Mountbatten resolved to fill in the blanks with a full disclosure. Speaking appropriately enough in Jersey at a star-studded charity gala which featured Morecambe and Wise, Rolf Harris and Larry Grayson, he acknowledged for the first time in public his father's affair and illegitimate child. She was, he explained, the result of a *coup de foudre* between two highly attractive individuals: "[Lillie] had charisma as well as beauty...My father was not a bad looking chap. The romance was pretty serious - it must have been since they had a baby daughter - Jeanette [sic]."[6]

In front of more than three hundred guests (including Prince and Princess Michael of Kent), he made it clear that he felt no shame or embarrassment about the affair: "my father met her six years before his marriage. It was something to be hushed up then, but today we admit freely that these things go on". He went out of his way to deny that he was the main whistle blower: "My family never gave the secret away and nor did hers. But a wealthy man called Chips Channon did so in his diary."

No one knows what prompted him to set the record straight there and then. It could have been the location - in that Jersey was Lillie's homeland - or perhaps it was to do with timing - he wanted to pre-empt some revelation that he thought imminent. At the time, a big budget ITV drama series "Lillie" with Francesca Anis in the title role had caught the public imagination - something he cleverly interweaved into his speech: "Are you watching the TV series about Lillie?...How they will portray my father's romance in the series I do not know." Laced with his usual charm and wit, his indiscreet speech managed to upstage many of the professional entertainers at the gala winning, according to one press report, the biggest applause of the evening.[7]

This very public announcement motivated Jeanne Marie's daughter, the well known BBC television announcer Mary Malcolm, to write Mountbatten a letter of thanks. In November 1978, he replied with an invitation to stay at his Hampshire estate of Broadlands since, in his view, it was high time that the matter came into the open.[8] By all accounts, the weekend went well and after Mary was asked to plant a tree in the grounds, she wrote again hoping it might be the start of a fruitful relationship. But within six months Mountbatten was dead - blown up by the IRA while on a boating trip in Ireland.

In the final months of his life, there was one last twist to the tale. A distant relative of Mrs Langtry discovered in a Jersey attic a cache of intimate letters between Lillie and the man who accompanied her to Paris, Arthur Jones, indicating that they were lovers. Later when the full correspondence was combed through by Lillie's biographer, Laura Beatty, and discussion of a possible abortion was discovered, it was suggested that Jones may even have been the father of the child. Lillie certainly gave him the impression that he was the father but of course she did the same to Prince Louis. It is perfectly plausible that the wily Lillie who in addition to two husbands had a legion of lovers and sugar daddies could have duped the credulous Jones into thinking he was the father so that he would support her during the loneliness of giving birth to an illegitimate child in a foreign land. In the absence of any DNA material, it is impossible to establish the matter conclusively one way or the other. But the balance of evidence suggests that Arthur may well have been the true father and if so, it is also possible that Lord Louis was told about this and so had nothing to fear from making his will available to public scrutiny.

Chapter Four
The Princes At War –
1936 -1945

"The profession to which I was born has been losing ground for centuries. I have better cause than most to make provision for a rainy day. For me, as for Noah, it would mean a deluge"
The Duke of Windsor

The death of King George V at Sandringham at 11.55 pm on 20 January 1936 appeared a master class in succession planning. It was handled with the same meticulous timing and forethought that went into ensuring that all the clocks on the estate were set exactly thirty minutes ahead of Greenwich Mean Time. Earlier in the day his physician Lord Dawson gave advance warning of the death by arranging for the BBC to broadcast in its evening bulletin the message that "the King's life is moving peacefully to its close." The king lingered longer than expected and later that evening Dawson resolved to hasten the inevitable by injecting 0.75 grams of morphia and

1 gram of cocaine into his jugular vein. Much later still he explained that the timing of the death was designed to coincide with the print deadline of certain newspapers so that the announcement could be made in the respectable morning titles as opposed to the down-market evening ones. He even rang his wife to ask her to inform The Times, regarded at the time as the voice of the nation, that they should hold back the next edition as a final bulletin on the king's deteriorating health was imminent.

The Duchess of York, the future Queen Mother, was unable to attend the deathbed vigil as she was herself in bed having succumbed to a bout of influenza that turned into pneumonia, but the Prince of Wales, the future Edward VIII, was there along with the Duke of York, Queen Mary, the Princess Royal and the Duke and Duchess of Kent (the Duke of Gloucester was ill). Edward's overt display of grief surprised many onlookers. According to the king's private secretary, Lord Wigram, the Prince of Wales became "hysterical" and began crying out, while in the view of Helen Hardinge - a lady in waiting and wife of the future Edward VIII's private secretary - his "frantic and unreasonable" reaction went well beyond that of his three brothers, even though they had loved the king as much as he had.[1]

The reason why the succession process did not go like clockwork is that, for the Prince of Wales at least, the king had died several months too early. By all accounts, the premature death had upset his plans to renounce the throne. Alan Lascelles, George V's assistant private secretary and a former private secretary to the Prince of Wales, believed that he planned to forsake the crown for a new life with Mrs. Wallis Simpson. He was now so besotted with the American divorcée whom he had first met in 1931 at the home of his then mistress, Lady Thelma Furness, that he was determined to marry her regardless of the constitutional improprieties. Lord Hardinge is also of the opinion that had George V lived for another six months, the Prince of Wales would have opted out of the line of succession. Much later in 1994-5 the Queen Mother revealed in a private taped conversation to Eric Anderson, the former Eton headmaster, that George V had even expressed serious doubts to her and her husband that the Prince of Wales would ever be king.[2]

On the evening of January 24 the new king was in for another shock at Sandringham when his father's will was read out by the royal solicitor, Sir Bernard Halsey-Bircham. Also present were Queen Mary and Lord Wigram who left a detailed account of the scene in a personal memorandum. He records that King Edward became agitated when he learned that his father had left him a life interest in Sandringham and Balmoral but no money. His four siblings - the Dukes of York, Kent, Gloucester and the Princess Royal - each got a lump sum of three quarters of a million pounds. His response to the news was an anguished cry enquiring about his rightful share of the pot. Apparently, he was the last to know.

Wigram and the solicitor tried to explain that the old king felt that during his twenty-five years as Prince of Wales he ought to have built up a nest egg out of the revenue from the Duchy of Cornwell and as such there was little necessity to provide for him. For the same reason, Edward VII had never left his eldest son any money.

When the new king protested that it was unfair that he had got nothing while his siblings had got large sums, Wigram tried to persuade him that he would not endure any financial hardship since he could save money from the Civil List and the Privy Purse as his father had done.[3] In passing it should be noted that this was the first official confirmation of what had long been suspected – that, monarchs made a profit on the Civil List. In theory, this may have amounted to if not an abuse then certainly a bending of the rules concerning the use of public funds since certain designated classes of the Civil List payments were supposed to cover the wages, salaries and expenses incurred by members of the royal family in the performance of their official duties and were not to be used for capital accumulation. But in practice the Treasury turned a blind eye to any surplus being transferred to the monarch's privy (i.e. private) purse as it could be justified as simply a way of putting money aside for their grandchildren. Using select committee statistics, one royal chronicler later calculated that during his twenty-five year reign George V made a total saving of £487,000. The value was further enhanced by the fact that since 1910 Civil List payments to the monarch were tax-free.[4]

Wigram's invitation to raid the public purse did little to assuage the new king's worries. He stormed out of the room and strode down the corridor - according to the old king's private secretary, Alan Lascelles - with a face like thunder. He then shut himself in his room and telephoned Mrs. Simpson with the bad news.[5]

Lascelles who knew Edward's true nature better than most having been his assistant private secretary for almost all of the 1920s believed that the reading of the will may have been a key moment in the abdication crisis. Up until that time the king's intention - in Lascelles's view - was to give up the throne almost immediately. He would inherit from his father the fortune he had promised Mrs. Simpson and he could take her away (perhaps to his ranch in Canada) where he could afford to keep her in the manner to which she was accustomed. The king in fact told Lascelles in the summer of 1936 that he did not want to be king, while Owen Morshead, another courtier, recorded a remark from George VI to the effect that Edward never wanted to take the job on but the sudden death of his father upset his plans to renounce the throne while he was still Prince of Wales.[6] But having been disinherited by his father Edward was now determined under the urging of Wallis to stick it out and amass as much money as he could from the situation. This meant not just realising every asset but also cutting costs.[7]

One of the earliest targets for the chop was the Sandringham estate - which he regarded as a "voracious white elephant" that ate up £50,000 a year in running costs. As a mark of the changing of the guard, his first act as king was to turn all the clocks back thirty minutes so that they ran to normal time. He decided to cut the raising of game on the estate and ordered the Duke of York to produce a blueprint to reduce costs further. He recommended that one hundred of the four hundred employees be made redundant. Through a combination of redundancies and pay cuts, the wages bill in 1936 was reduced by £6,150.[8] The cost of food at Sandringham and the other royal residences was cut from £45,000 a year to £13,500. Edward also arranged for the sale of Anmer and Flitcham, two farms adjoining the estate.

The new king kept his younger brother in the dark about his long term plans to sell the family home. Although separated by little more than a year in age, the two siblings could not have been more different in character. The dashing "David" was the epitome of urbanity: charming, fashionably dressed and obsessed with money; while the plodding "Bertie" with his love of the outdoors had more modest tastes, being content with a quiet family life having married his soul mate Elizabeth Bowes Lyon. In private David and Wallis referred to her as "Cookie" on account of her ample figure. The mutual dislike of the "Queen Wallis" and the Duchess helped drive a wedge between the two brothers. This social divide would become, as the abdication crisis deepened, a financial chasm.

Balmoral did not escape the king's axe either. There the wage bill was cut by £1,330 and the remaining staff worked under the looming threat of further redundancies.[9] The Duchess of York noticed a much less warm atmosphere at Balmoral than prevailed under George and Mary.[10] During a visit in October 1936, legend has it that when Mrs. Simpson tried to act as hostess at one dinner, the duchess snubbed her saying that she had come to dine with the king and left early after the meal.

The reverse side of Edward VIII's ferocious economy drive was his unrestrained expenditure on Mrs. Simpson - or as one hostile conservative MP put it, "lavishing" jewellery on his mistress, while at the same time "getting rid of his father's servants."[11] When she turned down the free use of the Duke of Westminster's yacht for a Mediterranean cruise, the king was obliged to charter Lady Yule's more luxurious 250-foot Nahlin for five weeks. It came complete with a swimming pool, gymnasium and dance floor.

In the previous two years he had showered her with a fortune of jewellery, on several occasions withdrawing more than £10,000 from the Duchy of Cornwall accounts for the purchases. When Mrs. Simpson began to appear in society wearing familiar-looking rubies and emeralds, tongues soon wagged.

Had Edward given her the royal jewellery he had inherited from Queen Alexandra? Much later - on December 3, 1936 at the height of the abdication crisis - her old friend and travelling companion Lord Brownlow recorded in his diary that she left London for the seclusion of the south of France with £100,000 worth of jewellery in her luggage. It was the talk of the town that the collection included Queen Alexandra's jewels.

The Duchess of York, the future Queen and Queen Mother, was conveniently absent from the main drama in the abdication crisis. Throughout the first fortnight of December she was confined to bed at her London residence of 145 Piccadilly with one of her "traditional chills", since at times of family crisis - whether Princess Margaret's separation from Peter Townsend or Prince Charles's divorce - she had a tendency to play ostrich.

On the day Edward VIII signed the Instrument of Abdication, he also tried to change his father's will. Much of December 10 was taken up with heated negotiations about the financial settlement. The two bones of contention were: how the private residences of Balmoral and Sandringham were to be transferred from Edward VIII to George VI and how the former king was to be provided for after the abdication.

The talks took place at Edward VIII's other residence, Fort Belvedere, the 18th century mock castle on the fringes of Windsor Great Park where at the swimming pool away from prying eyes he liked to entertain Mrs. Simpson and his circle of friends. It was his sanctuary and in the interwar period he spent thousands of pounds refurbishing the residence. Present on that chilly winter day in the octagonal drawing room along with Edward were two legal advisors, his solicitor George Allen and his legal *éminence grise* Walter Monckton, and two financial advisors, Ulick Alexander, the Keeper of the Privy Purse, and Sir Edward Peacock, a former chairman of the Bank of England and receiver general of the Duchy of Cornwall who took on the role of the king's personal consultant on finance. The Duke of York, the future king, was there for much of the day and helped by his solicitor Sir Bernard Halsey Bircham and Sir Clive Wigram, the former private secretary to George V who had been called out of retirement to advise the future king. The other presence in the room was Mrs. Simpson who although one thousand miles away in a villa in the south of France was able to voice her strong opinions to her future husband down a crackly telephone line. According to Peacock, the king's obduracy derived from her repeated urging on the phone that he should "fight for his rights" and that he would prevail due to his popularity as king.[12]

The December 10 meeting which in many respects echoed the reading of George V's will almost a year earlier began with an impassioned plea from Edward stating how badly off he would be and requesting that his father's will be changed so that he might fully benefit from it. He later insisted that the new king buy his life interest in Balmoral and Sandringham. In addition, according to Wigram, he clearly told his brother that he did not think he had £5,000 a year claiming only to have £90,000 as his total fortune.[13] Wigram himself felt compelled to interrupt, angrily reminding Edward that he should respect his father's testamentary wishes. He went on to point out that when the will was drawn up, there was no way abdication could have been contemplated or even provided for. Repeating what he had said the previous January he emphasised that the will had taken into account that Edward as Prince of Wales had been able to save money in a way that was not available to his brothers and sister.

The new king later likened the occasion to a horrid lawyer interview. In a nod to family harmony, he generously offered not to change a thing in Fort Belvedere (apart from taking the American power mower from the garden) so that it could always be used as his brother's private residence.

After much wrangling over the legal status of the private estates, it was left to Sir Edward Peacock to break the deadlock. Sensing that matters were getting overheated, he took the Duke of York and Sir Bernard aside for short private talks and tried to simplify some of the legal technicalities that were proving a sticking point. The final proposal he offered was that Edward would sell his life interest in Sandringham and Balmoral for an agreed sum in return for dropping any claim to the royal heirlooms.

The agreed sale price would not be handed over as a lump sum but the new king would pay him £25,000 a year if parliament declined to grant the money. However, the king would not be liable to underwrite the agreement if the reason for parliament's refusal was due to his conduct from that date.[14]

After the two camps split into separate rooms, they eventually agreed to make a number of minor changes to George V's will and the financial settlement document was signed by both the new and the old kings. The agreement also included a commitment by the future George VI to pay the pensions of his brother's staff and a promise by Edward VIII that he would gift His Majesty the total contents of Sandringham and Balmoral belonging to him, the live and dead stock at Windsor and any other effects inherited from his father.[15]

When Edward informed Wallis of the precise details in a phone call that evening she was far from pleased. He later compared the hurried negotiations to a fire sale.[16] For his part, the Duke of York remembered the meeting ending harmoniously due in no small part to the advice of Sir Edward Peacock.

Unfortunately two linked developments conspired to undermine the agreement - and ultimately to sour relations between the two brothers for the rest of their lives. First the mood in parliament - particularly among Labour MPs who formed part of the coalition government's majority - began to turn against Edward. Originally the government had been sympathetic to the view that Edward should be granted funds from the Civil List to allow him to live in a style appropriate to a former sovereign - with Baldwin famously responding to one dissenting colleague "but you can't let him starve." But in the months after the abdication - as Mrs. Simpson's divorce case dragged through the courts - attitudes to the king began to harden. Perhaps anticipating a change in public opinion and a backlash from Labour coalition MPs, Neville Chamberlain, the Chancellor of the Exchequer, now became distinctly chilly about granting the king £25,000 a year and as chairman of the parliamentary select committee responsible for Civil List payments his opinion held much weight.

Secondly - and more significantly - it was discovered that Edward had lied about the true state of his finances. Although in December 1936 he claimed to have less than £100,000 in capital, around mid February 1937 it was discovered that that his total fortune was closer to £1m. Wigram believed he had accumulated considerably more than one million sterling[17] and Sir Edward Peacock put the figure at £1.1m (including a portion settled on Mrs Simpson), although more recently the royal chronicler Michael Bloch, who had full access to the Windsors' papers calculated that his investment was at least £800,000.[18] This last sum, however, does not appear to include his ranch in Canada or his collection of jewellery.

In retrospect, Edward was a fool to lie. His official biographer Philip Ziegler takes this view and then attempts to be charitable arguing that his mind may have been disturbed by the emotional impact of the abdication and that he was worried that he would let down the woman he loved by failing to secure the funds he thought she deserved.[19] But the fact of the matter is that he was devious and greedy. Indeed, he was unabashed about his obsession with money, often remarking that in his precarious profession he had good reason "to make provision for a rainy day."[20]

As a result of the new information, the parliamentary committee did not grant him the promised Civil List money and the Belvedere agreement had to be renegotiated. On February 10, 1937 the representatives of the government and the former king met again. Edward's solicitor, George Allen, insisted that the Belvedere agreement was a legally binding contract that must be honoured. Warren Fisher, the permanent secretary of the Treasury, reminded him that Edward had failed to disclose the true extent of his private income - a point that was repeated in a letter a day later from George VI to his brother. Negotiations over the financial settlement dragged on for another year - with the threat from Edward's camp that he might prevent the court moving to Balmoral that summer unless there was a satisfactory agreement. They did not accept what they saw as the government's low valuation of Sandringham at £146,000 and Balmoral at £90,000 (later the estates were revalued so that their total value was set at £300,000).

In the end, it was decided that the revenue from their sale should be invested in war bonds and the annual income (around £10,000) should be paid to Edward. Since he had been promised a revised total of £21,000 instead of £25,000 a year, this left another £11,000 a year which would have to come from George VI's own pocket rather than parliament. Even for the king of England, this extra payment put a strain on his finances which had already been stretched by the need to reverse Edward's proposed sale of thousands of acres of farmland neighbouring Sandringham and his other cost-cutting reforms. For his part, Edward was unhappy that he now had to pay for the pensions of his former staff which under the Belvedere agreement had been paid by his brother.

※ ※ ※

Edward's disputed financial settlement would sour relations with Bertie for the rest of his reign and the new king's anguish was deepened by the fact that the unexpected abdication meant that he had little preparation for the job. No "gentle glide" like today's handover to Prince Charles which even provides special constitutional tuition for Prince William, this was the most bumpy of succession processes. When Edward sprang the news of his imminent announcement to abdicate, the future king rushed to his mother's sofa at Buckingham Palace and broke down in tears on her shoulder.[21] Seeking further family solace, he confided to Lord Mountbatten that his only training was as a naval officer and he was totally unprepared for the new job.[22] At the back of his mind too must have been the appalling prospect of delivering long formal speeches with a permanent stammer.

In 1942, however, the squabbling siblings were briefly brought together in grief by an accident to their youngest brother, Prince George. On August 25 the Duke of Kent as part of his duties as Chief Welfare Officer of the Royal Air Force Home Command boarded a Sunderland flying boat at RAF Invergordon in Scotland bound for another RAF station in Iceland. Flying conditions were poor due to a thick mist that had descended on the neighbouring mountains. After take-off at 1.30 pm, the plane failed to reach a height above seven hundred feet and in the fog flew straight into the hillside at Berriedale. All but one of the fifteen men aboard were killed and the prince's mutilated body was identified from an ID bracelet that read: His Royal Highness the Duke of Kent, The Coppins, Iver, Buckinghamshire. The fact that the one survivor, Flight Sergeant Andrew Jack, never disclosed what had happened fuelled speculation that it might have been a case of pilot error and that the prince might have been at the controls himself flying the plane too low. But new evidence now suggests that the most likely cause of the crash was instrument failure as the gyro-magnetic compass failed to show the correct height. A recent authorised royal biographer has also argued that the plane should never have taken off in such poor visibility and that the pilot may have been partly to blame for the accident.[23]

George VI was less than seventy miles away on the moors of Balmoral shooting with his other brother Prince Henry, when the crash happened. He took the news badly, almost broke down at the funeral four days later in St George's Chapel and was only consoled by the fact that his brother had died in active service (later underlined in the official probate records that cite that he died "on war service"). Eager to be given some military duties to perform, the Duke of Kent had been created an air commodore in the Royal Air Force and made responsible for inspecting RAF facilities in the UK and abroad. Hence his trip to an air station in Iceland.

Edward was on the other side of the Atlantic in Nassau serving as Governor of the Bahamas when he learned of the death. On receiving the telegram he was so distraught that he was barely able to cable back a message to his family. Despite being eight years his junior, "Georgie" had been his favourite brother and in their bachelor years in London they had lived in each other's pockets - and for a time under the same roof. When the continual round of partying left the Duke of Kent addicted to cocaine, Edward came to the rescue by moving him into his own apartment at York House and acting as "doctor, gaoler and detective combined" before a stay in a rehabilitation clinic finally got his brother off the habit. Unable to attend the funeral, he received a tender letter of condolence from his mother Queen Mary in which she thanked him for all the kindness he had shown to "Georgie" and which after six years of estrangement he interpreted as a thawing of the ice.[24]

The Duke of Kent was survived by his thirty-five-year-old widow, Marina, and three young children. Svelte, sophisticated and always impeccably groomed, the beautiful duchess was the Diana of her day - a thorough-bred clothes horse who brought a European chic to the House of Windsor's frumpy wardrobe. In the thirties - in much the same way as would happen in the sixties to Princess Margaret and in the eighties to Princess Diana - she was built up by the popular press as an arbiter of fashion with her trademark pillbox hats and her British-made blue cotton outfits being splashed across the front pages. The society photographer Cecil Beaton also captured her glamour in a series of film-star like portraits. Her sense of style had been cultivated during her adolescence as an exiled princess in 1920s Paris where she mixed with couturiers and boutique-owners and even modelled in advertisements for skin care products earning her pin-money of £50-£100 for each photographic shoot. Her good looks and high cheekbones (not to mention her pronounced accent and penchant for Russian cigarettes) had been inherited from her Danish-Russian ancestry. She was the daughter of Prince Nicholas of Greece and Denmark, the son of George I of Hellens, who had been put on the Greek throne briefly after the Danish royal family had been chosen to provide an overseas sovereign, and the brother of Prince Andrew who married Alice, the daughter of Lord Louis of Battenberg, who in turn gave birth to Prince Philip, the later Duke of Edinburgh. Her mother was Grand Duchess Elena of Russia, daughter of the Grand Duke Vladimir (uncle of Tsar Nicholas II) and grand-daughter of Tsar Alexander II. So despite her image as a "Greek princess", she was two thirds Russian and one third Danish and possessed not one drop of Greek blood.

She met her future husband through her eldest sister Olga who was married to Prince Paul of Yugoslavia, a close friend of both the Prince of Wales and the Duke of Kent. Although the dashing heir to the throne initially had his eye on Marina, it was his younger brother who soon fell for her charms marrying her in a full state ceremony at Westminster Abbey in November 1934, less than a year after their first formal introduction at a London lunch party. Rejecting the proposed suitors arranged by his straitlaced parents, he was determined to marry for love and proposed to her during a summer vacation at Prince Paul's holiday home in Yugoslavia. Up to that point, "Georgie" had been the wild boy of the House of Windsor. Having turned his back on the naval career favoured by his father, he worked intermittently at the Foreign Office and Home Office and developed a passion for flying, fast cars and derring-do (Marina's willing embrace of his breakneck driving was one of the things that especially endeared her to him).

In the free and easy Jazz Age of the twenties and thirties, a royal prince could live recklessly in a way that would be impossible in today's intrusive media world. Described by one member of his raffish set as "weak but charming"[25] and another as a "narcissist", he had a string of affairs with unsuitable women including the good time girl "Poppy" Baring, the black singer Florence Mills and most disastrously the American adventuress Kiki Whitney Preston who got him hooked on cocaine and morphine. He also had male partners. Tall, with neat brown hair, deep blue eyes, thick sensuous lips and sharp aquiline features, he was a natural magnet to many men - including the bisexual Chips Channon who noted: "The Duke of Kent followed, blue-eyed...insinuating, and - to me - though not to Honor [his wife] altogether irresistible."[26] His name was linked with the Kaiser's grandson Prince Louis Ferdinand, the art historian Anthony Blunt and the playwright Noel Coward. Later in a London nightspot a well-known gay South American whispered in Marina's ear: "you don't know me but I was your predecessor."[27]

Marriage to Marina brought much-needed stability to George's life, although he never totally lost his wandering eye. They rented a town house at No 3 Belgrave Square, redecorated its spacious reception rooms and threw glittering dinner parties for the cream of London society. They also acquired a country retreat in Buckinghamshire more suitable for a young family. Their first child Edward was born in October 1935, followed by a daughter Alexandra in December 1936 and a second son Michael in July 1942 - just six weeks before the duke's fatal crash.

The sudden death of her husband caused not just emotional turmoil for Princess Marina - for a time all photos of him had to be hidden from her view and his name not mentioned to staff - but also severe financial hardship. She had turned down a RAF widow's pension of £398 a year - presumably on the assumption that she could live off the duke's Civil List income. Unfortunately the payments ended with his death due to an inexplicable oversight by which no provision was made for widows of the sons of the king. She also had the unenviable distinction of being among the few war widows who paid death duties.[28] His estate of £157,735 was liable to estate tax of 26-30% and after the further deduction of debts the net amount came to £79,148.

This five figure sum seems remarkably small for a prince who six years earlier had inherited £750,000 in cash from his father and who in each subsequent year had had received a £25,000 annuity from the Civil List. In 1936 he also inherited a country house (valued at £400,000 in 1974) from his maiden aunt "Toria," Princess Victoria, the second sister of George V. Coppins - a two-storey, gabled Victorian mansion set in one hundred and thirty-five acres of Buckinghamshire countryside - provides a clue as to where the missing million may have gone. Finding the redbrick property too dank, dark and cluttered for his tastes, he splashed out on a major conversion, turning the library into a music room with two pianos including a new Ibeck which he liked to play over cocktails before dinner. He also built a nursery, modernised the reception rooms and spent a small fortune on furnishing the house with *objets d'art*, antiques, and a collection of fine clocks, including an exquisite golden French timepiece in the main room.

After seeing how luxuriously he filled his two residences with "their houseful of treasures", his friend Chips Channon joked that he might be spending as much as "£500,000 a year" on his London shopping sprees.[29] Channon knew from personal experience as the son of a shipping magnate and the husband of a Guinness brewery heiress that if you were fortunate in the thirties to possess great wealth you spent it - recording in his diary on 27 September 1935 that "it is very difficult to spend less than £200 a morning when one goes out shopping." In 1936 he spent £6,000 redecorating a single room, employing the world's foremost interior designer Stephene Boudin to transform his dining room into a luxurious replica of the famous Amalienburg pavilion in Bavaria complete with silver fittings and blue rococo decor. His next door neighbour at No 5 Belgrave Square was the Duke of Kent who became a frequent dinner guest and in an upper class equivalent of keeping up with the Joneses the aristocrats of Belgravia competed with one another to possess what Channon regarded as "London's loveliest room."[30]

George too had an eye for beauty. By far the most intelligent of the five siblings of George V and Queen Mary, he inherited from his mother a passion for fine art and in the interwar years amassed an impressive collection of furniture, silver, porcelain and paintings - none of which came cheap.[31] The highlight of his collection were three paintings by Claude Lorraine that he snapped up at the beginning of the war. He also had works by the Italian master Giovanni Pannini and fine porcelain from Meissen. It is hardly surprising that the Keeper of the Queen's Pictures later described him as "the most distinguished royal connoisseur since George IV."[32]

Marina was - according to one report - left nothing in her husband's will.[33] This may be a slight exaggeration as one would have expected George to make some provision for his young wife despite his shortage of cash. Some money was probably placed in a trust fund for the three children but what is certain is that the Coppins house was held in trust to be inherited by his eldest son, Edward, on his 21st birthday. Meanwhile, it was left to Marina to pay for the upkeep of the property and the upbringing of her young family. School fees alone would have been a considerable outlay as Edward moved from his prep school at Ludgrove in Berkshire to Eton College (where his brother Michael would later join him) and Alexandra was sent away to Heathfield School in Ascot - earning her the distinction of being the first British princess to go to boarding school.

Despite an official allowance from George VI, the young widow soon found it impossible to make ends meet and had to resort to what one observer called "a royal car boot sale."[34] In November 1943 she auctioned a batch of antiques left to George in 1939 by his great aunt Princess Louise, Duchess of Argyll, as part of her massive £247,671 estate. Selling her husband's chattels was made less of a wrench for Marina by the knowledge that he never much liked the old furniture which eventually fetched £20,000.

The second auction at Christie's in March 1947 was a more public and humiliating affair. Marina was forced to swallow her pride and sell some possessions closer to her husband's heart - including furniture, porcelain, *objets d'art* and more than sixty paintings and drawings. The loss of the three Claude Lorraine pictures was partially eased by the fact they fetched more than double the price that George had paid for them just seven years previously, while a prized Queen Anne sofa raised £1,700 guineas. Altogether, the three-day auction realised £92,341 - enough to keep the wolf from the door of Coppins, at least for the time being.

One of the lasting ironies of George's estate is that even though every effort was made to keep it secret by sealing the will, much of its contents ultimately became public thanks to the forced auctions.

Had he not been third in line to the throne, one wonders whether George's modest estate would ever have warranted being locked away from public inspection. But reduced financial circumstances forced Marina to open the lid on his treasure trove of artworks. As we shall see later with the estate of George's elder brother Prince Henry, the Duke of Gloucester, this would not be the last time that royal heirs would have to put the family silver up for auction.

Although financially stretched, Marina managed to hang on to her Coppins country home. There she liked to entertain theatrical friends such as Noel Coward, Cecil Beaton and Sir Malcolm Sargent and members of her extended family including her sister Princess Olga, Princess Katherine of Greece and the Tsarina's sister Victoria Milford Haven. One frequent visitor in the years immediately after the war was her first cousin Prince Philip of Greece, another was the young Princess Elizabeth who lived nearby at Windsor Castle. Marina was very close to Philip who had gone to great trouble as a boarder at Gordonstoun school in Scotland to attend her London wedding (at which Princess Elizabeth was a bridesmaid) and then stayed regularly at Coppins during the school holidays. It became one of his favourite places - a retreat from the turbulence of his family life which had seen the separation of his parents, his mother's committal to a sanatorium and the death of his sister in a plane crash. Marina treated him as her protégé and is said to have encouraged his romance with the young princess. Another house guest, Chips Channon, observed presciently in October 1944: "As I signed the visitors' book I noticed 'Philip' written constantly. It is at Coppins that he sees Princess Elizabeth. I think she will marry him."[35]

Chapter Five
The Princesses Of Nothing – 1948-1952

"Princess Helena Victoria - of what?"
Sir Henry "Chips" Channon's verdict on the princess's royal pedigree

The wedding of Princess Elizabeth and Lieutenant Philip Mountbatten on 20 November 1947 was memorably captured in a group photograph that showed all forty members of the royal family clustered around the happy bride and groom. To the right of the smiling princess are her mother, Queen Elizabeth, and her father, George VI, while just behind the future Duke of Edinburgh is the stern figure of his grandmother-in-law, Queen Mary, and at the back Louis Mountbatten, his tall and handsome uncle, characteristically manages to get into the picture, towering above the bejewelled Princess Marina. Just squeezed in on the right at the corner of the frame is a frail elderly woman seated in a wheelchair and holding a stick. She is dressed in a white gown cut by a royal sash with a fur stool across her shoulders and a beret-type hat with a small brooch half hiding her curly locks. Unlike other members of the family she ignores the camera and seems lost in a world of her own. Her name was Princess Helena Victoria, a distant cousin of the bride, and the wedding would be her last major public appearance. She died four months later on 19 March 1948, aged seventy-seven and unmarried.

Helena Victoria would have gone to her grave a footnote in royal history but for her one claim to fame: her will. If you inspect the records at the London Probate Registry, her name appears 19th on the list of the royal wills sealed by order of the president of the Family Division. Her entry sits between that of HM Queen Mary and the Rt Hon Maud Countess of Southesk but in one significant respect it differs from the thirty-two royals on the list. The recorded details for Her Highness Princess Victoria Louise, Sophia, Augusta (otherwise known as Princess Helena Victoria) read: Probate London 28 May 1948 - £52,435 12s 9d. No order made for the will to be sealed.

The list as we have seen gives the names of all the senior royals you have died since 1910 and records that with this one exception all their wills have been sealed. So, how did Princess Helena Victoria slip through the net? Why did her executors not follow the example of the thirty-two other royals and make an order for her will to be kept secret? What was special about this forgotten princess?

She was born Princess Victoria, Louise, Sophie, Augusta, Amelia, Helena in Frogmore House near Windsor Castle on 3 May 1870. Her mother was Princess Helena, the third daughter of Queen Victoria and her father was Prince Christian, the third son of Duke Christian August of Schleswig-Holstein. They had married in 1866 after Queen Victoria gave her consent apparently on condition that her daughter continued to live close to her in England. Until her marriage, the docile Helena (known as Lenchen) seemed content to play the role of dutiful daughter to her grieving and demanding mother. Not blessed with beauty and forever struggling to keep her weight down, the twenty-four-year-old princess was in danger of being left on the shelf until the thirty-five-year-old prince from Schleswig-Holstein appeared on the scene. With no family money of his own, he was delighted to receive a £30,000 dowry from Queen Victoria.

The couple moved into Cumberland Lodge in Windsor Great Park where Prince Christian was given the honorary post of ranger and Helena set up home for her growing family. Helena Victoria - as she became known to distinguish her from her mother - had a younger sister, Marie Louise, and two older brothers - one of whom died in the Boer war. During the fighting her mother started the military nursing service and founded the Prince Christian Nursing Home in Windsor in memory of her lost son.

Despite her German-Danish pedigree, Helena Victoria was regarded as a fully paid up member of the British the royal family. She became close to her grandmother Queen Victoria and often visited her at Balmoral. When she wanted to arrange an afternoon tea with friends in the gillie's cottage in the outer grounds she first had to get the permission of her grandmother who meticulously vetted the guest list.

The queen always referred to her granddaughter as "Thora" (a contraction of Victoria) but the rest of the royal family knew her as "Snipe" on account of her lengthy nose and elongated doleful features. As the twenty or so photos in her collection at the National Portrait Gallery clearly testify, she was no oil painting. One taken in 1885 at the wedding of Prince and Princess Henry of Battenberg shows a plump, plain-looking teen-ager. After her younger sister, Marie Louise, married Prince Aribert of Anhalt in 1891, her parents were desperate to find her a husband and earmarked Prince George (the future George V) as a possible match.[1] But the prince had already been paired with another German royal, Mary of Teck and in a crowning irony that much annoyed her mother Helena Victoria was made one of the ten bridesmaids at their wedding in 1893.[2]

Mary of Teck had originally been engaged to George's older brother, Prince Albert, the Duke of Clarence, but in January 1892 just weeks before the wedding he caught the flu and died suddenly. When it came to finding a bride for Prince George, Mary was the obvious choice since her suitability to be a royal consort had already been approved. Although an arranged marriage, it proved – according to one royal biographer - a relationship of lasting strength and affection.[3]

Left on the shelf with no husband after a brief flirtation with the Duke of Hesse came to nothing, Helena Victoria devoted much of the rest of her life to charitable work. This sense of duty had been drummed into her from an early age, being taught as children, as her sister highlights in her memoirs, to work for the sick and the distressed.[4] She became president of a number of charities including her mother's hospital in Windsor but her name was most closely associated with the Young Men's Christian Association. On the outbreak of the First World War she founded the YMCA National Women's auxiliary force (which consisted of 40,000 volunteers under her charge) and as casualties mounted she travelled to France to see for herself the shocking conditions in the camps and hospitals.

Later in the war a bombshell from a *royal* provenance dramatically changed her status. In July 1917 - in a response to the growing anti-Kaiser feeling in the country fuelled by the war's horrendous death toll - George V changed the name of the British royal family from the House of Saxe Coburg Gotha to the House of Windsor. It was a shrewd move to reconnect the king with some of his potentially alienated subjects. At a stroke all German-sounding connections were shed - although a veil was drawn over the fact that his wife Mary still spoke with a slight German accent. He ordered a root and branch renaming of royal relations in England - so that not only did the Battenbergs become Mountbattens as we saw earlier but Mary's Teck relations adopted the name of Cambridge. For Princess Helena Victoria and her sister Princess Marie Louise, this meant that they could no longer use the territorial title "of Schleswig Holstein" and instead had to be called "Her Highness Princess" Helena Victoria or Marie Louise. The two sisters were left in a curious royal limbo of being princesses but not princesses of any family or monarchy. George V never formally granted them the title of Princess of Great Britain and Ireland, even though they were both British citizens and for all intents and purposes treated like any other member of the royal family. In effect, they were – as Princess Victoria, the Marchioness of Milford Haven, rather mockingly put it - "princesses of nothing."[5]

In 1917 her eighty-seven-year-old father died and in 1924 her mother aged seventy-seven also passed away. It is unclear what she inherited from her parents as neither of their wills is available to the public. But it is unlikely that she received much money as her father was known to be penniless when he married her mother.[6]

It is known that under the settlement of their mother's estate both daughters were granted a right to use their parents' London residence, Schomberg House, which in due course became their home for the next two decades earning the distinction of being the last house in Pall Mall to be used as a private residence. Sitting at No 78 on the south side of the club-lined avenue, Schomberg House is today an elegant 18th century four-storey mansion with a rich history. After the death in 1719 of its first owner the Duke of Schomberg, it was rented by fashionable artists of the day, most notably Thomas Gainsborough. When two centuries later the two sisters took over the lease, they were keen to continue this artistic tradition and Helena Victoria, an accomplished pianist in her own right, became a patron of music. Her beautiful drawing room which had acoustics to rival those of Covent Garden was used as a private venue for some of the leading singers and instrumentalists of the day. Leon Goosens, regarded as the finest oboist in Europe, often took to the stage and the sisters were able to wallow in their love of the music of Wagner. With more than a suspicion of her own suppressed passion, Marie Louise recounts in her memoirs listening in raptures to the great Wagnerian soprano Frieda Leider singing the Liebestod from Tristan and Isolde.

Of the two sisters Marie Louise was the more artistic and individualistic, once admitting that despite their close attachment they were totally different in temperament.[7] If Helena Victoria was closer to Princess Elizabeth, the reserved and dutiful future queen, Marie Louise was Princess Margaret, the pleasure-seeking younger sister. Like her distant niece, she loved music and liked to surround herself with actors and the show business crowd. The renowned actor-manager Sir Henry Irving was a frequent guest as was his commercial partner and grand dame of the London stage, Ellen Terry. Like Princess Margaret, she enjoyed holidaying in the Caribbean and her wanderlust stretched to trips to South Africa, Rhodesia, Ceylon and Burma. On her journeys across Europe, she pursued her bizarre hobby collecting anything to do with Napoleon: carved ivory figures, bronzes and even snuff boxes. Her habit was in part inspired by her nominal connection with the emperor. As an eleven-year-old boy her father, Prince Christian, had the honour of being the dinner guest of Napoleon's wife Empress Marie-Louise and later - having dined off the story for a decade or more - decided to name his daughter after her.[8]

Like Princess Margaret she had a failed marriage – but in her case it was unconsummated. In July 1891 she wed Prince Aribert of Anhalt, a cousin of the Kaiser Wilhelm II who helped to arrange the match. They managed to stay together for another nine years but the marriage was as joyless as it was childless. In her memoirs she makes no attempt to hide her bitterness about not being wanted by the man she refers to throughout as simply her husband. The final rejection came in a letter from Aribert informing her in a matter of fact fashion that he was a young man and wanted to live his own life. It was rumoured that the prince was homosexual and had been caught in flagrante with a man either by Marie Louise or her father-in-law. What is certain is that he got his father to exercise his sovereign right as Duke of Anhalt to declare the marriage null and void in 1900. Despite this legal fiat, she still regarded her marriage vows as binding. In later life her main male companion was Edward Voules, an openly gay writer who privately published a book about the royal family called "Free of All Malice." It was left to Edward VII to sum up the plight of his niece: "Ach, poor Louise," he is widely reported to have said. "She has returned as she went - a virgin."

The two "spinster" sisters began the Second World War defiantly encamped in Schomberg House. But their home on Pall Mall was dangerously close to government buildings and as the German bombers started to hit their targets, they reluctantly had to move to the relative tranquillity of a friend's house at Englemere near Ascot. It was just as well since soon after moving four incendiary bombs hit Schomberg House and burnt out most of the dining room.

After the war, they moved again into the queen's Berkeley Square flat at 10 Fitzmaurice Place. The fourth floor premises although far from cramped were much less grand than Schomberg House but Helena Victoria was now very frail and confined to a wheel chair. After a spell in her mother's hospital in Windsor, she finally died in the new flat on 13 March 1948 aged seventy-seven. Her funeral was conducted at St George's Chapel Windsor and she was laid to rest in the Royal Burial Ground at Frogmore.

The Times obituary of March 15 records that "her death severs one of the few remaining links with the family life of Queen Victoria whose example of public duty she so worthily followed." Probate was completed two months later on May 28 and an estate duty of £12,437 4s was paid by her executors - her sister and Coutts bank. So why did they decide to fly in the face of royal convention and make the will available to the public?

One obvious explanation is that because she was not a true royal her will was not royal either. As we have seen, in 1917 due to the actions of her uncle George V Helena Victoria had lost not only her geographical designation of Schleswig Holstein but also her royal title, ending her life being known simply as Her Highness. It should be added that George V was so concerned about the great number of descendants from Queen Victoria that he clarified what was meant by royal, decreeing that only the children of the sovereign and the children of the *sons* of the sovereign could be called royal. Hence Princess Margaret was strictly speaking correct when she famously said that "my children are not royal; their aunt just happens to be queen." In accordance with her grandfather's ruling, Lady Sarah Chatto, as the daughter of the Queen's sister, has no title, whereas HRH Princess Beatrice of York, the daughter of the Queen's son, Prince Andrew, has the royal title.

So if one follows this argument losing the HRH title also entailed losing the privilege of having your will kept secret. The only problem with this line of reasoning is that when Helena Victoria's sister, HH Princess Marie Louise, died her will *was* sealed even though she too had lost her royal title. In fact, of the thirty-one sealed royal wills on the Principal Registry's list ten do not have a royal highness title before their name. Even the royal who set the ball rolling in 1910, Prince Francis of Teck, was only his Serene Highness. In normal usage - despite the attempt of George V - the term royal is commonly applied to members of the House of Windsor who are not direct descendants of the sovereign.

So, if losing your royal highness title is no bar to having your will sealed are there any other reasons why Helena Victoria's will slipped through the net? Another plausible explanation is clerical error: the elderly Princess Marie Louise simply forgot to place an order for the will to be sealed. If this indeed had been the case, one would have expected that at a later date the error would have been discovered and her executors would have put in a retrospective application. When the author first discovered on the royal list that Helena Victoria's name had been omitted, he presumed that when he came to request a copy of the will, it would be withheld because the error would have been rectified. But to his surprise, the royal will was delivered to him in the same way as any commoner's will. So, the fact that the will was not resealed at a later date suggests that there was no error and the will was deliberately made open to the public.

If that was indeed the case, why was there such an un-royal-like desire for transparency? Why in this instance did the House of Windsor not want to protect their privacy? One clue lies in the size of the estate - £52,435 - which although not a paltry sum in 1948 was in royal terms relatively modest when you take into account that five years earlier Prince George, the Duke of Kent had left £153,735 and a year before that Prince Arthur, the Duke of Connaught and Strathearn, bequeathed £150,677. Traditionally, one of the alleged reasons why royal wills were hidden was to hide the size of their wealth and to minimize death duties. So, if as in Helena Victoria's case the estate is small and the resultant tax liability is small, then there is much less cause to hide the value and nature of her assets.

A second traditional reason for sealing wills, as we have seen with Prince Francis, was to hide skeletons in the closet - embarrassing mistresses, illegitimate births or details of which offspring got what share of the estate. Since Helena Victoria died unmarried, childless and possibly a virgin, she had no heir whether legitimate or not to whom she could pass on her assets. Moreover, apart from her sister, she had no other surviving close relatives. Both her parents were long dead. Her elder brother, Prince Christian Victor, died childless in 1900. Her other brother, Prince Albert, the titular Duke of Schleswig-Holstein, had died unmarried and heirless in 1931.

One is forced to conclude that because Helena Victoria had few assets - and even fewer relatives to give them to - her executors decided there was nothing to hide and no need to seal her will. Indeed, as we shall see, her executors were forced to look outside her family to find suitable beneficiaries.

But what was actually in the will? The four-page document is dated 23 June 1943 and begins by appointing as both executors and trustees her sister Marie Louise, her banking accountant John England and her solicitor John Nairne although the latter two are replaced by Coutts bank in a codicil dated 10 June 1945. Her first bequest is to her sister. This consists of the bulk of her chattels – including books, furniture, china and jewellery. Her sister was further instructed to make gifts from the chattels to anyone named in a memorandum left with the will or her papers. No memorandum was attached to the will and it is not known whether one was found in her private papers, although it is a well established method for wealthy testators to distribute their possessions without making it public in their wills. It is likely that one of the unnamed beneficiaries was Prince Henry, the Duke of Gloucester as his estate when put up for auction included many personal items of furniture (such as a dressing table and a mahogany stand branded "PRSS H.V") once owned by Helena Victoria. As we shall see later, Princess Diana did something similar with a letter of wishes.

The rest of the will concerns another testamentary vehicle commonly employed by both royalty and the rich - the trust. In clause four, Helena Victoria instructs that all her remaining property be sold and the proceeds placed under the control of the two named trustees. Once the funeral expenses and debts had been paid, all the trust income was to be divided equally between Alexander Arthur Ramsay and Prince Michael of Kent.

As a commoner, Ramsay might be regarded a strange choice. He was the only son of Lady Patricia Ramsay who was Helena Victoria's cousin and whose loss of a royal title mirrored that of the two sisters. She was born Princess Patricia of Connaught, the daughter of Prince Arthur, the Duke of Connaught and Strathearn and the third son of Queen Victoria. Her mother was Princess Louise Margaret of Prussia. With such a royal pedigree and statuesque good looks, everyone expected her to marry into one of the great European families. Her name was linked to Grand Duke Michael of Russia as well as to the future kings of Spain and Portugal. To the horror of crustier courtiers in the House of Windsor, she chose a commoner, Alexander Ramsay, a naval commander and one of her father's aides-de-camp. This was – as The Times diplomatically put it - a complete break with tradition. She had to get special permission to wed from King George V and before the ceremony it was announced that she had relinquished the title of royal highness and taken up the style of Lady Patricia. So, like Helena Victoria, she became technically a non-royal but also like her cousin, she was in de facto terms treated like a member of the royal family being invited to attend all the set-piece royal events like weddings and coronations.

As patron of one of London's leading interwar salons, Helena Victoria would have been naturally drawn to Lady Patricia for artistic reasons. "Patsy" was an honorary member of the Royal Institute of Painters in Watercolours on account of being a gifted semi-professional artist who painted in the advanced style of Gaugin and Van Gogh and who Marie Louise described in her memoirs with a whiff of disapproval as altogether very modern. As patron of various nursing and wartime charities, Helena Victoria would also have taken an interest in the military career of her cousin's only son. After being commissioned into the Grenadier Guards, he fought in the North African campaign during World War Two and was severely injured in a tank assault in Tunisia, losing his right leg. The injury occurred in 1943 at around the time when Helena Victoria was drawing up her will. So, the most likely explanation why she left half of her "royal" wealth to a commoner is that as a naturally caring person with a professional track record of looking after the casualties of war, she would have wanted to help a war casualty in need.

So, why did she leave the other half of her residuary estate to a full-blooded royal? HRH Prince Michael George Charles Franklin was the second son of her cousin Prince George, the Duke of Kent, and Princess Marina. Michael was born on the Coppins family estate in Buckinghamshire on July 4, 1942 - six weeks before the air crash that killed his father and reduced his mother to selling the family silver.

So, the selection by Helena Victoria in her will of Prince Michael as a beneficiary is not really that surprising. It follows the same logic as the choice of her other relative Alexander Ramsay. Both were casualties of the Second World War and both were in need of financial help. When Helena Victoria signed her will on 23 June 1943, baby Michael was less than a year old and his mother was preparing for the auction a few months later to help pay for his upbringing. As the younger son, he would not inherit the title of Duke of Kent (and with it the Coppins estate) and with no family fortune to buttress a royal lifestyle, he would be beset by financial tribulations until well into adulthood with his business ventures. In crude terms, he could do with the cash.

⚜ ⚜ ⚜

As for Princess Marie Louise, she led an altogether more demure life. After the death of her sister, she relinquished any claim to live at Schomberg House and the contents of their home were sold at auction. She took over many of the charitable duties of her sister becoming president of the Canning Town Docklands Settlement and vice president of the YMCA. Despite the absence of a royal title, she was treated like the grand dame of the royal family with the young princess Elizabeth often quizzing her for her memories of past sovereigns.[9] In 1953 she was invited to Elizabeth's coronation - her fourth coronation in all - and photographers captured her almost regal wave from one of the horse-drawn carriages, an image reinforced later in the year in a more staged portrait by Cecil Beaton which shows in the old-fashioned Queen Mary-type pose her wearing a tiara, pearl necklace and fur stool. In 1956 she published her memoirs - "My Memories of Six Reigns" - which soon went into a second edition being lapped up by a public hungry after the coronation for more royal pomp and circumstance.

Its final chapter entitled "The Royal Task" offers an insight into her true character - or at least how she wanted to be perceived in the public imagination - and perhaps also a clue as to why she might have resisted pressure to seal her sister's will. She regarded the royal family and its members not just as some form of figurehead but as servants of the public who through their work could contribute something definite to the nation.[10] This explains why she and her sister devoted their lives to charitable work and also perhaps why when her sister died and left the bulk of her estate to two needy casualties of war she felt no compulsion to hide the fact.

Not all executors of royal estates shared her sense of duty or desire for transparency. When she died in December 1956 she left behind an estate valued at £107,644 11s. It is believed that she bequeathed a pearl and honeycomb bracelet to Queen Elizabeth and a diamond brooch to the Queen Mother[11] as well as a diamond tiara, a collection of ornate fans and a set of candlesticks to the Duke of Gloucester (who liked to send her fresh produce from his farm) but we do not know where the rest of her assets went as her will was sealed. All the official calendar at the Principal Registry records is that the executors were Coutts & co and Augustus Sindon, a retired bank official.

Marie Louise's funeral was a relatively low key affair at St. George's Chapel, Windsor with the congregation including not the cream of European royalty but three pearly queens and a pearly king from Finsbury who wanted to pay tribute to their patron. As a "princess of nothing," she did not merit a full state ceremony. There would be none of the pomp and pageantry that had been accorded the funeral of her more famous cousin, King George, four years earlier but perhaps at the end of the day that better suited her modest character.

Chapter Six
George and Mary's Legacy – 1952-3

"We have lost the rock in our family"
Anonymous member of the royal family on the death of Queen Mary

The weather was as grim as the faces of the mourners thronging the London streets as the cortege carrying the coffin of George VI wound its way through the heavy rain from Westminster Hall to its final destination at Windsor Castle. As the procession crawled into the Mall, Queen Mary's stern profile appeared at the window of Marlborough House. She whispered a last farewell and clasped tightly the hand of her friend Mabell Airlie.[1] The eighty-four-year-old queen watched the rest of the journey ending in her son's internment at St George's Chapel, Windsor Castle from the comfort of her home in front of the television set.

Although she had not felt strong enough to go to the funeral on that wet afternoon of February 15

1952, she had earlier attended his lying-in-state as the coffin was placed on the catafalque in the centre of Westminster Hall. A dramatic photograph captured her heavily veiled face, next to those of her mother and daughter: three queens bound together by their grief in a black shroud. For the third time in her life, the mother of the nation had found herself in the unnatural position of having to bury a son - first John, then George and now "Bertie". Queen Mary never recovered from this last blow. Just as in early 2002 the Queen Mother would only outlive her daughter Princess Margaret by a few weeks, so in 1952 Mary only survived her son by a matter of thirteen months.

Like her grandmother, Princess Margaret took the news badly. "He died as he was getting better" was reportedly her initial shocked response. She had been particularly close to her father - the apple of his eye - deeply loved and dreadfully spoiled. While Elizabeth was shy and young for her age, Margaret was extrovert and precocious. She liked to be centre stage with the family or "us four" as the king called them. A few days after his death she wrote to Queen Mary enclosing all of her and her father's customary Christmas cards, presumably in an attempt to keep her in the bosom of the family, and for months after, all her letters were bordered in mourning black.[2] Many believe that the loss of her father triggered the explosion of her affair with Peter Townsend, a man sixteen years her senior and a former equerry to the king.

George VI's early death was both a great shock and highly predictable. On February 5 he had gone out shooting rabbits on the Sandringham estate bagging a hare running at full pelt with his last shot of the day. After a relaxing evening with Queen Elizabeth and Princess Margaret, he retired to bed at 10.30. When his valet entered the bedroom at 7.30 the next morning, he found the king dead. A blood clot had stopped his heart sometime during the night. He was just fifty-six.

But for some time the king had, in Churchill's words, "been walking with death." Having survived the strains of the Second World War - with the support of too many cigarettes - he was diagnosed in 1948 with arteriosclerosis and then in 1951 with lung cancer. In September of that year his left lung had to be removed following the discovery of a malignant tumour. After that, there was little more his doctors could do.

After the car crash of the previous succession in 1936, wheels were set in motion for a less bumpy ride. It would be a smooth, Rolls Royce handover aided by an experienced driver in the shape of General Sir Frederick Browning, a decorated soldier in two world wars who acted as Princess Elizabeth's personal advisor in much the same way as today Sir David Manning counsels Prince William on affairs of state. The young princess was allowed to see state papers and she began to take on some of the ceremonial duties of her ailing father. She rode in his place at

Trooping the Colour, attended meetings of the Privy Council and welcomed visiting dignitaries. When in October 1951 she flew off on a state visit to Canada, it was significant that hidden under the seat of her private secretary, Martin Charteris, were the historic accession documents.[3] This time, nothing was left to chance.

As was the case with all recent sovereigns, George VI's will was sealed from public view. There was no probate to be granted nor death duties to be paid. The Royal Rich Report gives a figure of £20 million for his estate but offers no indication of how they came by this estimate. If at all accurate, it seems remarkably low - even allowing for the fact that this sum would not include all the inalienable Crown property: the official palaces, the Royal Collection and the Crown Jewels. But some sources close to the palace suggest that George VI was not as cash rich as many suspected. They point out that since he was never Prince of Wales, he was in stark contrast to Edward VII and Edward VIII unable to build up a financial nest egg from the Duchy of Cornwall revenues which go to the heir to the throne. Andrew Roberts, the historian and erstwhile luncheon guest of royals, has written that the Queen Mother regarded herself as relatively badly off. She told him at one of Woodrow Wyatt's lunches that "the King had to buy out the Duke of Windsor at the time of the abdication.... It left us terribly short but otherwise we couldn't have had Balmoral and Sandringham."[4] This is given credence by a royal courtier who is quoted by his biographer Sarah Bradford as saying that the pay-off had left them with virtually nothing.[5] Roberts goes on to suggest that Queen Elizabeth "inherited relatively little cash from her father in 1952." This could well be true in terms of a liquid or cash bequest although it should be remembered that the king had in the thirties set up a trust fund for both his daughters from savings made from the Civil List. As part of the post-abdication settlement he was also exempted from paying income tax.[6]

King George VI could afford to put money aside for his children because he shunned a lavish lifestyle. His one indulgence was shooting on his beloved Sandringham marshes or out on the grouse moors near Balmoral castle. With little interest in the arts, he showed no desire to add to his collection of paintings (he did collect stamps but not on the same scale as his father who amassed one of the greatest collections of Commonwealth stamps). He was – in the view of one biographer – at heart a "private shy man" who was reliant on his immediate family for "happiness and support."[7] Some accused him of lacking imagination and being slow-witted but it is possible that he saw how his two brothers had wrecked their lives through high living and decided instead to tread a simpler path. At the end of the day, the most valuable thing he bequeathed Queen Elizabeth may have been his frugality.

Today the Queen is known for her down to earth approach to jewellery, wearing the same family jewels repeatedly and unlike her grandmother, buying very few new items. Nevertheless she did receive from her father an immensely valuable collection of private jewels. Some would have come through his estate (of which we know little) but others were gifted to her well before his death (of which there is some limited record). As photographs clearly show, the nine-month-old princess was given a string of pink coral pearls by her parents just before they departed on a long royal tour of Australia and New Zealand. Twenty years later, on her wedding day they gave her a double string of pearls as well as a pair of chandelier diamond earrings.[8] It should be remembered that the king also gifted Princess Margaret many valuable jewels at similar rites of passage dates in her early life.

When it comes to landed property, we know for certain that King George bequeathed to Elizabeth his two private estates of Balmoral and Sandringham. Their precise value in 1952 is not known but given that they were valued at £300,000 in 1937 the figure is likely to have been well in advance of half a million pounds. It is probable that he bequeathed the bulk of his wealth to the future queen (including his father's stamp collection worth several millions pounds), although he would have been expected to pass on a few family heirlooms to Princess Margaret and his widow, Queen Elizabeth.

It is unlikely, however, that King George would have bequeathed any valuable heirlooms to his mother, Queen Mary who at the time of his death was eighty-five years old and in deteriorating health. After his funeral, she spoke for almost the first time of her own mortality, admitting to a close friend that she must compel herself to keep on going to the bitter end.[9] She put her last weeks to good use by doing everything in her power to ensure a smooth succession.

One urgent thing she needed to do was rewrite her will. She had done this twice before - after the death of her husband, George V, in January 1936, and after the abdication of her eldest son, Edward VIII, in December 1936. Now, she had to decide who was to replace her Bertie as the beneficiary of what she termed her interesting things. Highly practical to the end and without any hint of morbidity, she set aside days in March and April of 1953 to work on the catalogues of her many possessions and trace different family connections. She was determined that her death should leave behind it no remnant of ambiguity or confusion.[10]

"Mama" tough but failing was how the Duke of Windsor characterised his mother at his brother's funeral and over the next twelve months her health steadily declined.[11] She fell ill in April and was consigned to her bed for five weeks. By the summer she was well enough to go to Sandringham but by the time she returned there in winter her days were numbered. She told her friends she did not want to go on living as an old crock. In February she began suffering severe abdominal pains and for the next three weeks took to her bed in Marlborough House where she managed to hang on in considerable pain and barely conscious. She finally died on 24 March 1953, aged eighty-five.

Her passing marked the end of an era. Some compared it to the disappearance of a national monument, while her biographer described the nation as mourning the unique.[12] To the diarist Chips Channon she was "above politics, a kind of Olympian Goddess… her appearance was formidable, her manner - well, it was like talking to St. Paul's Cathedral"[13] but within the House of Windsor, the overriding mood was best summed up by one unnamed relative: they had lost the rock in the family.[14]

Queen Mary, of course, always had a soft spot for rocks. Uncharitable voices suggested she showed more passion for her jewellery collection than her close family. A simple hobby turned into an obsession that dominated her life. It was estimated that she had assembled at the time "a greater collection of priceless jewellery than any previous queen of England."[15] Yet in her early years her family was on its uppers and she lived from hand to mouth due to the generosity of her fellow minor European royals.

So, how did an impecunious and imperfectly royal princess come to possess one of the richest jewel boxes in history?

From the outset it is important to point out that the vast majority of her valuable jewels came to her relatively late in life and not from her immediate family. Her father, his Serene Highness Prince Franz, Duke of Teck, had neither wealth nor pure royal blood. He may have married the granddaughter of George III and first cousin of Queen Victoria, the statuesque (not to say monumental) fifteen-stone Princess Marie Adelaide of Cambridge, but his personal royal credentials were tainted by the morganatic marriage of his father to a Hungarian countess. As a result he lost any claim to be heir to the principality of Wuerttemberg - and with it any inheritance. This did not stop him from aspiring to a royal lifestyle. He kept residences at Kensington Palace and at White Lodge in Richmond Park and ran up large bills catering to the expensive tastes of his wife and growing family. On many occasions he had to be bailed out by his in-laws, the Cambridge family, but when the debts reached astronomical heights, royal generosity began to ebb away. Even Queen Victoria decided enough was enough.

Heavily in the red, the family was forced to depart London court life in 1883 and lead a more modest existence in a rent-free villa in Florence. There the sixteen-year-old princess developed her taste for precious objects, visiting every day the Pitti Palace and marvelling at the Titians, Van Dycks and Raphaels. She frequented other art galleries and churches and with her parents' encouragement took painting lessons, learnt Italian and perfected her German. When not in Italy, she often stayed by the Swiss lakes or with her German cousins in Wuerttenberg. Thanks to this peripatetic childhood, she was better educated and more cultured than many of her royal contemporaries, some of whom may not have taken kindly to her superior airs. Her early financial instability must also have taught her the importance of acquiring wealthy possessions.

On her marriage to Prince George in 1893, she received a cascade of wedding gifts worth £300,000, including a diamond brooch from her friend Alice de Rothschild. At the ceremony she wore a diamond riviere given to her by the Prince of Wales. The death of her mother in 1897 and her brother in 1910 brought her more diamonds and some of the Cambridge emeralds but these family heirlooms had as much sentimental as monetary value. She had also inherited from her mother ("fat Mary") her statuesque looks (without, thankfully, the weight). In the eyes of many her fuller figure and perfectly proportioned neck and shoulders made her well suited to the wearing of jewels - particularly when she was dressed *à la décolleté*. In France, she acquired the nickname "*soutien-Georges*" - a play on words for her support for George V and the French term for bra (*soutien gorge*). She also had to wear dresses with a reinforced lining to accommodate the extra weight from the jewels.

Her first major acquisition of jewellery came in the aftermath of the Boer War. As a token of their loyalty to the crown, the people of the Transvaal gave Edward VII cleavings (or chips) from the Cullinan Diamond, the largest diamond in the world that had been discovered by a mineworker in 1905. Just before the king's death in 1910, the South African government gave the future Queen Mary one hundred and two cleavings from the diamond. She turned Cullinan III and IV - known as the Lesser Stars of Africa - into a spectacular brooch which is today Crown property and the most valuable jewel owned by the Queen. She later set Cullinan VII into another brooch and Cullinan IX into a claw ring.[16] With typical royal understatement her younger relatives always referred to these magnificent jewels as "Granny's chips". They are thought to be worth £29 million.

More gifts from the empire flooded in after the coronation. In December 1911 she was acclaimed Empress of India before tens of thousands at the Delhi Durbar and presented with the finest gems from the Maharajahs' palaces. The most valuable probably came from the Maharani of Patiala who gave her a magnificent set of emerald necklaces, pendants and brooches.

The death of Queen Alexandra in November 1925 brought further riches. As we saw earlier, she died intestate and a quarter share of her personal jewellery passed to Mary and George V. They picked out several royal pieces given to Alexandra on her wedding to the future Edward VII in 1863 and a few bequests from Queen Victoria in 1901. It is known that Mary acquired two expensive wedding presents - the Dagmar Necklace, an historic Danish jewel, and a valuable diamond necklace presented by the City of London. As for the state property, she also inherited some of the remaining Cullinan diamonds that Edward VII had given to Alexandra.

It was Alexandra's unruly younger sister, the mischievous "Minnie" described in Chapter Two, who was to be responsible for Queen Mary's biggest windfall – the fabled Romanov jewels. The daughter of King Christian IX of Denmark, she married Tsar Alexander III of Russia in 1866 and took up the title Empress Marie Feodorovna of all Russias. Her son Tsar Nicholas and his family died at the hands of the Bolshevik revolutionaries at Ekaterinburg in 1918 but she was protected by White Russian soldiers in Crimea and on the urging of her sister and with the help of a gunboat sent by King George V, she managed to escape to the west, eventually ending up in her native Denmark. She bought with her a large leather jewellery case containing some of the finest gems in the world: ropes of pearls the size of cherries, globular cabochon emeralds, deep blue sapphires and a fistful of large rubies.

George V tried to take control of his aunt's finances as well as the jewels that had been valued at half a million pounds. He granted an annual pension of £30,000 for the empress and her daughter Grand Duchess Olga to live in the luxury they were accustomed to in their Copenhagen Palace and provided a further stipend of £2,400 a year and a grace-and-favour cottage in Windsor Great Park to her other daughter Grand Duchess Xenia who had earlier lost £20,000 worth of her personal Romanov jewels to a conman. When the empress finally died in October 1928, the king decided that her collection of jewellery should be sent to Buckingham Palace for safe keeping.

Once all the family had been reunited in London, it was agreed that the gems should be sold discreetly so as not to flood the market and the money put in a trust for the two grand duchesses. The royal jewellers Hennell and Sons valued all the items and eventually sold them for a reported sum of £350,000. What was not known in court circles at the time - when all attention was directed on the ailing King George who had earlier promised to organise the sale - is that Queen Mary had an inside track in the process. Back in 1921 she had managed to buy a diamond tiara from Grand Duchess Vladimir and now she had the pick of the Romanov jewels for herself - including the empress's stunning sapphire brooch surrounded by two rows of diamonds with a pearl drop. "She bagged all the best," was how the socialite Lady Pamela Berry summed up the selection process in which the two duchesses also participated. Later it was also questioned whether she had actually paid the full valuation price.[17]

A clearer picture only emerged in the mid-sixties after the publication of the memoirs of the Grand Duchess Olga which alleged that she and her sister,

Xenia, had received a fraction of the money from the jewels. Further investigations strongly suggested that just £100,000 of the reported £350,000 figure had been paid of which £40,000 went to Olga and the rest to Xenia. It also emerged that Mary herself had paid a mere £60,000. In her defence it was argued that some of the jewels were not sold until 1933 by which time the world recession had depressed gem prices and some of the missing £250,000 could be explained by her husband recouping the considerable financial support he had given to the empress and her family. If this had indeed happened, no one told the Grand Duchess Olga or her two surviving sons - Guri and Tikhon - who demanded an explanation from Buckingham Palace. A team of lawyers was engaged to sift through the documentation and weigh up the competing arguments. In 1968, according to the jewellery expert Suzy Menkes who after the death of Guri was in close contact with Tikhon, any outstanding debts were finally settled.[18]

But how could Mary have afforded to buy the Romanov jewels in the first place? Although she did not pay the full price, she still had to find £60,000 – a significant amount in anyone's money. It has been suggested that due to illness George V was not fully aware of what his wife was up to. It is true that the removal of a near fatal abscess on the king's lung forced him to take a six-month convalescence in Bognor in 1929, but overall he was clearly mindful of his wife's passion for collecting. Even Mary's official biographer - who glosses over any mention of the Romanov jewels - admits that her collecting was an interest of which he did not disapprove.[19] In fact, on many occasions the king added to her collection of jewels - beginning with a diamond anchor before their wedding in 1893 and more recently giving her for Christmas 1928 a stunning topaz and diamond pendant.

So, how could George himself afford to fund his wife's hobby? At the start of his reign his finances were in a fragile state with the sprawling Sandringham House, farm and its stables haemorrhaging £50,000 a year. On the advice of friends in the countryside, the estate was reorganised and following the counsel of some city contacts his investment portfolio was put on a surer footing. By 1935 the annual losses of the farms at Sandringham, Balmoral and Windsor had been reduced to £12,650 a year.[20]

But the biggest bonus came from changes to his Civil List payments. In 1910 he managed to persuade the Treasury that for the first time they should be tax exempt. This important concession allowed him to accumulate money for his own personal use that had been allocated not just for his Privy Purse but for the general running of the Royal Household. According to Treasury figures, he saved £643,133 gross (on average £25,725 per annum) from the Civil List in the first 25 years of his reign.[21] As one Treasury mandarin observed wryly, "King George was a very careful person in money matters."

As we saw in Chapter One, he did not let the exigencies of World War One get in the way of picking up bargains for his stamp collection – on several occasions enlisting the support of the Foreign and War Offices to track down rare specimens in territories captured by British forces. During the fighting he also snapped up the prized stamp collection of the Earl of Crawford for a modest price (and many of these items were sold at auction in 2001 for £625,000).[22] He benefited from the fact that his passion for collecting stamps was known throughout the empire and even though he claimed not to accept unsolicited gifts (unless official presents), he was prepared to make exceptions, as in the case of the rare stamps from St Vincent sent to him by a Mr H Vaux in the West Indies. In 1911 at the Coronation Durbar he had the opportunity to add to the collection when after being asked whether he wanted a souvenir of the occasion, he said he would like to visit the archives of the Postal Department. According to the story told by Sir John Wilson, the Keeper of the Royal Philatelic Collection in the 1930s, he spent a fair amount of time there with a pair of scissors and as a result there are now items in the Royal Collection that are not represented in Delhi.[23]

Apart from his stamp collecting and shooting, the king spent relatively little on himself. He bought his furniture from Maples on the Tottenham Court Road and hung on his walls reproductions from the Royal Academy. Diffident by nature and distasteful of public ceremony, he shunned the smart set and what he called the intellectual "eyebrows", rarely going out to private parties and entertaining little at home. A typical evening would see the king dining alone with his wife - although for the sake of appearances she always wore a tiara.

While George waged his war on the twentieth century (as the Duke of Windsor memorably put it), Mary fought hers on waste. In the eyes of her relatives, she was famous for being generous in spirit but exceedingly mean about money.[24] On one occasion when she moved out of Buckingham Palace to Marlborough House, she took with her all the silk wall coverings from two sitting rooms - at a cost of £550 to the public purse. From her childhood in Florence she learned the importance of making economies and she extended this to her collecting. If a beautiful item took her fancy when visiting relatives or friends at their country home, she would drop a none too subtle hint that they might wish to sell it to her at a discounted price or even give it to her for free. Other acquaintances would be drafted in to act as "spotters" or "shoppers" in her quest for jewels and antiques.

By now she had got the itch for collecting antique furniture. She regularly called on *antiquaires* and even in her later, frailer years, she would often visit the top London showrooms and dealers. Sometimes she acquired furniture simply through inheritance. When Lord Farquhar, the wealthy banker and steward of the royal household, died in August 1923 he left her the complete contents of his home at White Lodge along with a Louis XVI commode.

One of the great ironies of the queen's obsession with jewels is that she had so little occasion to show them off. In part this explains why she was reduced to wearing them while dining alone with her husband. Allergic to long distance travel, the king managed in the interwar years just two state visits abroad, visiting fellow sovereigns in Belgium and Italy, while at home he kept state pageantry to a minimum. His wife had many more jewels than she could ever hope to wear and so most of the time they remained locked away in the store room at Buckingham Palace. She spent hours cataloguing all her collection and writing labels on the jewels. Often she gave them personal names like the "Surrey" tiara, the "Kensington" bow brooch and the "City" collar.

It has been suggested that her collecting - particularly in later life - became a displacement activity for her children. Unable to show overt love for her offspring, she poured her passion into her jewels. One of Prince Charles's earliest memories is visiting his great grandmother ("Gan Gan") in Marlborough House and not being allowed to touch her priceless collection of jade that was displayed around the room in cabinets.[25] It has also been argued that her collecting was a form of revenge against more snobbish relatives who looked down on her imperfect royalty. In a sense, she found true regality in her royal jewels. But perhaps the real roots of her mania go back to her childhood and the penury of her parents. She once let slip that her interest in fine objects came from her aesthetically-inclined father – who sadly was poor and did not have the means to buy them.[26]

When she died in March 1953, Mary was regarded as the richest royal, with a fortune estimated at £3 million. Bearing in mind her fabulous treasure trove of jewels, this might seem an undervaluation. But when probate was finally granted in August 1953 following the sealing of her will, her estate was valued at just £406,407 9s 8d. In principle if it had been treated as a normal private estate falling in the band of £300,000-£500,000 it would have been liable to death duties at a rate of up to 60% leaving a tax bill of around £240,000 - although if her estate had been valued at £3 million, it would have fallen into the higher band rate of 80% leaving a liability in the order of £2,400,000 - a difference of a neat £2 million.

Any attempt to answer the question what happened to her "missing millions" must first distinguish between crown property and personal property. Obviously the crown jewels as inalienable property would not have been included in her personal estate - most would have passed to Queen Elizabeth (the consort of George VI) in 1936 after the abdication of Edward VIII. But the wider category of crown jewellery (including gems given as public gifts or through official bequests) is less easy to pin down. "It's a grey area," admitted Dickie Arbiter, the former palace press secretary. But the writer Leslie Field who had access to the Royal Archives for her book "The Queen's Jewels" believes that Mary left a list to the present queen cataloguing which jewels belonged to the crown for perpetuity and which were family heirlooms[27] and Sir Hugh Roberts, the former director of the Royal Collection, has indeed viewed an unpublished inventory of Mary's jewels.[28] As gifts presented to the crown, the Cullinan diamond from the Transvaal and the Ladies of India emerald necklace from the Delhi Durbar were both classified state property, whereas the Vladimir diamond and pearl tiara which was bought with Mary's own money would have been deemed private property.

But tracing Mary's missing millions is complicated by her tendency to recycle and shape shift her jewels. She loved to acquire one piece and convert it into something else. For instance, she took the large sapphire which was the centrepiece of the diamond tiara bought from Empress Marie Feodorovna's estate and turned it into a separate brooch. She gave this to Princess Margaret and the stripped-down tiara to Princess Alice. The accompanying diamond chain link necklace in the collection was further divided into two bracelets.

Sometimes she converted raw gems into finished pieces. When she visited South Africa in 1901 as part of an official tour of the empire, De Beers presented her with a magnificent cache of diamonds. On her return to England, she turned some of the gems into an ornate tiara with a diamond set in each of the seven arches, although when she later became queen she never wore it and it disappeared into the vaults of Buckingham Palace. Similarly, she reportedly turned the Cambridge emeralds inherited from her mother into a delicate choker and late reworked it (possibly with the addition of some of the Romanov emeralds) into a fashionable Art Deco design.[29] As a result of this shape shifting, on some occasions private gifts might become crown property and on others "state gifts" might become private property. Whichever way they went, the effect would be to muddy the waters of provenance.

Mary in her will, according to Elizabeth II's biographer, left the bulk of her estate to the Queen.[30] This of course ignores what she gave her before her death which in part may explain the low probate valuation. We know that on Princess Elizabeth's marriage to Prince Philip in November 1947 she gave her twenty-five wedding gifts including furniture, silver salvers and nine pieces of jewellery.[31] One of the most valuable pieces was Elizabeth's first tiara (the so-called "granny's tiara") which had been made from the De Beers diamonds given to Mary in South Africa. Two other items were gifts Mary had received on her own marriage in 1893: a pair of pearl button earrings and a ruby and diamond pendant. She also gave her the Duchess of Teck's corsage brooch, the Rose of York ruby bracelet and two diamond studded Indian bangle bracelets that she had been given in India in 1907.[32]

ROYAL LEGACY

The wedding gift seemed a favourite transmission belt by which Mary passed on her jewels to her family and avoided death duties. When her fourth son, Prince George, the Duke of Kent, married Princess Marina in November 1934 she gave the couple a pearl and diamond choker and an antique sapphire and diamond parure. When her third son, Prince Henry, Duke of Gloucester, married Lady Alice Montague Douglas Scott in 1935, a similar hoard of jewels was passed on. This time the parure of matching jewellery was made of turquoise and the rest of the gem case consisted of two necklaces of Indian pearl and emerald, two wide diamond and emerald bracelets, a baroque pearl brooch and a pair of diamond stud earrings. In the years after the wedding, Prince Henry's family were to receive many other gifts - not just jewels, but silver and furniture - from his mother. Henry had become a serious collector of antiques (see Chapter Sixteen) and Mary obviously saw him as a chip off the old block.

We are able to get some indication of the scale of the transfer thanks to an auction in January 2006 of some of the late Duke of Gloucester's possessions. When it comes to the provenance records, Mary's name dominates. The auction also allows us to put a price on the items - the twenty-one lots once owned by Queen Mary fetched £137,580, the two most expensive items each went for £31,200. One was a late 19th century French rosewood table which was branded on the underside with the queen's initial "M" next to a crown. The other was a Victorian Silver cup and cover which had been given as a christening present to Prince Henry's son William in 1942, with a card from her godmother, Her Majesty Queen Mary.[33]

Most of the gifts were given at key rites of passage such as a christening or confirmation. The latter had always been a significant date for Queen Mary because when she was growing up in the late 19th century you could not be presented at court or come out in society until you had been confirmed and the occasion was normally accompanied by the giving of jewellery and other presents by senior members of the family. The seventeen-year-old Mary had been given precious gems by her uncle and grandmother.

Prince William of Gloucester's confirmation present was a George V Silver Tray (worth £7,800 today) made in 1912 and owned by his godmother and grandmother, Queen Mary. Of the twenty-one lots, silverware was the favourite gift, accounting for seventeen items ranging from a set of silver dessert spoons (£660) and a silver sauce ladle (£1,920) to a silver coffee set (£6,000) and a silver basket (£13,200). The four remaining items were furniture or household goods - including a gilt wood stand (£2,880) and a maple oak chest (£4,560).

The later Christie's auction of Princess Margaret's possessions also revealed another destination for Mary's missing millions. As we shall see in more detail in Chapter Eleven, her granddaughter received £782,000 worth of gifts at birthdays, Christmases and confirmation. These were only the presents that were put up for auction. We know that she also received from Mary the sapphire from the Romanov tiara but it is likely that there were other valuable items given by her grandmother that were never publicly disclosed.

It would be simplistic to assume that Mary's gift making was driven by a single motive. As a generous matriarch she would have wanted to provide for her children and grandchildren and as an upholder of royal tradition she would have thought it appropriate to pass on jewels and precious objects to them at key family milestones. But as someone who was financially astute from an early age, she would also have been aware of how her fortune could be eaten away by death duties. In all likelihood she would have taken financial advice on the subject and it is notable that the man she chose as her executor, Lord Claud Hamilton, would have known many of the financial hazards having been Comptroller and Treasurer in her household for twenty years. The other executor, Charles Vivian, Lord Tryon, had also learned the financial ropes as Keeper of the Privy Purse and Treasurer to the Queen. It is believed that Mary may have set up trust funds for some of her close relatives: Princess Marina certainly received an annuity from her and the Queen Mother may also have been a beneficiary of her largesse.

Mary found other discreet ways of disposing of her valuables. Well before her own death, she gave to the London Museum all the mourning jewellery she had collected over the years. This included not just personal items such the Prince Francis brooch carved in memory of her dead brother but all the black royal jewels that the widowed Queen Victoria had amassed and the jet diadems that her mother, the Duchess of Teck, had helped acquire for Princess Alexandra after the passing of Edward VII.

On the whole, however, Mary preferred to keep the valuables in the family rather than give them to outsiders. Even her exiled son, the Duke of Windsor, was remembered with a several boxes and a set of candlesticks. When more details of her will leaked out, one friend was shocked that she had left nothing to her faithful lady-in-waiting, Lady Cynthia Colville. But this was normal behaviour for royals. Even Princess Diana left no cash bequests in her will for friends or charities. Her butler, Paul Burrell, gives an interesting insight into how Queen Mary's estate may have been divided amongst her family. In the aftermath of the death of Diana when all her personal property had to be listed, he claims that the Queen told him that when a royal passed away there was often a tendency to earmark personal items before they disappeared. She recalled that when her grandmother died she went across to Marlborough House and found stickers on everything. They had all descended on Mary's personal possessions like vultures.[34]

One thing we know for sure about Mary's will is that it included clear instructions about what should happen if she died before the coronation of Queen Elizabeth. In such an eventuality, mourning for her should be kept to a minimum so as not to disrupt the big day. Her wishes were faithfully followed and ten weeks after her death, there were street parties up and down the land to celebrate her granddaughter's succession to the throne.

In death as in life little was left to chance. There would be a seamless succession. Not for nothing did Prime Minister Winston Churchill in his parliamentary tribute call Queen Mary "practical in all things."

CHAPTER SEVEN
THE DUCHESS AND THE COUNTESS – 1960-1968

"Like so many wealthy people, particularly those of royal blood, he [Lord Mountbatten] was always convinced he was poor"
Brian Hoey, biographer of Lord Mountbatten[1]

On her death Queen Mary left her daughter-in-law, Marina, Duchess of Kent, a small personal allowance to supplement some of the fabulous Romanov jewels she had given her earlier as a wedding present. These were the sapphires and diamonds that she had bought in 1921 from the estate of Marina's grandmother Grand Duchess Vladimir, the daughter-in-law of the Tsar.

It was a welcome windfall. A widow at thirty-five with three young children, Princess Marina was still struggling to make ends meet. Despite a new £5,000 annuity from the recently crowned Queen Elizabeth, she was seriously strapped for cash and having to rely on the thrifty habits (including the ability to make her own clothes) learned as an impoverished exiled Greek princess in Paris in the 1920s. She cut staff wages to the bone (causing one bitter former employee to lambast her as "a beautiful and spoilt woman"), borrowed dresses from fashionable designers for one evening's wear only and even recycled floral gifts.[2] Her butler (who was paid a mere £225 a year) tells the story of how on receiving a bouquet of red roses from her friend the conductor Sir Malcolm Sargent, she substituted the card with one in her own name and forwarded the flowers to Princess Marie Louise.[3]

In the end she was obliged to auction some of her Russian heirlooms. In June 1962 a few pieces by Faberge and other *objets d'art* went under the hammer to realise a much-needed £12,426 bonus to the household purse. By this time she had vacated the Coppins country home in Buckinghamshire for her newly married son Prince Edward and daughter-in-law Katharine and moved into a grace-and-favour apartment at No 1 Kensington Palace. She was now benefiting from financial guidance from Philip Hay, her former Private Secretary who became Comptroller of her finances, confidant and ultimately her lover. A friend of the family described him as "the pivot of her life" - although he remained married to Margaret, a former lady-in-waiting to Princess Elizabeth, with whom he had three sons.[4] Reliably discreet, he was on hand to give emotional support to a widow at thirty-five who never remarried despite retaining her good looks and attracting many suitors from the world of show business, including the comedian Danny Kaye. During his twenty years of service, the Harrow-educated courtier also acted as a much-needed financial advisor to her son, Prince Michael, and dutifully accompanied her on long and tiring royal tours of South-East Asia and South America. He had many of the hallmarks of a royal consort, his stately bearing was - in the eyes of Marina's butler - reminiscent of the Duke of Windsor.[5]

Over time Marina began to acquire a significant international profile based on her work for the Commonwealth. In 1957 she represented the Queen at the independence celebrations in Ghana and then in 1966 she performed the same role when Botswana and Lesotho became independent. As a travelling ambassadress she enjoyed a more affluent lifestyle abroad - on one tour of Canada she was accompanied (much to the derision of some members of the press pack) by two ladies-in-waiting, one aide-de-camp, three maids and one secretary.[6] At home, she had to make to do with a butler, sub-butler, head housemaid, two ladies maids and three housemaids. They took personal pride, according to one staff member, in helping her "dress to kill" and present a glamorous image to the outside world. Wearing her hat as President of the All England Lawn Tennis Club, she became known to television viewers round the world as the duchess who handed out the silverware at the end of Wimbledon fortnight. In July 1968 she presented Billie Jean King with the women's plate for winning the singles final.

In the same summer Marina started to notice a weakening in her left leg. She had long had a limp caused by a birth defect which left one leg slightly shorter and thinner than the other but recently she had begun to lose her balance and stumble in a more troubling way. After being admitted to hospital for tests, she was diagnosed on July 18 with an inoperable brain tumour and her children were told that she had six months to live, although *she* was not informed of the seriousness of her condition. After a visit for tea on July 25, Noel Coward wrote in his diary how shocked he was about her deteriorating condition.[7] By now she had returned to her Kensington Palace home where on August 26 she had a fall in her bathroom, cracked her head and sank into a coma. She died the next morning at 11.40 with her doctors at the bedside. She was just sixty-one. Following a private funeral attended by royalty from all the great European houses, she was buried on August 30 next to Prince George in the royal plot at Frogmore.

On October 17 it was announced that she had left an estate with a gross value of £54,121 which after tax and debts was reduced to £17,398. One biographer described it as "one of the smallest fortunes" ever left by a member of the royal family.[8] Another argued that it proved to any who doubted it that Marina "had not been as rich" as her position might lead one to predict.[9]

Although Marina was not flush with cash, she was hardly leading a life of penury in her palace apartment surrounded by antique furniture and fine art. Her silver safe, according to her butler, was chock a block with jewellery and jade work, as well as the more usual tableware.[10] She had a circle of affluent and famous friends - including Cecil Beaton, Frederick Ashton and Douglas Fairbanks Jr - and enjoyed travelling to official engagements in her blue Rolls-Royce and sometimes by helicopter.

Noel Coward had been a friend since 1923 when she and Prince George met him backstage after a performance of the play "London Calling" and following the death of her husband he often acted as a chaperone on visits to the races or theatrical and film premieres. She still cut a glamorous figure with her elegant clothes and stunning jewels. At one glittering first night with Coward, on hearing a familiar drum roll begin to rumble they both stood up for the national anthem and all the audience dutifully followed their cue only to discover after a minute or two that the music was in fact the overture to that evening's entertainment. The two sat down sheepishly trying in vain to stifle a fit of giggles.

But in an echo of Queen Mary there remains the mystery of what happened to her family jewellery - and in particular the Romanov jewels which she inherited not just from her mother-in-law but also her own mother, Princess Nicholas, daughter of Grand Duchess Vladimir of Russia - and which given their great monetary value could clearly not all have been included in her small estate. The only explanation for their absence is that despite the suddenness of her death she had the foresight to gift them during her lifetime to her three children: Prince Edward, Prince Michael and Princess Alexandra. According to one authority on royal jewellery, Suzy Menkes, she is believed to have followed the Greek tradition of leaving jewels to her sons rather than daughter on the basis that sons of the family have wives to support,[11] although another jewellery expert, Leslie Field, suggests that Alexandra may have received a diamond necklace, an emerald brooch and other gems from her mother's jewel box.[12]

For all her outward show of informality and sense of fun, Marina was at heart a blue-blooded duchess of the old school, a dedicated upholder of royal tradition. She could never approve of her brother-in-law marrying a twice divorcée like Mrs. Simpson and refused to visit the couple after their wedding, earning her the lasting mistrust of the Duke of Windsor. Even the wife of her other brother-in-law, Elizabeth Bowes-Lyon (the later Queen Mother) was famously dismissed as "that common little Scottish girl" on account of her lack of royal pedigree. She is also thought to have harboured reservations about her son Prince Edward, the Duke of Kent, marrying Katharine Worsley, a commoner (although well-born) and therefore insufficiently schooled in Windsor protocol.

If Marina was in need of advice on how to dispose of her precious possessions in the most appropriate fashion, she may well have turned to her loyal courtier Sir Philip Hay who had been knighted in 1961 and served from 1962 as Treasurer to the Duke and Duchess of Kent. A fellow stickler for protocol and a highly cultivated man, he had worked in the picture department of the auctioneers Spinks before he joined her household and would later be appointed a director of Sotheby's. Left in a state of utter misery by her death, he was given the unenviable task of putting her papers and belongings in order and closing down her apartment at Kensington Palace.

Despite the fact that her will was sealed, it is now widely believed that the bulk of her estate went to her eldest son Edward, the Duke of Kent. One valuation of his inherited wealth estimated that he owned £10.25 million worth of jewellery and heirlooms - of which some may have come from his father, but much must been passed on by his mother.[13] His wife, Katharine, has been identified wearing one of the most stunning of the Romanov jewels - a pair of antique diamond chandelier earrings that had once belonged to the Grand Duchess Vladimir. The Duchess of Kent has also been seen sporting a magnificent diamond necklace that had been George V's wedding gift to Marina, a diamond bandeau tiara that Queen Mary gave to Marina and a pearl and diamond pendant brooch once owned by Marina.

Some of Marina's other jewellery was left to Prince Michael of Kent. Although he was unmarried at the time of her death, it is believed that she made provision for his future wife. Princess Michael of Kent whom he wed in 1978 is known to possess a large oval diamond brooch which was bought by Queen Mary in 1929 from the estate of the Dowager Empress of Russia and given to Marina, a diamond and emerald three-leaf brooch - again given by Mary to Marina - and a favourite ring of Marina's featuring a large pearl and cluster of diamonds.

Asset-rich but cash-poor, the Kents have long been regarded as the "poor relations" of the House of Windsor. Unable to afford its huge maintenance costs on his army pay of £3,000 a year the Duke of Kent was forced in 1974 to sell the Coppins, his parents' family home, to the businessman Eli Gottlieb, for £400,000. For no doubt similar financial reasons in 2006 his brother Prince Michael sold his country home in Gloucestershire, Nether Lypiatt Manor, for £5.75 million. At the time, Princess Michael famously told a reporter: 'For the first time that terrible word came into my life when our private secretary said, "Ma'am, you have to downsize." It was the worst word I'd heard in ages.'"[14]

Their London residence also became a financial burden. Around this time the peppercorn rent of £69 a week on their five bedroom apartment in Kensington Palace was raised to a real market rate of £120,000 a year.[15] With no money available from the

Civil List, Prince Michael was obliged to earn his own living, setting up a business and public relations consultancy, Cantium Services, which earned him criticism for trading on his royal name but no sustainable income. In November 2009 both brothers decided to auction at Christie's in London some two hundred family heirlooms that once belonged to their parents. The sale realised £2.1 million including £187,000 paid for the highest priced item, a pair of mahogany hall benches dating to the reign of George III. A few minor pieces of jewellery went under the hammer - including a Victorian diamond brooch and a torque necklace - but significantly nothing from Princess Marina's valuable collection of Romanov gems.

So, at least as far as jewellery is concerned, the secrecy of her estate was preserved. But the Duke of Kent could have opted for transparency. As executor of her estate, he was equally entitled *not to* apply to the family courts to seal her will. To understand better this alternative avenue, it might be useful to compare Marina's estate with that of Edwina, the Countess Mountbatten and wife of Earl Mountbatten of Burma.

At first sight, the parallels are remarkable. Both were great beauties who married into the British royal family. Both were disliked by the matriarch of that family, the Queen Mother, who dismissed Edwina as a bit of "a rake" and, according to Cecil Beaton, hated Marina – at least until her death.[16] Both became close friends of Noel Coward and Douglas Fairbanks Jr.

and both died suddenly in the 1960s within a year of their sixtieth birthday.

The differences, however, lie in the scale of their wealth and how they handled it. One was exceedingly rich and a spendthrift, the other relatively poor and thrifty. But the one who had had every reason to hide her huge wealth decided not to do so and in due course had to pay a small fortune in tax. In short, it shows what can happen if you turn your back on estate planning.

When the Rt Hon Edwina, Countess Mountbatten of Burma, died on 21 February 1960 in the town of Jesselton on an official visit to British North Borneo, she left behind an estate of £589,655 and after a massive £335,153 had been deducted in tax and probate granted on 21 March 1960 to her three executors, Lord Mountbatten, the Marquess of Camden and (Baronet) Sir Harold Wernher, her proven will was made available for inspection to any member of the public. For the widow of such a prominent member of the royal family - the quintessential pillar of the establishment - it is a remarkably candid and comprehensive document running to eleven closely typed pages including two codicils.

The first striking feature is its date - 8 February 1939 - more than two decades before her death. It must have been written with the possibility of war and an early death at the forefront of her mind since one of the first clauses names two guardians for her children (Mountbatten's mother, the Dowager

Marchioness of Milford Haven and the Earl of Brecknock) in the event of both her and her husband dying. At the time, Lord Louis was a captain in the Royal Navy in command of a flotilla of destroyers and within a year, he would narrowly escape death when his boat HMS Kelly was struck by a German torpedo (an incident that would be immortalized in the film "In Which We Serve" co-directed by his friend Noel Coward). It was only after the outbreak of the war, according to Edwina's biographer, that she told him of her intention to leave him her landed estate - which would suggest that he had not seen the will at the time it was drawn up and signed.

Mountbatten later moaned that he received relatively little in his wife's will. In a letter to his actor friend Douglas Fairbanks Jr, he calculated that he would be left with just one shilling in the pound of Edwina's fortune after the deduction of death duties at 80% and the division of assets among other family members.[17]

It is true that there was a large tax bill to pay (and perhaps Edwina who became increasingly left-wing as she grew older did not mind sharing her wealth with the state) but on closer reading of the will, it appears that he did not do too badly out of her estate - particularly when it came to landed property. In a codicil written on 26 August 1939 to take into account the death of her father, Baron Mount Temple, seven weeks earlier, she left her husband a life interest in the family's country estate - Broadlands near Romsey in Hampshire. Should he die it would pass to their eldest daughter Patricia and then to the younger one, Pamela. Edwina also left him free of tax all her valuable personal possessions in the household.

The bulk of the non-landed estate involved a trust fund established by Edwina's grandfather. In the main body of the will she left her husband an one third share of the income from the fund with equal shares going to her surviving children. But in the codicil dated 26 August 1939 she changed how the fund should be divided amongst her two daughters. The residue should be split into eight portions of the fund, with five equal shares going to Patricia and three to Pamela. Presumably the extra weighting for Patricia was designed to recognize the fact that as the elder sibling with no male heir she would ultimately inherit the Mountbatten title and with it the landed estate and its accompanying overheads.

The amount of money in the family trust fund was monumental since it was the legacy of Sir Ernest Cassel, the wealthy banker who bailed out the finances of Edwina's godfather's Edward VII at the turn of the century and went on to amass a fortune greater than any possessed by a British royal. Like an Edwardian Warren Buffet, he had the golden touch when it came to picking the right investment at the right time. When he died in September 1921, he left behind such a huge estate that its original valuation had to be revised upwards. The official record at the Principal Registry states in type - probate London

7 October...effects £6,000,000 - and then in long hand is added - resworn £7,333,411. If any additional proof were needed this confirmed what many already suspected that he was one of the wealthiest men in Europe.

We know who inherited his assets because his will - like his granddaughter's - was never sealed. He left a life interest on his valuable London residence - Brook House on the corner of Park Lane and Upper Brook Street - to his sister Wilhelmine which on her death would pass to Edwina.[18] Edwina also received the lion's share of the residuary estate which was split into sixty-four parts. She inherited 25/64ths, her sister Mary 16/64ths and her aunt Anna 8/64ths. In cash terms, her portion was worth £2,900,000 earning her the soubriquet "the richest girl in Britain."

Edwina Ashley was Sir Ernest's favourite granddaughter. When his only daughter, Maud, died early he transferred his affection (and wealth) to her beautiful elder daughter. This, though, did not prevent him from attaching strings to Edwina's inheritance. As a successful financier who knew the value of having a diversified portfolio, he insisted that no single investment in the trust fund should exceed £100,000. Edwina would have to wait until her 21st birthday before some of the money came on stream and her 28th (or if earlier, her marriage) for the rest.

In fact, she got married to Lord Louis not long after her 21st birthday on 18 July 1922 in an opulent ceremony at St Margaret's, Westminster where the

Prince of Wales was the best man and King George V and the cream of European royalty made up the congregation. Although they had been friends for almost two years, their relationship had recently been cemented by shared grief – within the space of a month, Louis lost his father and Edwina her grandfather. Not long after the wedding, the groom discovered more restrictions on the bride's trust fund. Under statute, she was denied access not only to some of the capital, but also to its accrued interest. Never one to be put off by an insurmountable legal obstacle, Lord Louis set about lobbying parliament to change the law. A draft bill amending the legislation on trusts failed at an early stage in the Commons, but a second bill did eventually get the royal assent enabling the Mountbattens to get closer to their money. Lord Louis later admitted to his daughter Pamela that in the immediate pre-war years he and Edwina had difficulty spending their annual income of £60,000 which in today's money amounted to over £5 million a year.[19]

She splashed out on a Silver Ghost Rolls-Royce as a wedding gift for her husband. Unable to wait months for the Berkeley Square showroom to deliver the desired cabriolet design, she purchased a second-hand model from the Prince of Wales for £2,000 and then lavished another £2,000 on customizing its interiors (the new owner was eight inches taller than his predecessor). Lord Louis also spent a small fortune redecorating the private suite of his Brook House

London mansion. As befitting someone with a life-long passion for the sea, he turned it into a replica of his naval cabin: the ceiling was lowered to ship's specifications; the bed was replaced with a bunk and the windows with a port hole; and the bathroom was decorated with shells, fish and seaweed to evoke an underwater feel. To add a touch of authenticity, a generator was installed to replicate the throbbing of the ship's engines.

Edwina was able to dispose some more of her surplus wealth on the poorer relations she had acquired through marriage. She gave a helping hand to the family of Dickie's sister, Princess Alice who had to flee her Greek home after her husband Prince Andrea of Greece was sentenced to death on trumped up charges following a coup. She eased the financial hardship by renting their Corfu villa "Mon Repos" where their son Prince Philip had been born in June 1921 on the dining room table. As we shall see later, she and Lord Louis also gave generous financial support to Philip as a boy and until his marriage to Princess Elizabeth.

After the war some of the Mountbatten wealth was poured into a costly four-year restoration of another country retreat - Classiebawn castle, a near derelict turreted Victorian manor house set in 1,500 acres of rugged terrain in Mullaghmore on the west coast of Ireland. Edwina had inherited the property on the death of her father in 1939. She does not refer to it by name in the codicil to her will that was necessitated by his death but in one of the added new clauses she stipulates that all her remaining property (which presumably includes Classiebawn) should be treated in the same way as the transfer of the Broadlands estate. In other words, a lifetime right to the castle should go to her husband and on his death, it should pass to her eldest daughter and after that to her younger one. Indeed on Edwina's death - as confirmed by a recent biographer of Mountbatten who was given full access to the family archive - a life interest in the property was bequeathed to Lord Mountbatten.[20] By 1962 the property was haemorrhaging money at such an alarming rate that he seriously considered selling it. In one year the estate's net loss was £1,800. But when he realised the economic hardship the sale could cause the local community, he was forced to explore a less drastic remedy. He attempted to rent it to holiday makers and even approached the prime minister of the Irish Republic offering to make it available rent free in return for the state paying the rates and other overheads. The Taoiseach politely declined the offer saying that he appreciated "the generous gesture and the friendly feeling towards Ireland." In the end, he found a local businessman, Hugh Tunney, who in 1976 was prepared to pay for a twenty-one year lease, fund most of the running costs and allow Mountbatten access to the castle for the month of August.

On 27 August 1979 Lord Louis was relaxing aboard *Shadow V* on a fishing trip close to Classiebawn when the IRA blew up the boat killing him, his fourteen-year-old grandson, Nicholas Knatchbull, the eighty-three-year-old Dowager Lady Brabourne, as well as the fifteen-year-old shiphand Paul Maxwell, and leaving his daughter, Lady Patricia Brabourne, his son-in-law, Lord Brabourne, and his grandson, Timothy Knatchbull with horrific injuries. The IRA claimed he had been "executed" as an act of war against "the English ruling class" and its "imperialist heart." Ironically papers in the Dublin national archive later revealed that Mountbatten had long advocated a united Ireland.[21]

Although such a violent end was beyond his wildest imaginings, Mountbatten had planned meticulously for his death, to such an extent that he surpassed even Queen Mary in his succession planning. This was illustrated not just in the long lists dividing the chattels in his estate but also in every detail of his funeral set down in an "informal note" to the Lord Chamberlain running to eleven pages and a more detailed family file several inches thick. On the day of his burial on September 5, his naval commands were obeyed to the letter - down to the prescribed dimensions of the tablet that was to be placed over his grave at Romsey near Broadlands.

The earlier service at Westminster Abbey attended by the Queen, King Olaf of Norway, the Queen Silvia of Sweden, King Juan Carlos of Spain, Prince Rainier and Princess Grace of Monaco and heads of state from all over the world had all the pomp and pageantry of a state funeral. Mountbatten's one great regret in planning his farewell parade was that he could not be there himself. Being such a showman and self-publicist, the grand old Earl had few inhibitions about his private life and thus would have been expected to want to display the contents of his will and his overall estate to the general public. After all, in the last months of his life he had gone out of his way to disclose that his father had had an illegitimate child and that there was no shame in sharing family secrets.

But - as the formality of his funeral revealed - there was another side of his personality that loved tradition and royal protocol. In accordance with protocol for a member of the royal family, he had wanted his body laid-in-state in the Chapel Royal at St James's Palace. By the same token, he should have requested that his will be automatically sealed. So, which side of his character would prevail? What would it be transparency or secrecy?

The typed entry in the probate register for "Mountbatten of Burma, Earl Louis Francis, Albert, Victor, Nicholas of Broadlands Romsey Hampshire" contains one annotation written in red ink "Royal will: Copy will not be opened to public inspection". His most recent biographer observes that as a member of the royal family he no doubt felt he was perfectly entitled to keep his private affairs confidential through a sealed will.[22]

Whatever the reasoning behind the decision it was not to hide the size of his estate or minimise death duties. The official calendar records that he left an estate of £2,196,949 - the third largest estate in the one hundred year history of sealed royal wills. It is not clear whether the probate figure is net or gross. If it is indeed after deductions of debts and other liabilities, then with the top rate of capital transfer tax in 1979 at 75% on estates over £2,010,000, his executors could have been faced with a six-seven figure tax bill. Clearly, Mountbatten was better at state funeral planning than estate tax planning.

Although Lord Louis's will was sealed, because his family have always been refreshingly open with biographers and in their own writing, it is not difficult to piece together the contents of his estate and how it was administered. From the list of sealed royal wills, we learn that there were three executors - Lord (John) Brabourne, his erstwhile aide-de-camp and son-in-law who became the son he never had and earned his complete trust, particularly since he was one of the few brave enough to stand up to him; Patricia, Countess Mountbatten, his elder daughter who with no male issue inherited his title and to whom such was his devotion that he spoke to her every day and once wrote to her that she was the only woman in his life; and Edwina Hicks, the daughter of his younger daughter, Pamela, who in a strange echo of a previous Edwina's relationship to her grandfather, was treated as a favourite granddaughter and showered with gifts and affection. In his choice of executors, Mountbatten had adroitly covered all the family bases - son-in-law, daughter and granddaughter.

Thanks to family records and testimony, we know what happened to Mountbatten's landed properties. In his memoir of his grandfather's assassination and his own narrow survival, Timothy Knatchbull discloses that his elder brother, Norton, inherited Broadlands and the title Lord Romsey in 1979.[23] The first born of Lady Pamela and Lord Brabourne, he was Mountbatten's eldest grandson and his most direct male heir.

Edwina's will laid down that in the event of Lord Louis dying a life interest in Classiebawn would pass to their eldest daughter, Pamela - and Knatchbull's book confirms this transfer did indeed take place.[24] But due to the security worries of her husband, she never again set foot in the castle she owned. In February 1991 it was sold to Hugh Tunney, the millionaire businessman who had leased the property for the previous fifteen years keeping open the option of the Mountbatten family using it for the month of August. But after the death of Lord Brabourne in 2005 she was persuaded by her son Timothy to make one last surreptitious visit to Classiebawn - sneaking in this time as a trespasser.

Timothy also reveals in his memoirs what happened to Mountbatten's personal possessions. A confidential letter from his grandfather disclosed that most of the valuable private property went to his grandson Norton and his heirs but he did leave "personal souvenirs" of him and the Mountbatten family to his other grandchildren.[25] In the last years of his life he had painstakingly catalogued and collected ninety boxes of memorabilia which were to be left with a personal note and a personal chart of his family tree to each of his grandchildren and his two grand nephews. Among the one hundred and forty-nine items in the eight boxes left to Timothy were a silver ash tray with coat of arms, a gold sovereign, various medallions and a set of three volumes on naval medals by Lord Louis of Battenberg. This was a seminal work on numismatics written by his great grandfather in his retirement years after he had been unfairly drummed out of the navy and later forced to sell his own collection of medals to make ends meet. Timothy was particularly touched to find among the items left to him a pair of gold and amethyst cufflinks with a note from his grandfather explaining they had once belonged to the first Lord Louis.

Despite his best efforts to avoid the charge of favouritism by standardising his gift-giving, each grandchild got a different set of Mountbatten memorabilia. Ashley, the first son of his younger daughter Pamela, was fortunate to receive some of his naval possessions - including his Morse code kit, the compass and sextant from one ship he served on and other instruments of navigation from his personal yacht. As a souvenir of his grandfather, Ashley also received a translation of an account of a visit that Lord Louis made to the Mikado on a tour of Japan in 1881. The fact that Lord Mountbatten went out of his way to leave two of his grandchildren relatively insignificant heirlooms from Lord Louis indicates the importance he placed on keeping his father's memory alive.

Since Lord Mountbatten's death his closest relatives have kept the flame alight by ensuring that the Broadlands Archive - the collection of family papers - was made widely available. In 1989 - on the tenth anniversary of the assassination - 4,500 boxes of photographs and documents were left on loan to the University of Southampton which after a grant from the National Heritage Fund bought the material in 2010. Today any registered online-user can have access to the Mountbatten database containing approximately 250,000 papers, 50,000 photos and quantities of recordings on audio-tape and video-tape - although no copy of his will.

Chapter Eight
The Burial Of Bad News – 1969-1971

"These figures [on the tax exemption for royal annuities] have been given to the committee but are not for disclosure and have been omitted from the evidence as printed"
Treasury briefing paper for the Chancellor of the Exchequer, 14 December 1971

On a humid rainy morning in June 1971 in the Treasury Chambers off Whitehall, the Chancellor of the Exchequer, Anthony Barber, met privately with two senior members of the royal household: the Lord Chamberlain, Lord Cobbold, and the Keeper of the Privy Purse and Treasurer to the Queen, Lord Tryon. Taking the minutes of the meeting was Barber's private secretary, Bill Ryrie, who marked his record of the discussions "SECRET."

Although there had been no royal deaths since Princess Marina's in 1968, royal inheritance in the form of the hereditary revenues was high on the agenda for the Treasury and the palace. It had been placed there by the crisis in the royal finances caused by the rampant inflation - the worst since Napoleonic times with prices rising 74% and wages 126% between 1953-70 - which had forced the Queen to dip into her hereditary income to make up for the under provision of the Civil List. As the Duke of Edinburgh famously lamented to an American television interviewer, if the royal finances go into the red next year and nothing changes "we may have to move into smaller premises, who knows?"

The meeting on the Civil List was not long under way before Anthony Barber raised the sensitive issue of the Queen's private resources. The Chancellor was worried that there "could be difficulties over this issue...Many reasonable people including government supporters felt that since Her Majesty and her predecessors had paid no personal taxation and estate duty, the private resources could not be regarded as private in quite the usual sense. It was at least reasonable that the facts should be known."[1]

It was left to Lord Cobbold, the more senior member of the royal household, to attempt to deadbat this tricky delivery. He had been Lord Chamberlain, in effect the non-executive chairman of the household of Windsor plc, since 1963 – the first holder of that office to be drawn from the professional world having risen through the ranks of the Bank of England from advisor in 1933 to Deputy-Governor in 1945 and finally Governor from 1949-1961. In total he served under six different Chancellors and by virtue of his personal authority and diplomatic skills maintained a constructive relationship with each of them. For all the individual warmth he exhibited in private, at work he was known to cultivate a certain aloofness. He was married to Hermione Bulwer-Lytton, the daughter and heir to the second Earl of Lytton, whose 15th century ancestral seat was Knebworth House in Hertfordshire (a generation later to be turned into a world-famous rock concert venue by their son, David). Educated at Eton and King's College Cambridge and holder of the Knight Grand Cross of the Victorian Order, Cameron Fromanteel, the First Baron Cobbold of Knebworth, possessed all the requisite establishment credentials to open the batting for Her Majesty.

Surprisingly, Cobbold opted for a front-on, open stance when it came to negotiating the inheritance bouncer. "Lord Cobbold said he did not know the Queen's mind on this matter," recorded minute six of the meeting, "but he thought she might be willing to make a statement not on her personal resources but on her inheritance." This would involve the three issues of: the inalienable assets of the Crown (such as her collection of paintings) which although valuable earned no income; the private residences of Sandringham and Balmoral that George VI brought from his brother which again could be shown to bring in no income; and her inheritance of financial assets (which was more problematical and might be dealt with by the Queen authorising him to confirm that this inheritance amounted to "not more than £X").

On the whole the Chancellor welcomed such a statement from the Queen, although he felt that the precise meaning of "inalienable" could be clarified. Known for his lack of pomposity, Tony Barber was cut from very different cloth to Lord Cobbold. A grammar school boy from the east riding of Yorkshire, he studied for a law degree in his spare time before becoming a barrister and later MP for Doncaster and then Altrincham and Sale. In 1970 Prime Minister Edward Heath - a friend and someone from a similarly unprivileged background - made him Chancellor of the Duchy of Lancaster with responsibility for EEC entry but when Iain Macleod, the Chancellor of the Exchequer, died suddenly a few weeks into office he was catapulted into the Treasury.

Some of his cabinet colleagues doubted if he was really up to the job – and even Barber wondered if he had the requisite Treasury experience, confiding to Heath's private secretary before the cabinet reshuffle: "I hope he's not going to ask me to be Chancellor."[2] Later he would become best known for the short-lived "Barber boom," an attempt to reflate the UK economy before joining the Common Market which due to the OPEC oil price rise ended in bust. A wiry prematurely bald man, his slight frame and thin voice belied a wry wit. He was the crafty spin bowler taking on the gentleman batsman from the palace, although anyone watching the game would have been forgiven for believing that at times they were actually playing for the same team.

The other presence in this game sitting well above the fray like a team coach in the home dressing room was Barber's boss, Edward Heath. The Prime Minister had made him Chancellor because he needed a trusted lieutenant who would do his bidding in one of the key offices of state. Although a moderniser when it came to the economy and the need for Britain to replace the Commonwealth with the Common Market as its main trading partner, on anything to do with the royal family and court ritual, Heath was, according to his biographer, "a convinced monarchist."[3] He greatly valued his weekly audience with the Queen ("you can speak with complete confidentiality to her. You can say things you would not even say to your number two," but unfortunately the feelings were not reciprocated.[4] Her Majesty did not find him an easy conversationalist (another courtier thought Heath "tricky" and that HRH was never entirely comfortable with him).[5] The Queen who went out of her way to forge personal relationships with all her prime ministers whether Conservative or Labour, found it almost impossible to penetrate Heath's famed carapace. With no small talk and little in the way of charm, he could appear brusque and impolite. "The monarch never succeeded in developing an easy relationship," wrote the journalist and political insider Hugo Young, "a failing that gave Her Majesty something in common with much of the human race."[6]

Royal Legacy

At the beginning of the round of bargaining over the revised Civil List, Barber had his doubts about the palace's case for a significant pay increase for the monarchy. He favoured an annual vote from parliament and no increase in the size of the annuities given to senior royals. For his part Cobbold advocated an index-linked grant of public money and a sizable increase in annuities. He was opposed to a separate plan to finance the spending totally from hereditary revenues, while his nightmare scenario was for the government to take total control of palace income and expenditure. But where they both appeared to agree was that the size of the Queen's wealth must be kept away from public scrutiny - at all costs embarrassing questions from parliament must be avoided.

There was also agreement on the related issue of whether the Queen's bankers should be allowed to give evidence to the select committee. Recently the press had been speculating wildly on the size of the Queen's bank account and other assets with figures ranging from £50 million to £100 million being touted. Sir John "Jock" Colville, a director of Coutts, the royal bankers, and a former personal secretary to the Queen when she was Princess Elizabeth, later wrote to The Times saying that £2 million was much nearer the mark and a palace spokesman seemed to confirm the ballpark figure. When this sensitive matter was discussed by Lord Cobbold, a former Bank of England Governor, Ryrie recorded that "it was agreed that firm resistance should be put up against any proposal to ask the Queen's personal bankers to appear or to ask Her Majesty to agree that they should give evidence."[7] Throughout the deliberations considerable thought was given to limiting the list of witnesses to a small, select and controllable group.

The real significance of the select committee inquiry into the Civil List was that it threatened to bring the sovereign's private fortune into the open for the first time. All previous Civil List reviews had been undertaken behind closed doors with no official records taken of the oral evidence. Barber was initially opposed to full disclosure but was forced to relent under pressure from MPs. As the Queen's biographer Ben Pimlott observed, "the committee put the Crown more seriously on the defensive than at any time since 1936...The emphasis, more than ever before, was on justifying, not merely expenditure, but also the need to incur it...The Queen, through her close advisors, had to present a convincing case that she gave value for money."[8] What happened during the eight months of select committee scrutiny was a struggle between parliament and the palace (often aided and abetted in private by the Treasury) to reveal the full extent of the monarch's inherited wealth. At times, it took on the character of not so much as a game of cricket but as a chess match with the courtiers thinking two or three moves ahead in order to thwart a gambit or outflank an attack on the Queen from MPs. At stake in the game was the financial independence of the monarchy.

As with all official inquiries, the composition of the committee was crucial. The issue had been debated at length even before the Conservative government took office. Back in 1969 the Labour Prime Minister Harold Wilson faced with growing pressure from the palace about the under provision of the Civil List had decided that the only way to resolve the funding crisis was to set up a new select committee and in an effort to avoid a row with parliament about "a pay rise for the Queen" and to take the politics out a highly combustible issue he got the agreement of the opposition leader Edward Heath that the establishment of the committee should be delayed until *after* the election. When the Tories surprisingly won in May 1970, Heath continued the bipartisan approach and had a quiet word with Wilson about what was the best way to proceed. We know from the released papers that Barber then wrote to Wilson on 8 April 1971 to arrange a meeting to discuss "how the problem might be dealt with...I think you will agree that it would be helpful to the work of the select committee if we were to have an exchange of views confidentially."[9]

They eventually met in May with Wilson being accompanied by Roy Jenkins, the deputy Labour leader, to discuss who should be on the committee and whether its evidence should be made public. While Wilson remained devoutly pro-monarchist and did everything in his power to expedite a favourable settlement for the palace, Jenkins, the former Chancellor of the Exchequer, was more sceptical about any pay rise for the Queen. In the wake of the election defeat, Labour was moving to the left and Jenkins was much more in tune with the mood of the party than Wilson, who was regarded by some backbenchers as an establishment lackey.

In the end, the selection of the select committee resulted in a Commons compromise. On the one hand, the palace would have been pleased to find many dyed-in-the-wool loyalists on the Committee - led by ultra-monarchist Norman St John Stevas, a friend of the Queen Mother, and ably supported by two establishment-minded men: John Boyd-Carpenter, whose family had close ties with every sovereign since Queen Victoria, and Sir Fitzroy McLean, who was another regular dinner guest of the Queen Mother and whose aristocratic wife was on first name terms with several senior royals. The committee which was chaired by a Conservative Chancellor with the assistance of the Leader of the Commons William Whitelaw would have a built-in Tory majority.

But to the dismay of the palace a few members of the awkward squad were also included. The most troublesome was Willie Hamilton, MP for West Fife and author of the forthright republican blast "My Queen and I" who achieved notoriety for a series of ad hominem attacks on members of the royal family (he famously described Princess Margaret as "an expensive kept woman," lambasted the Queen as "a middle aged woman of limited intellect" and dismissed her supporters on the committee as "diligent sycophants"). Hamilton was the son of a Durham miner and his visceral hatred of the royal family could be traced back to his experience as a schoolboy during the 1926 general strike and his parents telling him that the monarchy represented the pinnacle of "wealth, privilege and exploitation."[10] More sophisticated scrutiny could be expected from the experienced trio of Roy Jenkins with his wealth of knowledge from the Treasury, Douglas Houghton, who in the last Labour cabinet had been Chancellor of the Duchy of Lancaster and Joel Barnett, a skilled accountant and member of the Public Accounts Committee who would go on to become Chief Secretary to the Treasury.

On the credit side for the palace was the absence of one parliamentary troublemaker who had long taken a hostile stance on the Civil List review, Richard Crossman. Secretary of State for Health and Social Security in the previous Labour administration, the member for Coventry East had stepped down from frontline parliamentary politics in 1970 to become editor of The New Statesman where in an article entitled "The Royal Tax Avoiders" he nailed his republican colours firmly to the mast by launching a vitriolic attack on the royal family's financial privileges. He argued that you had to take into account the private inherited wealth of the Queen when assessing how much Civil List money was voted to her by parliament.

When his controversial cabinet diaries were posthumously published after a failed gagging order by the Civil Service, they revealed how several senior members of the government shared his republican sympathies and how they and other ministers were kept in the dark about secret discussions concerning a revised Civil List. In the entry for 11 November 1969 - just two days after the Duke of Edinburgh had caused a media storm by complaining about the inadequate state funding for his housing - he disclosed how Barbara Castle, the Secretary of State for Employment, and like him and the Chancellor Roy Jenkins a republican - was so enraged by Prince Philip's comments that she called for a special parliamentary committee to investigate the Queen's private wealth. Much to Crossman's amazement it emerged in the inner cabinet deliberations that discussions on the palace finances were already well advanced and unbeknown to the cabinet, the Prime Minister and his Chancellor had been plotting to try to transfer as much royal expenditure as possible away from the Civil List and into the budgets of government departments.[11] Crossman was particularly annoyed by the way a blind eye was turned to the sovereign's privileged inheritance position, namely the vital exemption on death duties which allowed her to accumulate so much wealth.[12] The Prime Minister seemed not remotely concerned about this tax free fortune – an oversight he attributed to Harold's strong royalist sympathies.

But one former Labour cabinet minister did throw a ratchet in the works of the well-lubricated machinery of the Select Committee. Using his knowledge gleaned as the Chancellor of the Duchy of Lancaster as well as chairman of the Public Accounts Committee and work with the Inland Revenue as its staff association secretary, Douglas Houghton came up with a proposal to turn the royal household into a government department - the Commissioners of the Crown. The Queen's staff would effectively be civil servants paid directly by grant from parliament like any other department. This would protect the palace from inflation since if a shortfall arose due to an increase in wages or prices parliament could vote through any additional funds in their annual grant. No one could accuse the Queen of getting a personal pay rise since under the new transparent funding arrangement it would be clear that funding was going directly into palace expenditure rather into her personal pocket. Public scrutiny would be guaranteed through a government minister responsible for royal expenditure and answerable to parliament.

In theory, everyone should be happy. Indeed, the plan got the backing of not just the Labour party where it was the official policy but also of a significant number of backbench Liberals and Conservatives. So, with this broad cross-bench support how would the palace respond?

On 30 June 1971 Lord Cobbold while residing in Holyroodhouse Palace in Edinburgh as part of the Queen's Scottish summer sojourn dispatched a remarkably blunt letter to the Chancellor voicing

Her Majesty's hostility to the plan: "The Queen has confirmed her view to me in no uncertain terms. Her Majesty would see grave objections both on grounds of management efficiency and on grounds of wider principle to transfer of the control of her Household staff out of the hands of herself and her officers."[13] Later the thinly veiled threat from Lord Cobbold was spelt out in a Treasury memo: "The whole scheme depends upon the willingness of the Queen and her Household to be reorganised along these lines, which Lord Cobbold indicated in evidence is unlikely. It is not clear for example that the Queen would wish to continue to occupy Buckingham Palace on these terms. If the Palace were in effect a government department she might well wish to live elsewhere in her personal capacity and appear at the Palace only for official functions."[14] So, now not only the Duke of Edinburgh but the Queen too was issuing threats to move house.

According to Cobbold's letter, Her Majesty's official objection was that the transfer to departmental control would undermine the independence of the monarchy: if a new Whitehall department were set up with authority over the royal household, then this would inevitably mean the presiding government would have to be involved which could weaken the non-political status of the Crown.

But behind this position of principle was the long-standing fear that it would result in the palace being financially beholden to parliament - and liable to the political whims of a future government which might be unsympathetic to the monarchy. This anxiety was revealed in an internal Treasury memo marked 'confidential': "it would be unlikely to be acceptable to the palace as it would leave the monarchy entirely dependent on parliament from one year to the next."[15] The same memo disclosed the real reason why the government was also hostile to the idea. The last thing it wanted was to take on the added administrative burden of running another Whitehall department: "it would entail the maximum Ministerial and Parliamentary involvement, since it would open up Royal Household expenditure to audit by the C and AG [Comptroller and Auditor General] and inquiry by the PAC [Public Accounts Committee]. In effect it would leave ministers permanently and directly responsible for all royal expenditure in detail." It also failed to address the separate issue of the individual annuities of members of the royal family, which had nothing to do with the cost of running the palaces.

Despite their deep reservations about the Houghton scheme, the government felt duty bound to comply with a request from the select committee to draw up a feasibility study. Confidential Treasury notes reveal how the delicate manoeuvring between Whitehall and the government was the stuff of a "Yes Minister" plotline. In the role of Sir Humphrey, Lawrence Airey, the Treasury undersecretary, wrote on the 19 July 1971 to the Chancellor's private secretary, Bill Ryrie, a note aptly entitled "Management - In confidence": "I have tried to make the description of the new department as plausible as possible since to put something which the committee could see was an understatement of the case would be likely to be counterproductive."[16] Although he does admit that "the main objection to this scheme from the government's point of view is the degree of detailed responsibility for royal expenditure which it would involve for ministers and the extent to which the expenditure would be questioned in parliament."

In passing, it should be noted that as Barber's principal private secretary, Ryrie had a duty not only to serve as the loyal servant of his Chancellor batting for him however sticky the wicket but also to act as an umpire in any turf wars between departments - oiling if not the bats then the wheels of the Civil Service machinery. This is precisely what the character Bernard Woolley, Jim Hacker's PPS, did in the "Yes Minister" series. As one Whitehall watcher graphically put it, the private secretary fulfilled the part of "shock absorber" in the departmental machine.[17] Traditionally the job of private secretary went to a Whitehall highflier and more often than not it proved a successful launching pad to much higher office with many occupants of that post going on to become permanent secretaries. Bill Ryrie - an Edinburgh-educated son of the manse who joined the Colonial Office in 1953 after serving as an intelligence officer in the Malaya emergency - finished his Whitehall career as Sir William Ryrie, KCB, CB,

Permanent Secretary at the Overseas Development Agency. He went on run the International Finance Corporation before dying in 2012 aged eighty-three.

Just two days later - on July 21 - Airey disclosed in a second memo the bad news that "the Chancellor told me this morning that the paper I put up on Mr Houghton's scheme was *somewhat too convincing* and likely to appeal to the committee in preference to his own scheme."[18] In the best Whitehall tradition, the civil servant offered to add "a few paragraphs emphasising the drawbacks," while in an attempt to cover his back he expressed his unease about taking sides since the paper was not designed "to argue the case for or against a solution on this sort" and then suggested that a better course of action might be "to leave the paper as it stands but not circulate it."

The Chancellor then appeared to reject this new strategy scrawling on the memo in a half-legible hand "...disadvantage is then made more [unclear/obviously?]. If you are happy publish & be damned!" In the end, all these machinations in "managing" the committee seemed to bear fruit since its final report concluded that the Houghton scheme was too costly and the Commons voted it down by three hundred votes to two hundred and sixty-three.

However, the government found it altogether more tricky killing off a second scheme - this time emanating from the ranks of their own party. John Boyd-Carpenter, the Conservative MP for Kingston-upon-Thames, former chairman of the Public

Accounts Committee and Financial Secretary to the Treasury responsible for overseeing the last Civil List review in 1952, put forward in the early summer of 1971 a scheme that in his view would be welcomed with open arms by both the palace and his Tory government. In a throwback to the 18th century arrangements, the whole of the Crown estates revenues would be made available to the Queen and the surplus would revert to the Treasury. For the Queen, this would avoid the embarrassment of going cap in hand to parliament in cases of under provision and for the government it would free the Treasury of the chore of administering palace income and expenditure.

To more cynical eyes Boyd-Carpenter might seem to fall into Willie Hamilton's category of one of the palace's "diligent sycophants." In his autobiography "Way of Life" he proudly records his family association with a long line of sovereigns. His grandfather, the Rt Rev William Boyd-Carpenter, the Bishop of Ripon and royal chaplain, was a close friend of Queen Victoria, knew both Edward VII and George V and confirmed George VI. As a young man, John Boyd-Carpenter dined with Edward VIII and later as a cabinet minister often met the Queen and her courtiers (Lord Cobbold was – in his opinion - the nicest of men.) His position before the royal family was always deferential: the Queen was a "courageous lady", while the Queen Mother was "physically incapable of being ungracious." His uncle, Sir Henry Boyd-Carpenter, a partner at Farrers, the royal family's law firm since

1789, was solicitor to the Duchy of Cornwall and later to the Queen personally.

Outside of the committee room, John Boyd-Carpenter argued his case through a number of personal interventions with the Chancellor. In one heartfelt letter addressed to "My Dear Tony," he explained that "I feel as strongly about this as I have ever had on any public issue" since "our real objective" must be that "the Queen...shall never have to take the initiative of asking parliament for more money during the rest of her Reign...particularly (although we cannot say this in committee) if this happens it may happen during a spell of Labour government."[19] In a most revealing aside, he outlined the secret strategy of his Labour committee colleagues: Roy Jenkins had used the Civil List review "as a lever to extract information about Her private fortune," Douglas Houghton "to try to get control of the Household through a government department" and Harold Wilson was trying to use it "to get his hands on the Duchies [of Lancaster and Cornwall]."[20]

Without realising it Boyd-Carpenter had touched a raw nerve at the palace. Although in theory they would have welcomed any scheme that would bypass parliament and offer them almost unlimited income from the Crown estate revenue, acceptance of the Boyd-Carpenter scheme opened up a can of worms in the shape of the hereditary revenues. If all the hereditary income from the Crown estates were made available to the Queen, then why should not the revenues from the Duchies of Lancaster and Cornwall be included in the pot? Lord Cobbold let slip this concern in a letter to Anthony Barber dated 24 September 1971 and marked "Personal and Confidential" (he also informed Treasury officials that he was anxious that no one but the Chancellor should see it) - "the point is taken that introduction of Crown estates revenues [the Boyd-Carpenter plan] into this picture might sooner or later add to pressures to alter the status of the two Duchies."[21]

His concern was put even more boldly in a letter four days earlier on September 20 from Barber to William Whitelaw: "Cobbold...would prefer our latest proposals to a link with the revenues of the Crown estates à la Boyd-Carpenter. His reason - which he would not want to give publicly - is that this might bring into issue the whole question of the revenues of the two duchies. I told him that this was what you had always feared."[22]

Later on December 14 this fear was spelled out in a briefing paper for the Chancellor prior to the House of Commons debate on the report: "the Lancaster and Cornwall revenues are in law the private income of the sovereign and the heir apparent respectively. Some members of the committee would regard them as being in a sense national property."[23] Indeed another Treasury memo noted in an echo of Boyd-Carpenter's warning of Harold Wilson's secret agenda that "traditionally...there have been attempts in a Select Committee to appropriate the Cornwall revenues in aid of the Civil List or otherwise to derive some public benefit from them."[24] This was indeed the openly-declared policy of one Labour member of the committee, Willie Hamilton who later made it a recommendation of his minority report.

What all these confidential comments revealed was the extreme importance the palace attached to the duchy revenues - Lancaster funded the Queen's affluent lifestyle, Cornwall Prince Charles's. This in effect was their bottom line - as was made crystal clear in a note from the Parliamentary Counsel, Sir John Fiennes, to the Treasury as early as 1 September 1970: "On all previous occasions one of the things which the palace has insisted on is that there should be no surrender of Duchy Revenues comparable to the surrender of the hereditary revenues of the Crown."[25]

The Treasury had their own reasons to oppose the plan. As a host of internal memos pointed out, the surrender of the hereditary revenues far from getting parliament off their back might lead to greater scrutiny from the legislature since the Treasury would still need to approve the expenditure of the palace in order to check how much had actually been surrendered and with the palace now having no incentive to economise, MPs might suspect collusion between the palace and the Treasury and "it might attract more rather than less annual attention in parliament." It also left unresolved the small matter of how you set the size of the annuity for individual members of the royal family.

With this ticking bomb lying in its in-tray, the Treasury had to find some way to persuade Boyd-Carpenter to defuse or dispose of his scheme without making too much of a commotion. After private discussions between Anthony Barber and Lord Cobbold, it was agreed that the Chancellor should write to Boyd-Carpenter explaining what was now their final position on the funding arrangement. Then, in order to let him down gently they could meet "on a Privy Councillor basis" (in other words, in secret) and Cobbold "would explain why he does not favour Boyd-Carpenter's proposals."[26] The confidential papers remain silent on how Boyd-Carpenter reacted to the killing of his plan but he did not appear to make a fuss. It might be a complete coincidence that around this time (and to be fair, the chronology of events is far from exact as he dates the event "in the latter part of 1971") the Prime Minister offered him the chairmanship of the new Civil Aviation Authority. Knowing that he was out of favour with the Heath administration which had failed to back his bid in 1970 to become Speaker, he accepted the position but since it was a salaried job he was obliged to resign his seat in 1972 ending twenty-seven years' service as the member for Kingston-upon-Thames. He died in 1998 after completing his autobiography. His three-hundred-page memoirs contains a whole chapter on his work with the CAA but not one word on the Select Committee on the Civil List.

The duchy revenues were the main bone of contention when another sensitive matter was discussed at the Treasury - what would happen if Prince Charles died prematurely. In most scenarios discussed in a paper bluntly entitled "The Death of the Prince of Wales" the Queen would then get the duchy money and she would deduct the same amount from her Civil List payments so that the outcome was revenue neutral. Although the monarchy does not gain materially from this arrangement, the sovereign does this to preserve the Duchy of Cornwall revenues for future sons of the sovereign. But if such a situation were to arise during the Queen's reign, hostile Labour MPs such as Willie Hamilton might use it to increase pressure on the sovereign to end this convoluted and outdated practice and surrender the duchy revenues to the Civil List once and for all. (Interestingly this was precisely the line of argument used by Margaret Hodge when in July 2013 she challenged a duchy official in oral evidence of the Public Accounts Committee).[27]

If this was the unspoken fear of the palace, then an equally jittery Treasury was prepared to express it in writing. One revealing internal memo raised the issue of the way a select committee on the Civil List might want to "appropriate the Cornwall revenues in aid of the Civil List...The Chancellor will wish to resist any change in this respect. Interfering in any way with the interests of the present Prince of Wales would make the ensuring legislation hybrid and there is no cause to overturn the 1952 arrangements in respect to another minority duke."[28]

To avoid any embarrassment, Whitehall and the palace agreed that if the select committee raised the issue of the surrender of the revenues from the duchies, a Treasury mandarin rather than the Chancellor of the Duchy of Lancaster, Geoffrey Rippon, would give evidence.[29] For some unexplained reason they feared that Rippon would not be a helpful witness. In the event, it fell to an official of the Crown Estate Commissioners, the luckless E.R. Wheeler, to face a grilling from Willie Hamilton. After reminding the witness that he had written recently to Mr Rippon about the duchy finances, he began probing its privileged tax status and then its history, in particular the surprising decision in 1760 not to surrender the two duchies along with the other hereditary landed revenues. Despite repeated inquiries and verbal jousting, Mr Wheeler could provide - to use Hamilton's words in his minority report - "no explanation... for this exclusion." All he could suggest was that the revenue from the Duchy of Lancaster was "already regarded as earmarked for the enjoyment of the sovereign."[30]

A possible explanation why the Duchy of Lancaster was overlooked can be found in one of the released Treasury papers that states it "only produced the derisory sum of £16 18s 4d in that year [1760]."[31] In other words, it slipped through the net because it was so small. However, if the government of 1760 had known that a century later Prince Albert would after a little reorganisation of rents transform it into a cash cow producing close to £50,000 a year they might well have had second thoughts and included it in the overall sum handed over to the public purse.

When they were not agonising over the fate of the Duchy of Cornwall, the Treasury and the palace were much preoccupied by the possibility of the death of another duke. A series of strokes in the late sixties had left the Duke of Gloucester a permanent invalid and unable to perform any royal engagements. In 1970 nearly all of his official duties were undertaken by either his wife, Princess Alice, or his younger son, Prince Richard (his eldest son, Prince William was otherwise engaged in work for the diplomatic service). On 6 August 1971 Lord Tryon, the Keeper of the Privy Purse and erstwhile executor of Queen Mary's estate, wrote to Lawrence Airey at the Treasury suggesting that "it may also be necessary in the event of the Duke of Gloucester's death to provide for Prince William and possibly in the course of time for other Members of the Royal Family - Prince Richard and Prince Michael. As we explained at our meeting, it is difficult to foresee the extent of royal duties which such Members of the Royal Family may carry out in the future but in our opinion a figure of £10,000 to £15,000 per annum should cover demands during the next five years." Given that minor members of the royal family were not customarily provided for specifically by name from the Civil List, some might have suspected that Lord Tryon was trying it on.

When in mid-August 1971 Chancellor Anthony Barber saw a first draft report of the recommendations proposing that the Duke of Gloucester's annuity should rise from £10,000 to £45,000 and the Duchess of Gloucester should now receive £20,000, he was far from pleased, scrawling on the text in an agitated hand: "Am I wrong in my understanding here? Is the idea that the duke's annuity is increasing [unclear] (although he performs no duties?) and that the Duchess should <u>forthwith</u> get £20,000?"[32] According to the Treasury files, a suitably chastened civil servant amended the recommendations and reported back to Barber's office "the Chancellor's suggestions have been all incorporated (p.27) [the Duke's annuity was now set at £20,000]. As regards the Duchess of Gloucester, the intention is certainly that her annuity of £20,000 will not be payable until she becomes a widow."[33]

Treasury mandarins were also keen to finesse another privilege linked to the duke's annuity. In the course of cross examination from the committee, the Permanent Treasury Secretary Sir Douglas Allen was forced to admit that most of the annuities of the royals - including that of the Duke of Gloucester - were tax exempt, since the sums were deemed a legitimate expense of their work. So embarrassing did the Treasury regard this disclosure that when it came to the publication of the oral evidence they decided that it should be censored - or to use the civil service euphemism "side-lined." A later

Treasury briefing paper for the Chancellor classified "Confidential - Not for disclosure" - revealed the full extent of the tax exemption: "The cases in question are Queen Elizabeth the Queen Mother, Princess Anne and Princess Margaret [100% exemption]. The Duke of Edinburgh is allowed 80% and the Duke of Gloucester almost 95%. These figures have been given to the committee but are not for disclosure and have been omitted from the evidence as printed."[34] Even today, more than forty years after the event, the online digital record of the testimony of Sir Douglas on this tax relief is blanked out by a series of asterisks.

Time and time again, the Treasury seemed to be acting in consort with the palace to spare their blushes. The Chancellor even proposed to Lord Cobbold and Sir Michael Adeane in their original meeting in June 1971 that the members of the royal household should offer some "suggested questions" with him "to open the proceedings."[35] A rather diffident Adeane dutifully sent to the Treasury a few days before he gave evidence five questions that the committee chairman might ask him, adding in a separate note: "I fear they are of a very general nature but if they are put they will, I hope, bring out such points that may be of use to the committee."[36]

Not surprisingly the questions were hardly penetrating - and certainly not in keeping with any serious scrutiny by a parliamentary committee. The first - "Has the Queen's work increased since she came to the throne - and if so to what extent?" - was indeed repeated almost verbatim by the Chancellor when he addressed Adeane in committee. "Mr Chairman I'm glad you have asked me the question in that form," responded the courtier with a straight face.[37] Shortly after, the third question drafted by Adeane - "What is the function of the Royal Archives?" - was asked word for word by the committee's deputy chairman William Whitelaw, who might have been expected to find weightier issues to address other than how the Windsors' personal papers were stored and catalogued.

Barber was also not above planting in the newspapers favourable information about his role chairing the select committee. No doubt he was seeking to recoup some political capital for all the personal effort he had invested on the marathon talks. In another Treasury memo reminiscent of a "Yes Minister" storyline, the Chancellor instructed his private secretary, Peter Middleton to ask the press office "whether it would be possible to get a favourable mention in the gossip columns of The Times, The Financial Times and The Daily Telegraph when the report on the Civil List is published. Mr Airey [the Treasury Undersecretary] would be able to supply facts about the number of sittings etc which would bring home that in addition to his responsibilities for the economy and the IMF situation, the chancellor had to spend a great deal of time chairing the select committee."[38]

The story that duly appeared in The Times' Diary of December 3 - and was placed in the Civil Service files alongside the request - could almost have been lifted from the original Treasury memo:

"The Commons Select Committee on the Civil List...held no fewer than twenty meetings – all of them presided over by the chancellor Anthony Barber. This compares with the nine meetings which were necessary to fix the Queen's salary at the time of the accession in 1952 and only four meetings when George VI came to the throne."

In fairness, the Chancellor had devoted considerable time and effort to the matter in a year when he was trying to keep the UK economy afloat. In public he tried to make light of the workload mentioning that the report weighed in at "more than two hundred and fifty pages" and that the committee had seen more witnesses and considered more schemes "than any other Civil List committee at least this century (and I would guess in the previous century as well.)"[39] But in private he admitted to his frustration in dealing with this Sisyphean task, writing in exasperation to his friend, the Prime Minister Edward Heath:

"From time to time I have told you of the interminable meetings and problems we have faced in the Select Committee on the Civil List. It has been a long haul and there is more to come."[40] Three weeks later when Barber sent the draft report to the Foreign Secretary Sir Alec Douglas Home, he added the personal comment:

"Dear Alec, I thought you would like to be informed of the "progress" since March and I'm writing similarly to other ministers concerned. The Lord President and I have had quite a time! Yours Tony."[41]

A week later the Foreign Secretary wrote back "Thank you for your letter about Civil List arrangements. I think you have achieved marvels. Alec."[42] In truth, it was the palace that had achieved marvels - or certainly achieved one of its key aims of keeping the size of the Queen's private fortune away from the prying eyes of the committee members. They hardly laid a glove on Lord Cobbold during his two long bouts in the committee room (a frustrated Willie Hamilton described him and Sir Michael Adeane as looking like two rich funeral directors intent on defending the status quo).[43] When in his second appearance Roy Jenkins pressed the Lord Chamberlain for more precise information about the Queen's private wealth, all he could do was to repeat Her Majesty's earlier assurance that the rumours of it being in excess of £50m were "wildly exaggerated." Slightly abashed, he acknowledged that he had said nothing new: "I accept, Mr. Jenkins, that that does not go all the way to answer your question you asked me. I hope it may be of some help, but I'm afraid that is as far as I can go," to which Jenkins could only reply: "It leaves certain problems to the committee but I would not wish myself to press further."[44] A former Chancellor of the Exchequer had clearly been bested by a former Governor of the Bank of England.

This victory for the palace was underlined in the opening paragraphs of the published report: "there is no foundation for the suggestions which have been made in some quarters that, apart for these items [the Royal Palaces, the Crown Jewels and similar inalienable property], the Queen owns private funds which may now run into such figures as £50 million or more. Your committee were assured that these suggestions are wildly exaggerated and have thought it right to incorporate this assurance in their report."[45] Interestingly the wording of this passage so troubled the Chancellor that he scribbled on his draft script: "Surely this needs amending [unclear?] in the light of Cobbold's later evidence? I thought he went out of his way to point out the £50m was "widely exaggerated". This important, & was certainly his contention. Stick to his words". But a later Treasury memo revealed who was calling the shots by explaining that at the end of the day the line had not been amended because "the references to the personal fortune has already been cleared with the palace and reflect very closely the evidence given on the subject by the Lord Chamberlain.[46]

The whole issue was clearly explosive as was revealed by a Treasury lobby briefing paper which recommended that the line to be taken by the Chancellor if asked about the Queen's private funds was: "the committee questioned Lord Cobbold on this and his replies are given in the printed evidence. For myself I do not expect the Queen to subsidise the expenses of state out of her private income any more than we should expect a Prime Minister - or Chancellor of the Exchequer - to do the same."[47] We know of course from the released papers of Barber's private meeting with Cobbold on June 11 that he did think that the Queen's personal wealth should be made known in order to reach a broad assessment of how much Civil List money should be granted to her. On this matter of disclosure, the Treasury Sir Humphreys seem to have won a small battle over their minister.

Even though Willie Hamilton could not have known what was going on behind the scenes in Whitehall, he came to the firm conclusion a little later that "the establishment" had succeeded in screening the royal family's private wealth from parliament and the people.[48] His Labour colleague on the committee Joel Barnett was so dissatisfied with the palace's failure to supply information about the Queen's private fortune and the extent to which it had grown since 1952 as a result of her income tax exemption that he refused to vote for the new Civil List. They found an unlikely ally in The Financial Times which in a leader at the time of the report's release complained: "the committee has not made any serious attempt to find out all the relevant facts about Her Majesty's private income and it has resorted to the practice of "sidelining" to censor from its pages such bits of evidence as it is officially thought right to conceal."[49]

We now know what really went on because more than twenty-five Treasury papers were released in

2002 under the thirty year rule and for the most part they confirm the suspicion of Hamilton writing back in 1975 that the role of the select committee was to put "a coat of democratic whitewash" over a process that was far from democratic.[50] But intriguingly one file was held back - Civil List Bill preparatory papers 1971-72.[51] By definition it is impossible to know the precise contents of the secret bundle of documents, but given that the numerically closest declassified file - T326/1629 - covers the issue of whether the Queen's private wealth should be taken into consideration when assessing the Civil List, it is possible that the closed document includes some sensitive material about the Queen and her family wealth, otherwise why not release it. Almost a decade after its closure all the National Archives catalogue will say about the missing file is: "temporarily retained by the department". When a request was formally made to the department for its release or some explanation why it was not declassified, the Treasury declined to respond. A cynic might judge that they had decided to hammer an extra nail into the lid of the coffin after the thirty year rule had let in too much daylight.

Based on the evidence of the Civil List documents that were released, the charge of some limited collaboration between the Treasury and the palace over suppressing details about the royal family's inherited wealth is hard to refute. Palace officials were without doubt deeply worried about the release of any embarrassing financial information and Whitehall was more than content to keep things under wraps. With no royal deaths in 1971, the only thing buried in that year was bad news.

Chapter Nine
The Windsors And Their Wealth
– 1972-1986

"Damn it. The money was his, not hers"
Lord Mountbatten on hearing that the Duchess of Windsor had rejected his plans for the Duke's estate[1]

In the later years of his life, that supreme planner Earl Mountbatten was at the centre of a protracted struggle for control of the Duke of Windsor's estate. When alive Edward VIII had thrown a spanner into the well-lubricated succession machinery and now in his grave he threatened to do the same thing again. At stake was the royal reputation in the form of a cache of documents and some family heirlooms.

After the death of his cousin in Paris on 28 May 1972, Lord Louis took it upon himself in his unofficial role as the ombudsman of the royal family to ingratiate himself with the Duchess of Windsor to ensure that any royal property was repatriated to England. He felt he had the blessing of the Queen as she had asked him to help her with the duchess since he was the only member of the royal family remotely close to her. He had served in the Royal Navy with her husband, made him best man at his wedding and later was wont to describe himself as "David's devoted friend." It was Mountbatten who was granted the royal seal of approval to make the official television tribute to the former king which on the eve of the funeral was watched by his widow and other family members at Buckingham Palace. "He was more than my best man, he was my best friend all my life," Mountbatten emoted with more than a touch of hyperbole.[2]

What Mountbatten did not realise was that the duchess had long disliked his overbearing manner, dismissing according to legend his decision to give his wife Edwina a naval burial: "what can you say about a man who throws his wife into the sea?" She had earlier been warned by the duke, who liked to refer to him as "Tricky Dickie," not to trust him. In truth, the embittered former sovereign had never forgiven him for failing to repay the compliment to be best man at his own wedding in the south of France in 1937 - a wedding that was conspicuously boycotted by the rest of the royal family.

When on Friday June 2 Wallis and her large entourage (which included a maid, secretary and hairdresser) flew into Heathrow Airport for the funeral, much to her dismay Earl Mountbatten rather than the anticipated Prince of Wales was waiting on the tarmac to greet her. He drove her to Buckingham Palace in the royal-crested Rolls-Royce briefing her about the protocol for the lying-in-state prior to the funeral on the Monday and assuring her that she would be welcomed with open arms by all the family. She told him that she was particularly worried about how she would be received by the Queen Mother whom she believed "never approved of her."[3] To combat her evident nervousness, Mountbatten accompanied her to St George's Chapel, Windsor where the duke's body was lying in state.

What the Windsors dreaded was that she might collapse under the strain of the occasion but on the day the funeral ceremony passed off without incident - due in no small part to Mountbatten's adroit handling of the situation. At the luncheon in Windsor Castle after the service, he and Prince Philip were conveniently seated next to her. Without beating round the bush they asked her what she intended to do with the duke's archives and other possessions and whether she planned to return to America. She reportedly told than that "I won't be coming back to England, if that is what you are afraid of, except to visit the grave."[4] When it came to the duke's papers, she only wanted to do what was considered right and after some prompting from her two luncheon guests she agreed that the documents should be sent to the archives in Windsor.

A week later on June 15 the first batch of the duke's papers along with his orders of chivalry and other decorations which had been deposited in a Paris bank were duly handed over to a librarian from the Royal Archives, Sir Robin Mackworth-Young. But Mountbatten felt obliged to pay several visits on his own to the duchess to tie up the loose ends. The first on June 30 was presented purely as a social call but he was really there to enquire about what would happen to the rest of the estate of the duke and duchess. After this softening up exercise which resulted in the removal of the second batch of papers by the archivist in December, in early February he was back in Paris with the duchess and over tea suggested that the duke's assets should be placed in a trust fund under the control of Prince Charles, his successor as Prince of Wales, who could keep his memory alive by distributing the money to worthy causes in Wales. In a letter to the duchess eleven days later confirming arrangements, he also offered his services as executor of the duchess's own estate.[5]

Far from weakening her defences, this bombardment of advice from the former Supreme Allied Commander only served to stiffen her resolve. She began to tire of his repeated hints that she might pass on some of her husband's gold boxes and other souvenirs to her "old friend Dickie" and in their next meeting insisted that her lawyer be present. Finally, she wrote him two terse letters: the first saying that she did not want to set up the proposed foundation preferring to use the money in ways she felt appropriate, and the second making it clear that he should no longer raise the matter of her and the duke's death as it was making her depressed.[6]

Meanwhile the judicial process of winding up the duke's estate was being completed with less drama. On 27 November 1972 probate was granted in London. As a former sovereign his will was sealed by right and the official entry at the Principal Registry records that he left £7,845 17s. This of course was just his English estate which most likely amounted to no more than a few UK bank accounts and investments made by his London stockbroker and did not include his French assets which would have been part of his French probate which was granted a week later on 4 December 1972.

For more than three decades France had been his home and one of the main reasons for this was its huge tax benefits. After the Second World War, he had considered moving to the United States, his wife's homeland, where he had many friends. It seemed the natural place to settle for a man who through his early impressionable visits to New York had been, according to court gossip, "Americanised" and "modernised" - to such an extent that he had begun to speak with a slight American accent.[7] His hope was to take up some diplomatic position helping to improve Anglo-American relations. But Walter Monckton, his lawyer and mentor, advised that the American tax laws were "strict and egalitarian" and that the US Treasury would be unlikely to grant an exemption to a former king with such a large fortune.[8] The duke had suggested that if he were granted diplomatic status in his capacity as some form of roving ambassador he would automatically be exempted from US tax, but this idea was soon quashed by the Foreign Office who took the view that the Americans would soon see through the appointment as a ploy to circumvent their tax regime.[9]

At this time, the duke seemed obsessed by the evils of taxation – not just in America but in Britain too. When his brother-in-law Earl Harewood died in May 1947, there was much talk about how his landed estate might be annihilated by death duties and other wealth taxes. Echoing Lord Crawford's warning that a national scandal was taking place before their eyes.[10] The duke lamented in a letter to Queen Mary how thirty years of Liberal and Labour legislation was wrecking a special part of national life – the country estate.[11] While there is an element of self-pleading to this observation, the duke nevertheless had a point. When combined with a seventy-year depression in land prices, the relentless rise in death duties from 15% in 1914 to a frightening 75% in 1948 had decimated the landed wealth of the British aristocracy. In the postwar years of Clement Attlee's welfare state socialism, Earl Harewood lost two thirds of his Yorkshire holdings, Viscount Portman had to dispose of all of his Dorset estate and the Duke of Argyll was forced to sell the Island of Tiree and much of Kintyre.[12] Although some of these estates were accepted by the Treasury in lieu of death duties, there was a limit to the number of mansions that heritage bodies like the National Trust could accommodate and between 1945 and 1955 four hundred country houses had to be demolished. By 1956 little more than one third of the peerage possessed a country estate.[13] At the back of the mind of any British royal – even an exiled one – was the worry that he might go the way of his aristocratic cousins. The only escape from such a fate was to be granted special treatment from the state.

In stark contrast to the United States and the United Kingdom, France had a long heritage of welcoming exiled monarchs to its shores and offering them generous tax concessions. After further inquiries to the French Treasury, it was learned that the duke would be granted diplomatic status, given police protection and exempted from many taxes. He would pay only modest property taxes, no income tax and many household purchases - including his television sets, vacuum cleaners and even cars - would be duty free. Even though the duke had no great love for France (during his thirty years in the country he never managed to learn the language despite his fluency in German), had almost no close French friends and liked to joke that the only thing wrong with the French countryside was that it was "populated with Frenchman"), he could hardly afford to live elsewhere given his lavish lifestyle and his aversion to paying tax.[14] Much to his delight in 1959 the Bank of

England confirmed his UK status as a non-resident for tax purposes.[15]

The tax privileges did not end with his death. Soon after his funeral, the duchess's lawyer negotiated a generous deal with the French state whereby she would pay no income tax and her husband no death duties. The latter was a considerable saving for an estate estimated to be worth well over £10m and the former was hardly necessary given that she would inherit the estate and enjoy the £5,000 annuity from the abdication financial settlement that her husband had persuaded the palace to pass to her on his death.

The duke had had plenty of time to put his financial affairs in order and prepare a smooth succession. After suffering for many years from a heart condition and other ailments brought on by his heavy smoking, he was diagnosed in November 1971 with throat cancer. He undertook an exhausting forty-one day course of cobalt treatment which brought little relief and was ended in January. On February 21 he underwent an exploratory operation that revealed that the tumour on his throat was inoperable and that he was unlikely to live more than six months. He did survive long enough to receive the Queen on May 18 on her state visit to France, much to the relief of the British Ambassador to Paris, Sir Christopher Soames, who had made it clear to his doctor that it would be a political disaster if the duke died during the visit.[16] Having fulfilled his duty in receiving his niece, the sovereign, the duke began to fade fast and died ten days later.

He had signed his last will and testament on 6 January 1972. On the advice of his long-standing English lawyer Sir Godfrey Morley and the French senator Jacques Roselli, he had decided to place all his assets in a trust of which the duchess would be the sole beneficiary during her lifetime. Should she predecease him, the following bequests would be given to his staff - $30,000 to his Bahamian valet Sydney Johnson, $20,000 his chef Lucien Massy, $15,000 to his driver Georgio Martin and $10,000 to his maid Giselle Deberry. Several other associates including the duchess's hairdressers Messieurs Alexandre and Edouard were each to receive $5,000, while his personal secretary John Utter was meant to get $10,000 but this was revoked by a codicil.[17] The amount of money that each received gives a clue to the importance he attached to them in the household and their loyalty of service. His trusted valet Johnson had been in his employ since his governorship of the Bahamas in 1940.

According to the royal chronicler Hugo Vickers who gained access to the will by virtue of his friendship with the duchess's personal secretary, the duke's clear intention was that the duchess should benefit fully from the estate during her lifetime but that on her death the residue would return to the United Kingdom and be donated to charity. A registered company had been created by Sir Godfrey Morley's law firm to channel the funds to this end. Morley was named as executor along with another English lawyer Ronald Edgar Plummer and the Windsors' French lawyer Suzanne Blum. For the will of a French resident to be valid in France, a French executor was necessary - although Maitre Blum was in no way involved in the drafting of the document or even notified that she would be executor. By all accounts, the duke deliberately kept her out of the loop.[18]

The duchess seemed in the dark too. On one occasion, Mountbatten went out of his way to confirm to her that the duke had indeed left her his *entire* estate.[19] This was not strictly speaking true since there was one other royal beneficiary. Mountbatten's eldest daughter, Lady Brabourne, was bequeathed an inscribed copy of a royal family tree which he had had printed privately and given to the duke.[20] This would appear to be the same personalised chart mentioned earlier that Mountbatten bequeathed to all of his grandchildren.

Although the precise value of the duke's estate was never made public, a breakdown of his assets - ranging from landed property to jewellery and other personal possessions - suggests that the duchess inherited a small fortune. Her most important inheritance in terms of both their monetary and sentimental value were the jewels. Here we need to unwind the love story to get an idea of their true worth. As was mentioned in Chapter Four, the Prince of Wales showered Wallis with jewellery from the very start of their romance in

May 1934 when Lady Thelma Furness found herself supplanted as the royal mistress. That summer on a cruise round the Bay of Biscay, he gave his new love a stunning Cartier diamond and emerald charm.[21]

In the months that followed the trickle of jewels turned into a flood. He bought her a magnificent pair of diamond clips ostensibly as a Jubilee present in May 1935 and by October of that year Lady Diana Cooper after dining at Fort Belvedere observed that Wallis was "glittering and dripped in new jewels and clothes."[22] When another leading socialite Mrs Belloc Lowndes innocently wondered whether they might be costume jewellery she was told in no uncertain terms that the prince had given her £50,000 worth of jewels at Christmas followed by another £60,000 in the New Year.[23]

Some saw this cascade of gifts as a reflection of the prince's emotional immaturity (one diamond bracelet came with the inscription "a boy loves a girl more and more and more"). Wallis who privately referred to the prince as "Peter Pan" wondered whether the infatuation might soon wear off, but with her own household income constrained by her husband's business problems, she was now beginning to get hooked on the royal high life and there was clearly an element of wilful financial entanglement on the prince's behalf in his extravagant gift giving. Just as he was emotionally dependent on her, so she would become financially dependent on him. In addition to the jewels, she received a more than generous income from the prince, believed to be £6,000 a year.[24]

After the abdication, he never recovered from the snub of being told in a letter from the new king that Wallis would be denied the title of "Her Royal Highness" – despite being the wife of a royal duke. The news came on the eve of their wedding on 3 June 1937 prompting the ex-king to retort: "what a damnable wedding present." In public he continued to address her as "Her Royal Highness" or "*son altesse*" and instructed his French-speaking staff to do likewise, as well as bow and curtsey in her presence. Some interpreted his gifts of jewels fit for a queen as a form of compensation for the royal title he could never give her. On 29 June 1937 he paid £6,320 to the jewellers van Clef and Arpels and a fortnight later wrote a cheque for £1,000 to their Parisian neighbour Cartier. The outbreak of war did little to dampen his ardour. Even in May 1940 as France was on the brink of falling to the Nazis, he found time to visit Cartier's showroom on the Rue de la Paix to buy her another hoard of jewels leaving detailed instructions for a special piece to be made – a flamboyant diamond brooch in the shape of a flamingo with tail feathers made of rubies, sapphires and emeralds.

At the time of the duke's death, Wallis's jewel box was locked away in the vaults of the Morgan Guaranty Bank in the Place Vendome and the secrecy surrounding its contents prompted rumours that it contained some crown property - a set of emeralds that he had inherited from his grandmother Queen Alexandra. To his dying day the Duke of Windsor always maintained that he had never given his wife any jewels that were royal property. He insisted he kept all the receipts for the duchess's jewellery, behaviour consistent with someone obsessed with money. There is some evidence to suggest that he was telling the truth. According to a letter from the socialite Maggie Greville, the emeralds did once belong to Queen Alexandra who left them to her daughter Princess Victoria who sold them to the London jewellers Garrard. King Edward VIII later bought the jewels from Cartier's in Paris who were acting as an agent for Garrard.

The only Windsor jewels that we know for certain made their way back to the royal family were some gems that the duchess gave to the children of the late Duke of Kent in memory of her husband's close bonds with Prince George. In 1977 some unspecified jewels were given to Princess Alexandra and the Duchess of Kent and in 1978 - following his marriage to Marie Christine von Reibnitz - Prince Michael of Kent was given a diamond brooch in the shape of the Prince of Wales's feather and a pair of panther shaped emerald earrings.[25]

The Duke of Windsor's liquid assets were believed to be worth well in excess of £3 million. A former financial comptroller admitted that when he saw the duke's portfolio of investments in the sixties it amounted to £3 million and since he was famously reluctant to dip into his capital by the seventies its value would have grown considerably if only by compound interest. The money had been built up from his savings as Prince of Wales from the Duchy of Cornwall revenues (£70,941 in 1936 alone),[26] his generous abdication settlement and income from his best-selling memoir "A King's Story" and two other successful royal books "The Crown and the People" and "A Family Album."

Always on the look-out for a quick profit, he had mixed while Governor of the Bahamas with a number of tax-exile tycoons (some with shadier pasts than others) whose financial brains he was not afraid to pick. Later on trips to the United States he took more formal advice from Charles Allen of the respected New York financial house Allen & Co, while his European-based financial affairs were placed in the hands of his personal banker Maurice Amiguet of Societe de Banque Suisse in Zurich. He also used a stockbroker in London, James Fitch at E.R.Lewis and Co, and judging by his UK probate it is likely that he had a small portfolio of shares in the UK. Such was his expertise in equities and his willingness to take calculated risks that the duke – as his official biographer pointed out – could have carved out a successful career as a stockbroker.

On the debit side, it should be pointed out that he lost a large sum of money on the foreign exchange market in the late fifties when it was discovered that his private secretary Victor Waddilove had been defrauding him on a long term basis. The scandal was hushed up to avoid embarrassment to the duke (and the extent of his knowledge of or even involvement in the embezzlement was never revealed), but in December 1958 Waddilove eventually admitted that he had operated illegally on the black market with his employer's money as part of a larger one billion franc crime ring. To stop him taking his story to the press "Mr Light Fingers" (as the duchess dubbed him) was reportedly paid off by the duke's advisors.[27]

When it comes to landed property, the duke was more secure. He owned the EP ranch in the hills of Alberta, Canada - and for a time harboured a dream of retiring there until it was eventually sold in the mid-sixties when he became too frail to enjoy it fully.[28] But his prized possession was the Moulin de la Tuilerie at Gif sur Yvette - better known as "the Mill." In July 1952 he paid the fashion designer and painter Etienne Drian $80,000 for this semi-derelict 18th century mill house set in twenty-three acres of woodland and semi-arable land in the valley of Chevreuse forty-five miles south of Paris. The money came in part from the proceeds of his book sales but in 1952 he also had to get special dispensation from Churchill's government to transfer from the United Kingdom an extra £20,000 (on top of earlier £80,000 remittance) which exceeded the strict exchange controls of the time.[29] For the next four years he spent a further $100,000 converting the stone-walled mill and the old wooden barn into a Fort Belvedere-like country house replete with English garden and babbling brook. Its *interior* decoration was less English – certainly in the view of Lady Diana Mosley who thought its apricot-coloured carpets and other bright features "more Palm Beach" than French or English. Much of this was the work of Stephene Boudin, the same designer that Chips Channon had hired in the 1936 to decorate his London home where he entertained the then Edward VIII and his brother Prince George. Although the design work was not to everyone's tastes – Cecil Beaton called it "overdone and chichi" - it nevertheless proved a good investment as in June 1973 the property was sold to the Swiss industrialist Edmond Artar for two million French francs (almost £400,000).

In the spring of 1953 he acquired a twenty-five-year lease from the city of Paris to No 4 Route du Champ d'Entrainement, an elegant turn-of–the-century mansion with a gatekeeper's lodge, garages and two greenhouses in its own two-acre park in the Bois de Boulogne. It was the former home of General de Gaulle and would be the Windsors' main residence for the rest of their lives. Thanks to the duchess's handiwork, it soon had all the trappings of a royal residence - from the driveway lamp-post topped with a gilded crown to the royal arms carved in wood in the entrance hall. Even the footman wore royal livery. In an echo of his buying her jewellery fit for a queen, he seemed to be building her a palatial home suitable for a royal highness.

Royal Legacy

Although the duchess tried to impose her own taste on the decor - spending a small fortune on upholstery and fittings as well as on her fine collection of china and porcelain - their home's valuable artworks and furnishings came from the duke's family. Full length portraits of Queen Mary and the duke in Garter robes, the abdication desk, the Garter standard and other heirloom treasures from his former English homes of York House and Fort Belvedere adorned the reception rooms, giving a further reminder as if any were needed of his royal ancestry. On a visit in September 1970, Cecil Beaton was struck by how the drawing room positively overflowed with royal souvenirs, wax seals and framed photographs of Queen Victoria and Queen Mary.[30]

It is difficult to put a price tag on the value of the mansion as the duke never bought the freehold but the exceedingly generous terms of the lease meant that after his death, the duchess was allowed to stay there for the remaining fourteen years of her life on a peppercorn rent. The French authorities also exempted her of income tax and death duties on her estate. As an expression of gratitude (or perhaps as part of the deal with the state) in March 1973 she donated her Louis VI furniture and porcelain to the Louvre and other French museums. Some of the remaining furniture was later bought by Mohamed Al Fayed for reportedly fifteen million French francs when he took over the lease and contents of the house.[31]

Despite inheriting such fabulous wealth, the duchess was worried about money. Convinced that she was living beyond her means, she felt obliged to reduce the size of her household from thirty-two (including two secretaries, two cooks, a butler as well as a valet, various gardeners and a gatekeeper) to a dozen key staff. Having always left financial matters in the hands of her husband, she knew little about running a tight budget and with her health now declining, she began to rely more and more on her lawyer Maitre Suzanne Blum to organise her affairs. Some have even suggested that Blum may have encouraged her worries about money in order to ease out staff and so increase her leverage over the duchess.

Just two years younger than the duchess, the Frenchwoman had strong American connections having studied law at Columbia University in New York and worked for the big Hollywood film studios representing Jack Warner, Charlie Chaplin and Rita Hayworth and gaining a reputation for being one of France's toughest attorneys. Her introduction to the Windsors came through her first husband, Paul Weill, who as the Paris representative of Sir Godfrey Morley's London firm of solicitors sometimes acted for the duke. Fiercely protective of her clients, Blum became the Windsors' bulldog - or as the wife of the British ambassador to Paris put it more diplomatically: "she defends the duchess like a lioness with her cubs."[32]

Maitre Blum was granted exclusive control of the duchess's legal affairs in January 1973 after the dismissal of her English solicitor. Blum managed to convince the duchess that Sir Godfrey Morley had been mismanaging the duke's estate and that the scheme to put all his assets into an English trust would be financially disastrous since it would be liable to 70% tax in France.[33] On 16 February 1973 the duchess rewrote her will that Morley had helped draft on 8 November 1972 to dovetail with the duke's estate and appointed Blum her executor instead of Morley. Further codicils were added on 4 December 1973 and 17 March 1977 which in their total effect with the new will overturned all the provisions to repatriate the duke's assets to England.

Almost everything was left to the Pasteur Institute, the renowned medical foundation in Paris. This was interpreted by Michael Bloch in his official biography as a show of gratitude to France for all the kindness and privilege the nation had shown to the duke and the duchess.[34] It should be pointed out that when choosing between countries she had no particular affection for the United Kingdom (where she was denied access for so long) and she had no siblings or surviving relatives in the United States. She was noted for having many homosexual friends (including the

Woolworth's heir Jimmy Donahue with whom she was rumoured to have had an affair) and she would have been sympathetic to the work of the Pasteur Institute in Paris which was at the forefront of research into finding a vaccine against AIDS.

Other biographers have hinted that the duchess's desire to leave everything to France might have been influenced by her French lawyer. In what he describes as "her takeover of the duchess" Hugo Vickers argues that Blum was motivated by "an irrational hatred of the English that developed during her sole visit to Britain [and]…extended to the royal family."[35] Not long after Blum rearranged the duchess's estate and organised the transfer of some the Windsors' furniture to Versailles and other French museums, she was made Commander of the Legion d'Honneur by the French state. In the view of Johanna Schuetz, the duchess's long suffering personal secretary who would soon be dismissed by Blum on the spurious grounds of being unstable, it was well merited since the *maître* had certainly served France well.[36]

As the duchess became weaker following a near-fatal intestinal haemorrhage in November 1975, Blum's influence grew stronger. Supposedly on doctors' orders the *maître* discouraged visits from friends and acquaintances and little by little the duchess became a prisoner in her own home - often eating too little and drinking too much. In October 1977 Blum was given power of attorney over all her affairs. With this seal of approval, she began to protect not just her client's wealth but also her image. On one level this meant using France's strict privacy laws to keep the paparazzi at bay, on one occasion exacting $30,000 in damages from Paris Soir for publishing illicit photos of an obviously distressed duchess being nursed in her garden but it also involved guarding her reputation and lasting legacy. Any biographer who had the temerity to suggest that the Windsors may have had carnal relations before their marriage would be threatened with a law suit. Caroline Blackwood who wrote an unflattering although largely accurate portrait of Wallis in her dotage - "The Last of the Duchess" - had to wait until the death of Blum in 1994 before it could be published.

By gaining power of attorney over the duchess, Blum also acquired control of the documentary record. She claimed that Wallis gave her written authorisation to publish some of her most intimate letters and papers, although she was reluctant to produce it to sceptical biographers like Hugo Vickers. To counter an unfavourable picture of the Windsors given in the Thames Television series "Edward and Mrs. Simpson" and several new hostile biographies, including "The Windsor Story" by two American journalists, Blum decided to release to the press some of their love letters that testified to the true depth of their feelings for each other. She also authorised her legal assistant, Michael Bloch, to write several books based on the Windsors' papers and putting forward their viewpoint.[37]

Blum now saw herself as guardian of the Windsor myth. As one royal chronicler observed after trying to interview her in 1980, "the duchess had always been a figure of myth and it was this myth that had captivated her old lawyer."[38] Johanna Schuetz was instructed to burn some of the duke's papers, while her predecessor as private secretary John Utter felt obliged to decline an offer to write a memoir about the Windsors on the grounds that anyone who destroys the myth will be despised.[39] Despite his loyalty, in 1975 he too was dismissed from the Windsor household.

By 1980, the duchess was confined to bed and in need of constant medical supervision. Now that her household staff had been reduced to four, her life was dominated by her nurses, her doctor Jean Thin and of course Maitre Blum. Crippled by rheumatism, no longer able to speak and only kept going by a life support machine, the widow of the former king of England was little more than a vegetable.

The duchess died two months short of her ninetieth birthday on 24 April 1986 and was interred next to her husband in the royal burial ground at Frogmore. A year later, on April 3 1987, Blum put the duchess's jewellery and other personal possessions up for sale. Sotheby's puffed the auction in its Geneva showroom as the "sale of the century" and enlisted buyers from round the world to take part in the bidding by satellite but even their wildest dreams were surpassed when the sale realised £31 million, six times the estimated price. The duchess's Mogul emerald engagement ring that the duke gave her on the evening after she divorced Ernest Simpson fetched £1.2 million, while the ruby and diamond necklace inscribed "My Wallis from her David" brought in £1.5 million. A diamond clip in the shape of the Prince of Wales's feathers given to her in 1935 was bought by Elizabeth Taylor for £350,000. The highest price paid was £1.8 million for the famous McLean diamond ring given to the duchess in 1950. But to the disappointment of hunters of the missing Alexandra emeralds there were no recognisable royal jewels among the two hundred and thirty lots.

A few antiques also went under the hammer. A 1910 gilt inkstand, an 1820 silver seal box and an 1823 desk set all commanded good prices - as did some of the duke's personal items such as tobacco boxes, clocks, swords and even a sporran. After the auction house deducted their premium, the Pasteur Institute was left with around £26 million. The bulk of the money was spent on a new building for research on retroviral diseases, including cancer and HIV (AIDS).

⚜ ⚜ ⚜

The world record proceeds from the auction give the lie to notion often propagated by the duke and duchess that they were ever short of money. Even if one allows for the fact that Sotheby's prices were inflated by the cachet of their royal name and romantic story, their combined wealth - including landed property, liquid assets and jewellery - would still be worth tens of millions of pounds at today's prices. The duchess's inheritance from the duke was further inflated by the exemption on any death duties. With no tax to pay, one would have thought that there was little to hide and therefore no reason to keep the duke's testamentary affairs secret. Yet his English will was sealed like other royals of his rank. Even though in his lifetime he rebelled against the monarchy and its cold-hearted customs that prevented him from marrying the woman he loved, in death he respected its protocols on testamentary secrecy.

What is unusual about the secrecy concerning the Windsor inheritance is that it concerned not just paper money but paper documents. The fact that within hours of the Duke of Windsor being buried, Lord Mountbatten and Prince Philip had reportedly asked his grieving widow what she intended to do with his private papers indicates how important it was for the royal family to control the documentary record. If there was anything remotely embarrassing in the duke's collection of letters - particularly relating to the abdication - then it was far better if it was all put under lock and key in the archives at Windsor Castle. This would explain why Mountbatten felt obliged to go to such lengths get the material back to Britain, even going behind the duchess's back to make an arrangement with the duke's staff. Suzanne Blum later alleged that two individuals acting on royal authority "burgled" the duke's filing cabinets without the knowledge or consent of the duchess. A small batch of documents were later returned "by mutual agreement" although the palace categorically denied any wrongdoing and it is now widely accepted that the *maître* may have embroidered the truth.[40]

The battle over control of the duke's image continued well after his death. In the early 1980s the palace authorised Philip Ziegler to write an official biography of Edward VIII and "by generous permission of Her Majesty" as he later acknowledged was accorded unrestricted access to the Royal Archives at Windsor.[41] This included access to the crucial memorandum of the king's private secretary Lord Wigram that revealed new details of George V's will and the duke's bitter disappointment at his inheritance. Many reviewers thought that Ziegler produced a less than flattering portrait of the duke.

The duke's camp provided their own version of events. Shortly after the duchess's death in 1986 her executor Maitre Blum authorised Michael Bloch to release a collection of her letters owned by the estate. In the preface to "Wallis and Edward: Letters 1931-37" Bloch explained that it was the duchess's clear wish that the letters be published on her death since she had been hurt by several recent biographies giving an image of their characters and relationship that she found "unrecognisable." She was thus keen that when the moment was right "the truth should be known to the world" via "the authentic contemporary record."[42] In 1996 Bloch went on to write a personal biography of the duchess that drew on the Windsors' correspondence and tried to set the record straight on "her much-misunderstood life." Most reviewers found it if not a hagiographic portrait then certainly one sympathetic to her viewpoint.

And what exactly was in the duchess's will? When the biographer Caroline Blackwood had the temerity to pose this question to her executor, Maitre Blum exploded: "If I have anything to do with it, the duchess's will is never going to be published. Never. Never."[43]

Chapter Ten
Diana's Estate Of War
– 1997-1998

"Basically not a lot of thought went into it. It has all the hallmarks of someone saying: 'You'd better make a will'"
A legal expert's verdict on Princess Diana's will

If in popular myth Wallis's marriage to the Duke of Windsor represented "the greatest royal love story" of the first half of the twentieth century, then Diana's "fairytale wedding" to Prince Charles played almost the same role in the second half. In their different ways, both stories ended tragically and so it was somehow inevitable that the only time their two trajectories crossed was in death. When Mohamed al Fayed's son Dodi died with Diana in the Paris car crash such was his grief that he decided to sell the contents of his Bois de Boulogne house that he had once dreamed might be their matrimonial home. That house was the Windsors' mansion in Neuilly which he had acquired through the duchess's executor Maitre Blum, paying £3 million to the Pasteur

Institute for its contents. These included - as the later auction catalogue showed - heirlooms passed down from George V, such as a set of silver dishes with the cipher of George III, the Garter banner of Edward VII and silver ashtrays from the royal yacht of Queen Victoria. The sale in February 1998 raised a total of £14.5 million which was donated by al Fayed to a charity in memory of Dodi and Diana.

A second - and more substantial - royal parallel to Diana is Princess Helena Victoria. At first sight, no two princesses could be more dissimilar. One was a global celebrity who dazzled the public with her model looks, stylish clothes and fabulous jewellery, the other was a plain Jane who liked to dress in sombre shades and hide her long face beneath voluminous hats. One married the future King of England, had two sons and seventeen godchildren - not to mention a string of lovers; the other had neither a husband nor children or indeed a single niece or nephew. One perished in a Paris underpass in the most publicised death of the 20th century; the other died almost anonymously in an obscure London flat.

Yet they shared one significant thing in common: they both left their wills unsealed and open to public inspection.

The first thing that strikes one on inspecting the two wills is how simple they are. Both leave almost all their estate to just two heirs: for Helena Victoria it was Prince Michael of Kent and Alexander Ramsay, while for Diana it was the two royal princes - William and Harry. With few beneficiaries, both wills are relatively short: Helena Victoria's runs to barely four pages, Diana's to six.

The second noticeable feature is that they both use trusts. Discretionary or will trusts are a typical device for royals and many other rich families to minimise death duties but in this case they were employed because three of the four heirs were minors. Prince Michael was just five years old when Helena Victoria died, while Prince Harry was twelve and William fifteen. Michael would have to wait until he was twenty-one before his trust fund came on stream; for Harry and William it was twenty-five, although this would be later changed so they could access funds sooner.

When it came to the matter of chattels or personal possessions, both wills use memoranda or a letter of wishes to govern their distribution. We saw earlier how Helena Victoria gave her sister total control over her jewellery and personal items, subject to any memoranda signed by her and left with her will or papers on her death. Similarly Princess Diana gave her chattels free of inheritance tax to her executors to dispose of according to any written memorandum or notes of hers. It would later emerge that she left behind a specific letter of wishes which - as we shall see - became the subject of legal dispute.

Attached to both wills was a codicil that altered the balance of executors in favour of an elder sister. In June 1945 - a few weeks before the end of the war in Europe and two years after writing her will

- Helena Victoria decided to replace two of her three executors (her solicitor John Nairne and a banking accountant John England) with the anonymous Coutts Bank leaving her sister, Princess Marie Louise, in the powerful position as the only named executor. In February1996 - two and half years after writing her will - Diana decided to replace one executor (her personal secretary Patrick Jephson) with her sister, Lady Sarah McCorquodale. For Diana, Sarah was the closest member of the family - just as Marie Louise had been for Helena Victoria. Her mother was named as the other executor.

So, Diana and Helena Victoria had more in common than meets the eye. One other significant bond is that they both lost their title or style and with it some of their royal status. As we have seen, during World War One Her Serene Highness Princess Helena Victoria of Schleswig-Holstein was divested of her German territorial title and never granted an English replacement or a fully royal style. Diana lost her royal highness title as a consequence of her divorce settlement in 1996. Without full royal status both princesses threw themselves into charitable work and the causes they adopted were remarkably similar. Helena Victoria worked tirelessly for her mother's Princess Christian Nursing Home in Windsor, while Diana championed the Great Ormond Street Hospital for Children in London. Helena Victoria helped the casualties of World War One through her YWCA work; Diana the casualties of civil wars through her campaign against land mines. Helena Victoria aided the destitute of the East End through her docklands charity, whereas Diana housed the homeless of central London through the charity Centre Point. By dint of this caring work, they swapped their royal status for a saintly one and became "a people's princess."

Where the two princesses differed, however, was in the size of their estates. Helena Victoria's was valued at £52,435, Diana's at £21,468,352. Probate for Diana's estate was finally granted on 2 March 1998 - six months after her death - following the payment of £8,502,330 in inheritance tax.

Within a few days of the granting of probate, Martyn Gowar, the senior partner of the city law firm Laurence Graham acting for the estate, agreed to release her will to the public. "The most disconcerting thing for me," he later admitted, "was that at the time we published all this [estate] information...I was being asked to do what I had always spent my life not doing, which was disclosing details to the public, and indeed the world, of a client's affairs."[1]

As the probate office in Somerset House prepared two hundred copies of the will in anticipation of a flood of requests from the general public for a soon-to-be 75 pence bestseller, just a stone's throw down the Strand Gowar handed journalists camped outside his office a press pack detailing all aspects of her estate. This strategy of full disclosure was designed to satiate the media's feeding frenzy: "If we had not published those details, they would have made the story run for weeks and weeks. By disclosing the information, the story became something of a twenty-four-hour wonder. That would not have happened if we hadn't bared body and soul."[2]

But Gowar wasn't the one who had decided to go for the Full Monty of testamentary transparency. "It was the decision of the family that the will should be made public. They felt it would be appropriate in view of the intense public interest." Two of the three executors were family: Diana's sister Lady Sarah McCorquodale and her mother Frances Shand Kydd, while the third was the bishop who confirmed her, the Rt Rev. Richard Chartres. They could have decided to be more discreet but that was hardly the Spencer way. Diana had a history of going public with details of her private life - first with her cooperation with Andrew Morton's book revealing the sham of her marriage, then the Panorama television interview with Martin Bashir which put the final nail in the relationship and finally with the details of her divorce proceedings which were leaked to the press. Her very popularity was based on the fact that she wore her heart on her sleeve. Even from the grave she seemed to be managing the media and her public image.

Lady Sarah too had once been famously indiscreet with the press. When she herself was having a relationship with Prince Charles in February 1978, she gave an interview to two tabloid reporters spilling the beans on her own battles with the bottle and anorexia nervosa and revealing according those reports how "I would not marry anyone I did not love whether he were the dustman or the King of England." The romance did not survive the interview. When she warned Prince Charles of its publication, his response was reportedly "you have just done something extremely stupid." Her mother Frances who had "bolted" from Earl Spencer to marry Peter Shand Kydd was understandably more wary of the press, but after Diana's death she went out of her way to collaborate with the journalist Max Riddington and his colleague Gavan Naden in a sympathetic portrait of her life - "Frances: the remarkable story of Princess Diana's mother."

If they had wanted to avoid publicity, the two family executors could have instructed their solicitors to make an application to seal Diana's will. This would have been done on the basis of the right of any member of the public to apply to the courts for greater privacy on the grounds that publication was "undesirable or otherwise inappropriate." They could also have tried to use the blanket royal prerogative that allowed all royal wills to be sealed as a matter of course - providing the standard summons was served on the Treasury Solicitor.

But why was it in the interests of the Spencer family to go out of their way to protect the privacy of the Windsors? It should be remembered that in the aftermath of Diana's death there was considerable bad blood between the two families. This was dramatically brought into the open by the funeral address of her brother Charles. In what was seen as a thinly veined attack on the Queen for taking away the HRH title of the princess, the Earl Spencer declared "she proved she needed no royal title to continue to generate her particular brand of magic...I pledge that we, your blood family, will do all we can to continue the imaginative and loving way in which you were steering these two exceptional young men so that their souls are not simply immersed by duty and tradition, but can sing openly as you planned." One royal chronicler interpreted the remarks as "the nearest thing you get in the late 20th century to an Act of Sedition."[3] Both Prince Charles and the Duke of Edinburgh were said to be so annoyed by the rebuke that they had to be restrained from making an official response.

Of course, the royal family could have tried to put pressure on the Spencers to seal Diana's will. The fact that she had lost her HRH title would not have necessarily prevented her testamentary affairs coming under the catch-all title of royal will. It was later confirmed that Buckingham Palace regarded her as a member of the royal family by virtue of the fact that she was the mother of the second and third in line to the throne and even after her death the palace seriously considered restoring her royal title. Both Her Highness Princess Marie Louise and Lady Patricia Ramsay had set a precedent of princesses who despite losing their royal title were still able to have their wills sealed.

The one person to whom the Windsors might have turned to put the case for sealing the will - or at least being as discreet as possible - was Patrick Jephson, Diana's initial choice of executor. Just a week after the princess's death the former naval commander declared in a newspaper interview that his first duty was to the monarchy and he later confirmed in his memoirs that he shared "an establishment outlook."[4] After eight years' service in the royal household - first as an equerry to the joint office of the Prince and Princess of Wales and then after the separation as private secretary to Diana alone - he was in a perfect position to act as a bridge between Kensington Palace and Buckingham Palace. Indeed, in his last two years in the job he had worked behind the scenes to "stitch together a rapprochement," trying to persuade the Queen's household that Diana could be a valuable asset to the royal family and trying to persuade Diana to curb some of her wilder comments and be more conciliatory to Charles. But all his efforts were torpedoed by the princess's interview to Panorama in which to his horror she suggested that Charles was not fit to be king and the monarchy was out of touch with the public. He only learnt of what exactly she had said by watching a video of the programme *after* its broadcast. Diana's refusal to keep him in the loop with her public statements proved the final straw in their disintegrating relationship. A few weeks later, he resigned as her personal secretary and executor of her will. With his departure went any direct leverage the Windsors might have had over the estate.

Even if they had found a sympathetic ear amongst the Spencers, any attempt to keep Diana's affairs secret would have met with opposition from the wider public. In the weeks following Diana's funeral, the mood of the nation was - if not exactly pro-republican then certainly hostile to the Windsors whose seemingly cold-hearted response to the death was symbolised by their refusal to fly the royal standard at half mast outside Buckingham Palace. When Prince Philip sought advice from his old friend Lord Brabourne on how best to respond to Earl Spencer's funeral eulogy, the media-savvy baron reportedly told him to do absolutely nothing. Similarly, when Charles learned that Diana's early death meant that legally he might be entitled to reduce his divorce settlement pay-off, his advisors pointed out that it would not be wise to be seen to be bending the rules in the current climate. Consequently, the royal family kept their heads down.

When the will was made public, the Windsors had to swallow some embarrassing details. The first page stated Diana's clear wish that should she predecease her husband he would consult with her mother with regard to the upbringing, education and welfare of their children. Written in June 1993 soon after the separation from the prince, this clause was interpreted as a snub to the parenting skills of Charles. In fact, this line is almost the only reference to her husband in the entire will. In many respects, the will is more interesting for what it does not include than what it does. There is no bequest to or mention of Paul Burrell, her long-serving butler who was portrayed as "her rock." Nor are there any bequests to any member of the Spencer family or any mention of the many charities she supported.

Was this act of omission deliberate or just sloppy? The simplicity of the will suggests that little planning went into its drafting. One legal source close to the estate was quoted as saying: "Basically not a lot of thought went into it. It has all the hallmarks of someone saying 'You'd better make a will'. It is just thoroughly unimaginative and pretty standard. But then to be fair nobody thought she would die."[5]

Indeed, Diana was brimming with life when she wrote the will in June 1993. She was about to embark on a solo tour abroad to Zimbabwe, having achieved what most people interpreted as a victory over her husband in the separation agreement. Quite apart from granting her a private office and staff and letting her keep her title Princess of Wales, it gave her the all-important access she wanted to her children - and "the boys" must have been uppermost in her mind when she hastily drafted a new will. Money matters would not have been a top priority since she owned no property and her Spencer jewellery belonged to her brother. At the time, her personal wealth was estimated at little more than £1m.

The divorce settlement in July 1996 changed all that. Thanks to the hard-bargaining of her lawyer Anthony Julius from the commercially-orientated firm Mischon de Reya and her own determination to face down the palace having seen how Sarah Ferguson had been bested by the Windsors in her divorce from Prince Andrew, she came away with a remarkably generous settlement. She would receive a lump sum of £15m and £400,000 annually for her office. She also got to keep her rent-free residence at Kensington Palace and Prince Charles agreed to pay the children's expenses and school fees. Her one reverse was to lose her HRH style, being known as Diana, Princess of Wales, but she would still be regarded as a member of the royal family and would have use of all the royal jewellery which eventually would be passed on to the wives of her sons.

In hindsight the time of the divorce is when she should have redrafted her will. Her personal fortune had suddenly skyrocketed from £1m to something approaching £20m and in such changed circumstances it would have been advisable to write into her will an interest in possession trust for her children. But amidst the turmoil of divorce inheritance tax planning must have been the last thing on her mind. Using the loss of her HRH status as an excuse, she announced without warning that she would prune her charity commitments from around one hundred to just six. Her media advisor Jane Atkinson promptly resigned. Diana also fell out with her close friends

Lord and Lady Palumbo, Elton John and Sarah Ferguson. The one financial decision she did make for her children was to follow Prince William's advice and auction her old dresses for charity. The star-studded New York sale in June fetched $3,258,750 - with one buyer paying $222,500 for the gown she wore when she danced with John Travolta at the White House.

When it later emerged that her sons would lose £8.5m of their inheritance to the taxman, Diana's inaction drew much criticism. Tax lawyers were amazed that she had not put the bulk of the settlement into a trust for the children. Such an arrangement was still liable to inheritance tax if she died within seven years, but this could have been mitigated by insurance policies against the estate paying tax within that period. It was also pointed out that the tax liability could be significantly reduced if Prince Charles appealed to the court to vary the terms of the divorce settlement. Available to him was the legal loophole established in the 1987 case of Barder v Barder in which a wife committed suicide shortly after her divorce settlement. The House of Lords ruled that in certain circumstances - and providing third parties such as the children were not adversely affected - the order regarding the divorce settlement could be overturned. It was reported that Charles's lawyers did for a time consider such a legal move involving a sum equal to the settlement money being put in a trust for the two princes but ultimately rejected it on the grounds that it might be portrayed in the press as a "raid on his dead wife's estate."[6]

In the end the will was changed - not by Charles or Diana but John Major in his capacity as special guardian. In November 1997 he had been appointed guardian for the financial interests of the two princes on the suggestion of the Prince of Wales who felt that they needed separate representation. The former prime minister was trusted by both sides. While at 10 Downing Street he had acted as an honest broker in the divorce negotiations between the Waleses and Diana later wrote him several personal letters to thank him for his advice. Again in his role as middleman, he helped organise a joint application by the lawyers representing the princes and the estate to vary the will and on 17 December 1997 the High Court granted the order. It ran to thirty-four pages – twenty-eight longer than the original will.

The main variation was to make it easier for the princes to gain access to their mother's money (or, as Martyn Gowar more elegantly put it, to ensure that they "were comprehensively accommodated"). Under the original will, they would have to wait until their 25th birthday before they could dip into the trust fund, but the new arrangement allowed them to use some of the interest from the capital. It also established a separate discretionary fund with a sum of £100,000, some of which could be distributed to them at the discretion of the trustees. A portion of the money could also go to charity, so answering the criticism that Diana had left nothing for good causes.

Paul Burrell who had also been forgotten in the original will was given under the new arrangement £50,000 free of inheritance tax. As butler, personal assistant and confidant to Diana for almost a decade, he was devastated by her death and on the eve of her funeral had insisted on maintaining an all-night vigil by her coffin in the hallway in Kensington Palace. In his memoirs he refers to Lady Sarah McCorquodale and Frances Shand Kydd as stating he was given the bequest as recognition of his duty and loyalty towards the princess.[7] Lady Sarah later confirmed that he had worked hard on Diana's estate and that her mother wanted to reward him for his years of service. But Frances Shand Kydd also told her biographers that he had begun to get ideas above his station and that his position might possibly have gone to his head.[8]

The variation also appointed a third executor to join Diana's sister and mother - Richard Chartres, Bishop of London. He was initially approached by Lady Sarah to take up the position. His direct connection with the royal family derived from his service since 1996 as Dean of Her Majesty's Chapels Royal. On the eve of Diana's funeral, he was with Paul Burrell sitting in prayer before her coffin. To underline his establishment credentials he was also a privy councillor and a member of the House of Lords. One reason for his involvement was the potential conflict of interest of the other two executors who were acting both for Diana's estate and the memorial fund set up in her name. They were competing for the right to use Diana's name in souvenirs, gifts and other products. "The relations between the estate and the memorial fund were very complex," the bishop later explained, "[and] it was thought useful and desirable that there should be an additional executor uninvolved with the memorial fund."[9]

A large part of the amendments to the will dealt with intellectual property, a matter that had been completely ignored in the original will. Indeed Gowar has suggested this was the prime reason behind the redrafting. Clause upon clause meticulously defined her moral rights, literary rights, performers' rights, copyright, audio and photographic rights and any rights linked to any sign or mark arising from her name. After her death it became apparent that the use of her name or image could be worth tens of millions of pounds. These rights were placed into the trust fund along with her wardrobe and wearing apparel. In hindsight, the estate was well advised to attempt to clarify her intellectual property since in 2004 Diana's image rights would be the subject of a costly legal wrangle when the Memorial Fund unsuccessfully tried to sue the Franklin Mint for exploiting her identity on its merchandise – an experience that might well have influenced the later decision of her two sons to set up companies to protect their own image rights.

The most controversial revision of her will, however, concerned the seemingly innocuous area of chattels. Clause four of the original will stated simply that Diana gave all her chattels to her executors who should distribute them according to any written memorandum or notes of wishes that she might leave behind. The revised arrangement deleted this clause and replaced it with more carefully worded instructions. The executors were given absolute discretion to select chattels from a list of items described in Part 1 of Appendix 1 and then distribute them to a list of godchildren named in Part 2 of Appendix 1.

The list of items in Part 1 was identified according to reference to Christie's Catalogue. The catalogue in question had in part been drawn up by Meredith Etherington-Smith, a marketing director at Christie's, who had after Diana's death been brought in to help Paul Burrell and the executors in the laborious task of listing and valuing all personal possessions before probate. She had already gained an intimate knowledge of the princess's property having spent many months in 1996-7 cataloguing her dresses for the Christie's auction in New York.[10] The sixteen catalogued items in the new will ranged from the infantile - a pen tray, china rabbit and a model harp - to the adult - a coffee service, carriage clock and a watercolour painting.

The list of seventeen godchildren in Part 2 was also a mixed bunch - and one that offered a fascinating insight into Diana's wide circle of friends. On the one hand, there were the titled aristocracy or royalty - such as HRH Prince Phillips of the Hellenes, the three-year-old son of the ex-King Constantine of Greece, Lady Edwina Grosvenor, the six-year-old daughter of the Duke of Westminster, and Lord Downpatrick, the nine-year-old son of the Earl of St Andrews and grandson of the Duke of Kent.

On the other hand, there were the offspring of some of her untitled friends from her teenage days. They included Leonora Lonsdale, aged eleven, who was the daughter of Laura Lonsdale (née Greig) who was at West Heath finishing school with her and whose twin brother Geordie Greig was the journalist who went on to be editor of the Tatler and the Mail on Sunday. Also a contemporary at West Heath and a flat mate during her pre-marriage Sloane period was perhaps her closest friend, Carolyn Bartholomew (née Pride). When she had a son, Jack, Diana agreed to be a godmother attending his christening and remembering him in her will. The ten-year-old Camilla Straker was the daughter of another former flatmate, Sophie Kimball, who married the old Etonian farmer Reuben Straker.

There were two other intriguing names. Master George Frost, who was the ten-year-old son of Sir David Frost and Lady Carina, the daughter of the Duke of Norfolk. Frost had been one of many television illuminati to whom she turned for media advice. Last on the list was Miss Dominica Lawson, the daughter of Dominic Lawson, the former editor of the Sunday Telegraph and son of the ex-Chancellor of the Exchequer, and Rosa, the daughter of Viscount Monckton and granddaughter of Sir Walter Monckton who had renegotiated George V's estate for Edward VIII. Rosa Monckton was almost a sister to Diana who allowed her to bury her stillborn daughter, Natalia, in the private gardens of Kensington Palace. Her other daughter Dominica who was named on the list suffered from Down's syndrome.

Lady Sarah duly carried out her duties as executor by distributing the chattels. She drove round the country in an estate car visiting the parents of the godchildren. Among the items she handed out were an incomplete tea service, a decanter inscribed to the princess from a Women's Institute and a framed print that had been a corporate gift from Argos, the high street catalogue store.

It later emerged that Diana had left a letter of wishes that in one significant respect differed from the way the chattels were actually distributed. Dated 2 June 1993 - one day after she signed the original will - the document stated that she would like her executors to divide her personal chattels at their discretion between her sons and godchildren. The division was to be three quarters in value to her sons and one quarter between her godchildren. But she wanted her executors to allocate all her jewellery to the share to be held by her sons, so that their wives, in due course, might have it or use it. She left the exact division of the jewellery to the discretion of the executors, although she selected sixteen special items for her seventeen godchildren.

It was thus the clearly stated wish of Diana that her godchildren should get a significant share of the *value* of the chattels and not just a few individual items specified on the list. The value for each godchild was later estimated at £100,000-£150,000.

This new information came to light in October 2002 when it was read out in open court at the Old Bailey by the barrister representing Paul Burrell. Diana's former butler had been charged with stealing three hundred and fifteen items belonging to Diana's estate - as well as to Prince Charles and Prince William - and the strategy of the defence counsel, Lord Carlile, the former Liberal MP, was reportedly to undermine the credibility of the evidence given by the Spencer family.[11] Lady Sarah was one of the early witnesses to take the stand for the prosecution and explained to William Boyse, the barrister acting for the Crown, that in the light of their age, it was better to give the godchildren a personal possession rather than a lump sum. In cross examination, Lord Carlile then asked her: "If the letter of wishes had been carried out the godchildren would have received much more than the 'memento' of Diana they got?"

Lady Sarah replied: "I think it was more than a memento, the things that were chosen." She went on to elaborate that she thought it made a difference that Diana wrote the letter of wishes three years before her divorce settlement: "Bearing in mind the age of the children which was very young that they would prefer to treasure what you call a memento rather than a lump sum." Lord Carlile then suggested that not all of the godchildren came from affluent backgrounds, to which Lady Sarah responded: "There are not many paupers in there."[12]

There had earlier been more revelations when the Bishop of London took the stand. Lord Carlile asked the sole non-family executor when he first became aware of the letter of wishes.

"I can't recollect being aware of these precise terms until now," he replied.

"So October 23, 2002, is the first time you have seen this letter of wishes?"

"According to my best recollection."

Lord Carlile continued: "Was the existence of this side letter ever mentioned to you by Lady Sarah McCorquodale or the Hon Frances Shand Kydd or by any solicitor?"

"I cannot say that it was," the bishop answered.

"If you had been aware of a letter of wishes by Diana, Princess of Wales, which plainly this letter is, that's obviously something you, as independent executor, would have considered very seriously?"

"Very seriously, yes," he replied.[13]

The trial revelations came as a thunderbolt to the children's parents. After a few of them voiced their misgivings in anonymous briefings, Rosa Monckton wrote an angry article in The Daily Telegraph attacking the executors for "not acting in an honourable fashion" by ignoring the letter of wishes. All her disabled daughter, Dominica, received as a memento of her godmother was "a tatty brown box containing some pieces of Herend china wrapped in old newspaper, accompanied by a curt demand for a receipt." With a final twist of the knife, she added: "Hijacking Diana's memory is one thing, her chattels quite another and both the executors, and Burrell in his more naive way, are guilty of this."[14]

The Tatler, the society magazine edited by Geordie Greig, poured further oil on to the flames with an investigation headlined "Betrayed: Diana's godchildren and their missing inheritance."[15] It spoke to several parents who felt that the last wishes of Diana had not been fulfilled and it claimed that even though the parents were not all interested in the money, each godchild might have received as much as six figures (perhaps even as high as £320,000). Patrick Jephson, the erstwhile executor, joined the clamour by expressing his amazement that the bishop knew nothing about the letter of wishes and stating in no uncertain terms that "I would not have hesitated to carry out her wishes in this matter, and I don't hesitate now to ask why they have not been followed."[16]

In fairness to the executors, the cited figure of £320,000 appeared to be based on a misreading of inheritance law. Presumably, the sum is derived by dividing one quarter of the *total* estate (£5.25m out of £21.5m) by seventeen (the number of godchildren). Legally, "chattels" only refers to movable possessions

ROYAL LEGACY

and not fixed assets nor cash and investments. So instead if you take the total for chattels alone (which would be at most £6.5m on the basis that the rest of the estate is taken up with the lump divorce settlement sum of £15m) and divide that by seventeen - each godchild might get a little less than £100,000. That is still a considerable sum, but Lady Sarah was correct - if a little undiplomatic - in stating that there were few paupers among the parents of the godchildren. One was on the Sunday Times Rich List.

From a legal point of view, the letter of wishes was not binding. Morally, the executors might have felt obliged to fulfil her wishes but not legally. Therefore, they were perfectly within their rights to go to the High Court to have it legally set aside as part of a wider redrafting of the original will. In defence of the Spencer family, Frances Shand Kydd's biographers have pointed out that by the time the executors made the changes considerably more money was at stake.[17] When Diana signed the letter of wishes in June 1993 her estate was worth little more than £1m but at the time of her death - following the generous divorce settlement - it had risen to over £20m. In the light of these changed circumstances, there was a case for altering the distribution of chattels.

But Frances's bona fides as executor were compromised by two other revelations from the trial. Under further cross examination from Lord Carlile, she was forced to admit that she had not even spoken to Diana in the last four months of her life. She explained this as "normal family behaviour" - part of the ebb and flow a loving mother-daughter relationship.[18] But Burrell claims that he overheard a telephone conversation where she strongly criticised her daughter's choice of male friends which ended with Diana in tears vowing never to speak to her mother again. Apparently, letters of apology to Diana were returned unopened, marked "Return to Sender."[19]

The defence counsel also pressed her on what had happened to some of Diana's own personal correspondence and documents:

Lord Carlile: "There was a lot of correspondence in the apartments where your daughter lived, and there was a shredder, and you spent many hours on many days shredding documents."

Mrs Shand Kydd: "Not many days...."

Lord Carlile said: "You shredded large numbers, no doubt properly in most instances, you shredded large quantities of correspondence."

Mrs Shand Kydd: "No, I shredded mainly a very small number of a very large amount of correspondence."

Asked how many documents she had shredded, she replied "between 50 and 100."[20]

Frances went on to say that no documents were from members of the royal family and that most were thank you notes from people like ladies in waiting. However, Rosa Monckton later wrote that "many of my letters and those from another close friend of hers, Lucia de Lima, were among those shredded."[21]

Paul Burrell claims that after hearing about the shredding he took away some of Diana's documents for safekeeping.

More embarrassing details were expected when Burrell - and possibly even the Prince of Wales - took to the stand. But just a fortnight into the proceedings the trial dramatically collapsed. William Boyce, the prosecution counsel, stood up in court one of the Old Bailey and announced that he would offer no further evidence and invited Burrell's acquittal. The main plank of their case was apparently that there was no evidence that Burrell had informed anyone that he was holding property belonging to Diana's estate. However, a few days earlier the prosecution had been told that the Queen had just remembered having a meeting shortly after Diana's death with Burrell during which he had told her that he had taken some of the princess's property for safekeeping.

Was Her Majesty's delayed recollection the real reason why the £1.5m trial collapsed? Following months of press speculation about the possibility of a royal conspiracy, Sir Michael Peat, Prince Charles' private secretary, was asked to examine - as part of a wider inquiry into the trial - whether there was anything improper in the conduct of the Prince of Wales's household in the termination of the case. After sifting through the testimony of dozens of witnesses (although not the Queen) Peat came to the conclusion:

"The disclosure made on 28th October 2002 of The Queen's conversation with Mr Burrell was properly made. Had it not been made, those advising Her Majesty and The Prince of Wales could rightly and strongly have been criticised. The suggestion that the disclosure was made for improper motive and in the expectation of preventing the trial continuing finds no support in the available evidence."[22]

Lord Carlile believes the Queen's intervention was just one of a number of factors in the collapse of the trial. In a newspaper interview a week later, he maintained that the overall case of the prosecution had been "severely undermined."[23] In court, the prosecution had succeeded in weakening the credibility of the Spencer side of the story and the Queen's intervention merely confirmed the general unreliability of the prosecution evidence. As a result, the Crown had no option but to throw in the towel.

The defendant Paul Burrell offers a slightly different perspective in his memoirs. He was amazed that so much significance was given to his meeting with the Queen since he had told her no more than he had informed Prince William in a letter, Prince Charles's officials in other correspondence and the Crown Prosecution Service in his defence statement. In his view, the written evidence was already available before the trial and he cannot understand why it came as such a surprise to the CPS.[24]

As for the Spencers, Frances Shand Kydd felt let down by the Queen's eleventh hour intervention. According to her biographers, she was incensed that others had been content to do nothing and observe the Spencers being humiliated in court and the press.[25] They go on to repeat the widely held view at the time that there was a strong element of convenient amnesia behind the Queen's delayed recollection and that she was worried that Burrell was about to expose embarrassing information in court about the royal family.

Burrell in his book hints strongly that he had much more information about Diana and the princes that he might disclose in open court and he makes it clear that his defence team were ready to call the Prince of Wales and even Prince William as witnesses. Lord Carlile later stated that "it was always our view that this case – however much we limited the scope of the evidence – had the potential for doing considerable damage to the Spencers and some collateral damage to the royal family."[26]

Thanks to the Peat Report, we now know for certain that the Prince of Wales was both "concerned" and felt "deep unhappiness about it all"[27] regarding the general prospect of him or Prince William being called as a witness. No member of the royal family had appeared in court since 1891 when another Prince of Wales (the future Edward VII) was called to the witness stand in a society scandal. Charles would have preferred if the trial could have been avoided.

He was worried that personal information about his family would be revealed and whether true or false, the disclosure would cause distress to his sons.

Although the Peat inquiry dismissed any suggestion that he instructed his lawyers to interfere in the prosecution process, the report did disclose one fascinating snippet of information about the behind the scenes discussions at St James's Palace. One meeting followed a conversation between Robert Seabrook QC, the prince's criminal law adviser, and John Yates, the Scotland Yard Commander in charge of the case, about the possibility of Prince Charles or Prince William having to give evidence.

"Mr Seabrook discussed this with the Prince of Wales on 28th February 2002, having previously been reassured by Commander Yates that the Prosecution would avoid their being called and going so far as to say, as Mr Seabrook, recalled, that 'the Prosecution would be stopped rather than doing that.' Commander Yates does not dispute that he may have said something to this effect."[28]

Even though the inquiry was clear that Prince Charles was not in any way involved in the collapse of the trial, this interchange would suggest that one actor in the case, presumably the Crown Prosecution Service, considered terminating the prosecution if members of the royal family were obliged to take to the witness stand. If this is indeed true, then it might have given the palace some peace of mind and explain why no one sought to stop the case *before* it came to trial. At the end of the day, whatever may or may not have happened behind the scenes with the prosecution case, information about Diana's estate and private life was kept safely under wraps.

The collapse of the court case left unsolved the mystery of what happened to Diana's personal possessions. By July 1998, the Kensington Palace apartment had been stripped bare - all the jewellery, furniture and paintings - having apparently gone back to the Windsors and Spencers. One unhappy parent of the godchildren speculated that most of the disputed chattels ended up at Althorp, the Spencer family seat in Northamptonshire, and indeed Diana's wedding dress - along with a few other personal possessions - were put on display in the museum dedicated to her memory and charging £12.50 entrance fee. It was rumoured that her BMW car was sent to a secret location to be destroyed in order to prevent it from being turned into a valuable relic.[29]

With the help of the Crown jeweller, David Thomas, Paul Burrell was able to provide the probate authorities with an inventory of Diana's collection of jewels.[30] He himself was given a pair of silver cufflinks from Lady Sarah McCorquodale and in his book records how some of the jewels given to Diana by Dodi were ultimately returned in boxes to Althorp.[31] This included all her earrings but some of the Spencer jewellery had been on loan. The family tiara she wore at the wedding had already been reclaimed by her brother, Earl Spencer.

It is less easy to trace what happened to the non-Spencer or royal jewellery. This is due in part to the secrecy surrounding the provisions of the divorce settlement relating to royal jewellery and in part to the ambiguity surrounding what is Crown jewellery and what is private property. It is believed that under the terms of the divorce agreement the jewels given to Diana by the Queen and the Queen Mother on her wedding and engagement were returned at her death (or earlier). These gifts included the pearl drop lover's knot tiara designed by Queen Mary around 1914 and handpicked by Her Majesty before the marriage in 1981 and the emerald and diamond choker that had been created by Queen Mary with some of the Cambridge jewels and then bequeathed to the present Queen. The latter was famously worn by Diana as a squaw-like headband while dancing with Prince Charles in Australia in 1985.

If these gems had been classified Crown jewellery they would have been automatically returned to the Buckingham Palace but according to Suzy Menkes neither item can be classed Crown property or a state piece. It is possible that the Queen reclaimed them as family heirlooms but it is more likely that they passed to their two grandchildren since according to Diana's letter of wishes all her jewellery should go the future spouses of the two princes.

Royal Legacy

So, what lessons can be learnt from Diana's unsealed will about the financial side of royal succession? The first thing that happens when a royal does not seal a will is that the full extent of his or her wealth becomes public knowledge and thus, a target for public criticism. When Diana's multi-million fortune was revealed, The Independent newspaper immediately asked "why does her pre-tax estate amounting to £21,711,486 not include a single penny for charity... surely this generous caring princess who devoted so much of her life to helping charitable causes could be accused of being heartless or mean?"[32] This is exactly the accusation that was soon made by Peter Tatchell, the gay and human rights activist, in another publication: "she was happy to do charity work for people with AIDS providing it didn't cost her anything. But when it came to parting with her own money she chose to keep it in her already super-rich family, rather than share it with those in need."[33]

The last line might be less than charitable in sentiment but it does point to a fundamental truth about royal succession: the wealth stays in the family. In the end - despite her letter of wishes - Diana left almost everything to her sons. The overriding fear of all rich families - whether royal, aristocratic or landed gentry - is that their wealth will be salami-sliced by outsiders. This was the unvoiced concern during the negotiations over Diana's divorce settlement with Buckingham Palace fearful that if Diana married again some of the Crown jewellery and family heirlooms might pass to a commoner or someone unsuitable. Similar worries were expressed during the abdication settlement of Edward VIII when there was a possibility that Wallis Simpson might end up with some of the family jewels.

Full disclosure of royal wealth also brings with it a massive inheritance tax bill. Here it might be instructive to compare Princess Diana's will not with Princess Helena Victoria's open will but with Princess Margaret's closed one. The two princesses were once close friends and neighbours in Kensington Palace and both were renegade royals who flouted convention in their social life. But while Margaret planned meticulously for her death, Diana's foresight did not even extend to wearing a car seat belt that would have saved her life. Consequently Diana's two children paid £8.5 million in tax and Margaret's two children paid £2 million.

A significant slice of the tax liability - perhaps as much as £5 million - applied to the value of the chattels. As we shall see in the next chapter, the executors (and possibly HM Revenue and Customs) were reportedly relatively conservative in their valuation of Margaret's assets underestimating the added value of the assets' royal provenance that later became apparent when they were sold at auction. Diana's estate was not so lucky. A year after her death, the Revenue reportedly began to challenge the executor's valuation. One report in The Times suggested the taxman thought that her possessions may have been "undervalued, with no account being taken of the higher prices they might face because of who she was," although officials claimed that such a reassessment was common practice with large estates of this sort.[34]

Diana's estate also revealed the importance of letters of wishes in royal wills. As we saw with Helena Victoria's will it is a traditional method to conceal the names of beneficiaries but when it came to Diana's will all was disclosed because her executors needed to rebalance the distribution of chattels. If it had all gone to plan, we would never have known that Diana wanted a significant share of her chattels to go to such surprise beneficiaries as the son of Sir David Frost and the daughter of Dominic Lawson. As a second layer of secrecy, the device of a letter of wishes also shows that even if a royal will were made totally public there would be other methods of obfuscation available to the royal family.

From Diana's open will we can see that she used a trust to set aside money for her two children until they were grown up. Again this was inadequately done and the executors had to alter the will to establish a more tax efficient discretionary trust. Altering the will proved a costly business since extra legal help had to be brought in to represent the independent interests of the princes. When the full charges of the solicitors Boodle Hatfield were leaked to the press - a figure of £543,000 was first reported which apparently was knocked down to under £400,000 - there were predictable howls of outrage from the media and John Major was blamed for not exercising proper cost control. This was probably unfair as he worked unpaid and St James's Palace quickly emphasised that the Prince of Wales was very happy with his work for the boys. But once again public disclosure brought public censure.

At the end of the day, whether they liked it or not, Diana's executors were obliged to use executors or advisors close to the royal circles or the establishment. This slide towards conformity and discretion was reinforced by the death of Frances Shand Kydd in 2004 which necessitated a replacement executor. In fact, she was replaced by three trustees – all with close ties to the establishment. One was Earl Home, the Eton-educated son of former conservative prime minster, Sir Alec Douglas Home, who was an executor of the Queen Mother's estate and later became chairman of the Queen's bank Coutts and Co. The second was Sir Nicholas Bacon, the Eton-educated barrister and baronet who was a page of honour to the Queen and was close to Prince Charles through his work on the Prince's council of the Duchy of Cornwall. But the most controversial choice was the Duke of Westminster, an old Harrovian and Britain richest landowner. In the bitter break-up of the Wales's marriage, he had clearly sided with Prince Charles's camp and friends of Diana suggested that his appointment as executor flew in the face of her expressed wish that

Prince Charles should not have sole control of her sons' upbringing. Now he would seem to be getting some influence over their inheritance. The Duchess of Westminster, Tally, was also close to Prince Charles and a godmother to Prince William. To complete the circle, the duke used to go out with Diana's sister and executor, Lady Sarah McCorquodale, as of course did Charles.

So it was that royal family had to pull out all the stops to clean up the mess left by Diana's inheritance. The overriding lesson from her open will was that if you fail to do any estate planning you open up a can of worms. Fortunately, there was no chance of her forward-thinking aunt making the same mistake.

Chapter Eleven
Margaret, Mustique and Money – 2002

"She is far too intelligent for her station in life. She often had a bad press, the usual fate of wits in society"
Gore Vidal on his friend Princess Margaret[1]

In the last decade of her life Princess Margaret made one important contribution to Princess Diana's legacy. She destroyed Diana's letters to the Queen Mother. Ordinarily such correspondence would have been deposited in the Royal Archives for future historians to pore over but on the princess's orders several large black bags of papers were removed for destruction.[2] Although the Queen Mother's official biographer has suggested that Margaret did this "to protect" her mother and other members of the family,[3] several commentators have wondered whether it was also to protect Diana from embarrassing her own family.

Andrew Morton, who famously collaborated with her on "Diana: Her True Story," has suggested that she might have confided in her grandmother-in-law her antipathy for her real grandmother, Lady Fermoy, who thought her an unsuitable match for a future king.[4] At the time of the destruction of the letters in 1993, Diana was still alive and expected to outlive everyone. Equally erroneously, the destroyer of the letters, Princess Margaret, was expected to outlive their recipient, the Queen Mother.

Shortly after 8.30 am on Saturday, 9 February 2002 Sky News's colourful graphics flashed with an alert about a royal death. A few minutes earlier Buckingham Palace had announced that at 6.30 that morning Princess Margaret had died peacefully in her sleep in the King Edward VII's Hospital for Officers, London with her two children, Lord Linley and Lady Sarah Chatto, at her side. She was seventy-one years old.

The news came as no surprise to anyone who had seen the princess at the 101st birthday celebrations for the Queen Mother the previous August. In one of her rare public appearances, the cameras captured the image of an erstwhile English rose as invalid. Her wheelchair was rolled out into the Mall with her legs hidden by a beige blanket that did not quite mask her swollen feet and her left arm hanging limply in a lilywhite sling. Her puffy cheeks and skin showed signs of someone on steroids, while the rest of her face was obscured by a large pair of wraparound sunglasses. She looked confused and the next day's papers ran shock headlines expressing "Concern for the Princess" and "The Queen keeps her eye on Margaret."

Her health had been deteriorating for almost a decade. After suffering a minor stroke in 1994 that forced her to curtail her official duties, she had a more serious attack after a dinner party on Mustique in February 1998 and had to be flown back to England for treatment at the King Edward VII's Hospital where she made a good recovery. A year later - again in her Caribbean home - she severely scolded her feet in an accident when she turned on the wrong tap on the shower and was only saved from greater injury from the boiling water by the intervention of her private detective kicking down the bathroom door. She never fully recovered from this accident. She suffered a third stroke on 4 January 2001 that plunged her into depression and a fourth on March 27 that had more serious consequences. As a result she lost sight in one eye and all movement in her left side. A few months before her death she confessed to a friend that she was so tired of being in pain and other acquaintances admitted privately that it was a pity she did not die earlier.[5]

A heavy smoker, Princess Margaret had long suffered from respiratory diseases and had part of her lung removed in 1985. Although she was forced to give up smoking late in life, the long-term effect of her nicotine habit may well have contributed to the final stroke that killed her in February 2002. She was far from being the first royal to die partly as a result of smoking and indeed, a strong case can be made that the last four British kings all died of smoking related complaints. Her father, George VI, died of lung cancer in 1952 after decades of heavy smoking. Her uncle, Edward VIII, died of throat cancer after smoking from a young age. The tobacco habit of her grandfather, George V, may have played a big part in the bronchitis, emphysema and chronic obstructive lung disease that led to his premature death in 1936. Edward VII too suffered from bronchitis - exacerbated by twenty cigarettes and twelve cigars a day before he died of a heart attack. Queen Mary smoked and encouraged her son George VI's smoking by giving him a cigarette case on his 18th birthday (Margaret's own gift collection - as shown from a single auction - numbers over fifty cigarette cases, holders and lighters, not to mention a dozen snuff boxes). Even the elegant Princess Marina was said to be inseparable from her Russian cigarettes (although it was not a factor in her early death), whereas Prince Philip only agreed to give up smoking on his wedding day. The Windsors' attachment to the weed is illuminated in a telling family photo taken at Balmoral in October 1945 which shows the fifteen-year-old Princess Margaret with a cigarette in her fingers, while her father George VI sits nearby with a teacup in one hand and a cigarette in the other.

Princess Margaret left precise instructions for her funeral service. Whether this was laid out in her will or in a separate memorandum attached to her last testament is not known. What is clear is that she gave considerable thought to every detail of the ceremony which she wanted in St George's Chapel, Windsor. She specified that it should be a private service for family and friends. On the day, the four hundred and fifty mourners featured almost every member of the royal family as well as a host of show business acquaintances which included Cleo Laine, Bryan Forbes, Maggie Smith and Judi Dench. As a reminder of her love of ballet, Tchaikovsky's Swan Lake was played on the organ in a prelude to the service. This was followed by music by William Croft and the choir singing Psalm 23. Later after a lesson from Romans 8, the congregation sang two of her favourite traditional hymns "Immortal, invisible, God only wise" and "When I survey the wondrous cross." Seated among the congregation was her centenarian mother, the Queen Mother, who was determined to attend despite her extreme frailty and the memories that the occasion prompted. Exactly fifty years ago to the day she had been in the same chapel for her husband's funeral. It would be the last time she was seen in public before her own death six weeks later.

True to her individualistic character, Margaret chose to go against royal tradition and be cremated rather than buried. This made her - according to one biographer - the "first senior royal since the dark ages" to be to be cremated, her only rival being the relatively minor Windsor Princess Louise who was cremated in 1939. According to another biographer,

her decision was in part influenced by her distaste for the royal family's private burial ground at Frogmore in Windsor Park which she always found "gloomy" and in part from a desire to be interred next to her beloved father in the King George VI memorial chapel. As a result, for a fee of £280 her body was turned to ashes in the anonymous setting of the municipal crematorium at Slough.

Meanwhile, in Farrers' law chambers overlooking Lincoln's Inn solicitors acting for her estate began to take steps both to prove her will and to prevent it from being made available for public inspection. It is not known whether the application to seal her will was made immediately after her death but it is likely that there would have been some delay since this request would have been linked to the application for probate which would have required some time to prepare a full inventory of her assets. This can often be a painstaking task as we know from the account of the royal butler Paul Burrell. After the death of Princess Diana, a team of valuers from leading jewellers including Asprey's had to be brought in to put a price on her jewellery collection.

We do know for certain that the application relating to her will was granted on 17 June 2002 and probate on 24 June. Although the contents of the will were kept secret, probate details are available for public inspection. They reveal that she left a gross estate of £7,700,176 and a net estate (after liabilities had been paid) of £7,603,596.

When this seven figure sum was first made public, many in the media suspected that it represented the tip of an iceberg. The Daily Mail suggested "it is likely to have been only a fraction of her true personal wealth."[6] Just one year earlier, its sister paper The Mail on Sunday had published a wide-ranging investigation into the wealth of the House of Windsor which ranked Margaret as the 11th richest royal (the Queen was top followed by Prince Charles, Earl Harewood and the Queen Mother) with a personal fortune of £20 million.[7] So - if this figure is in any way correct - what happened to the missing £12.4 million?

There is an element of guesswork about all valuations of the very wealthy - whether it is the Mail on Sunday's Royal Rich Report or the Sunday Times's annual and less regal Rich List. With no access to their personal tax returns or bank account details, valuers are left to speculate about the size of their assets. But when it comes to the royal family some of their assets – most notably their jewellery - are on public view and thus easier to value. Compared to her sister Margaret had a small jewel box, since traditionally the most important items are passed from sovereign to sovereign rather than to the sovereign's younger sibling. Nevertheless Margaret inherited a few particularly fine pieces thanks to the generosity of her grandmother, Queen Mary, who had some valuable gems left over after leaving the bulk of her estate to Queen Elizabeth. The most expensive gift from the "rock of the family" was a large sapphire surrounded by diamonds which had once belonged to the Russian Tsarina and which was valued at £495,000.[8]

Some of her jewellery was acquired through gifts on state visits. The most lucrative destination by far was South Africa which she visited in 1947 with the King, Queen and Princess Elizabeth and again in 1953 accompanied by her recently widowed mother. After a tour of the Kimberley diamond mines she was given a 4.5 carat blue-white emerald-cut diamond set in a ring - which today would be worth tens of thousands of pounds.

The value of some of her most precious items only came to light through the Christie's auction of her chattels in 2006: a ruby and diamond ring went for £299,200; the Queen Mary Diamond Riviere - bequeathed by her grandmother - was valued at £200,000 but on the day commanded £993,600; and the Poltimore Tiara which was bought for her wedding fetched £926,400.[9]

The auction records also reveal that Margaret possessed some valuable furniture and household items. One clock commanded £1,240,000 but it was no ordinary timepiece since Christie's catalogued it as a jewelled, gold mounted guilloche enamelled silver clock marked Fabergé. As can clearly be seen from the catalogue's provenance records, Princess Margaret inherited much furniture from Queen Mary - with one of the most valuable items being a chair used by her grandmother for the 1937 coronation which fetched £38,000 and which could be set in front of the Queen Mary mahogany display cabinet worth £19,200.

Margaret's art work is harder to value as much of it has been kept discreetly in the family rather than put up for auction. Her extensive art collection, according to some press reports, included paintings by John Piper, Patrick Procktor, Robert Heindel and Jean Cocteau, as well as highly collectable sketches by Oliver Messel and water colours by Bryan Organ. We know for certain that she owned the famous portrait of her by Pietro Annigoni since it was put up for auction and fetched £680,000. A portrait of her aged four in a pink bonnet from the less famous artist Frank Owen Salisbury realised £8,400, while a set of Picasso lithographs fetched £20,400 and a Russian icon £26,400. All in all, the Christie's sale of her furniture and artwork (as well as some silver) brought in £4,052,408.

We saw earlier how her sister, the Queen, received a small fortune in wedding gifts and she too benefited from a windfall on her marriage. One estimate puts their worth at a staggering £3m but when you take into account that the Snowdons reportedly received over two thousand presents that figure might not be too wide of the mark.[10] Of course many items - such as gifts from staff at Balmoral or from small Caribbean states - were worth only modest sums (less than £1,000), but some other items were of considerable value. A wedding present from the army - a 19th century mahogany dining table – was later sold for £18,000. The governments of old Commonwealth countries could be even more generous. For instance, a pair of silver kiwis from the government of New Zealand was auctioned for £36,000 while a set of gold presentation candlesticks from the government of South Africa brought in £31,200.

In September 1942 she received a surprise present when the society hostess Dame Margaret Greville left her a cash bequest of £20,000, a sizable sum for a twelve-year-old. But her biggest inheritance came a decade later in 1952 with the death of her father, George VI. The contents of his will remain secret but he would almost certainly have left her money - probably in the form of a trust fund. We know from letters dated as early as 1938 to his brother-in-law Sir David Bowes-Lyon, a director at Lazards Bank, that he wanted to use the surplus from his Civil List payments to establish an investment fund for his two daughters. According to Margaret's biographer Christopher Warwick on her 21st birthday she had access to such a trust fund at Coutts Bank. It is very possible that she also received a trust income from her grandfather, George V, since he is known to have spoken of the need to make savings from his Civil List income in order to provide for his grandchildren.

During her lifetime she also received valuable heirlooms from her parents. These were often given at important rites of passage such as key birthdays or Christmas. At an early birthday - probably her 2nd or 3rd - her mother gave her an antique diamond rose brooch worth £42,000 which was later augmented by an antique diamond and gem set bee brooch (valued at £33,600) that been her mother's own christening present and one of the first jewels she ever owned. For her 21st birthday her mother presented her with a valuable set of Persian turquoises. Her father George VI gave her a diamond gem set brooch (£38,000) round the time of her 8th birthday and at Christmas 1949 a gem set gold cigarette case bearing an inscription from Papa GR. It was later sold for £102,000. We also know that he gave her for her 21st birthday a diamond Colet necklace the precise value of which is unknown but likely to be in five or six figures.

The next big inheritance came a year later in 1953 with the death of Queen Mary. Again, the precise contents of the will are a mystery but the Christie's catalogue with its provenance records does reveal the extent and value of the items transferred from grandmother to granddaughter. As we have seen earlier, many of these took the form of valuable furniture but as one would have expected from one of the world's greatest collectors of gems, there were many items of jewellery. It is more than possible that many valuable heirlooms were also transferred before her death.

Yet despite this veritable waterfall of wealth, the two women were rumoured to dislike each other intensely. This was certainly the case in later life. Princess Margaret is known to have told her friend and biographer Christopher Warwick that they did not get on and that her grandmother was jealous of her more impressive royal lineage. The two princesses were daughters of a king, while the queen consort had merely married one. Some biographers have stated that Mary regarded her granddaughter as "spoiled" and unduly short. Margaret was just five foot one inch's tall and the towering five foot six inch Mary once tactlessly asked "When are you going to grow?" The patrician writer Nancy Mitford liked to refer to Margaret as the "royal dwarf."

When assessing the princess's wealth it is worth while considering whether she might have saved money from her Civil List annuities. In theory these were just payments to cover the expenses solely incurred in carrying out official royal duties, but in practice - as George V and Edward VII showed - it was possible in a good year to save from the allowances. After reaching twenty-one in 1952 she received a Civil List annuity of £6,000. A decade later this rose to £21,000 on her marriage to Anthony Armstrong-Jones. Clearly such state income was important to maintaining her lifestyle and some royal chroniclers have speculated whether it might have been a factor in her decision not to marry Group Captain Peter Townsend in 1955, after a year of frenzied rumours about an imminent wedding. In October Anthony Eden's government decided it could not justify spending taxpayers' money subsidising the household of Margaret and her divorced husband and his two children. If Margaret married she would have to renounce her royal status and with it her Civil List payments. The royal commentator Robert Lacey has pointed out that within four days of the Queen passing on the bad news, Margaret decided to give up Townsend.[11]

The Civil List payments continued and after the 1970-71 review, parliament granted her an uplift to £35,000 much to the ire of Willie Hamilton MP who branded her "an expensive kept woman" and a "monstrous charge on the public purse." But in 1993 her name was removed from the Civil List after a major reorganization of royal finances and she had to rely on the Queen for an annual payment of £219,000 for costs incurred carrying out her official duties.

During the four decades when she was on the Civil List she enjoyed considerable tax privileges. The expenses of all ordinary citizens are liable to tax but as was revealed in the chapter on the Civil List review Princess Margaret (as well as the Queen Mother) was allowed 100% tax relief on their royal annuities. Other less senior members of the royal family were only granted 90% or 80% tax relief – depending on the extent of their royal duties. It was a generous view to take that her annuity was fully used for official expenses. After her marriage to Lord Snowdon, she also benefited from public funds to the tune of £80,000 in the renovation of her private Kensington Palace apartment. It was turned into a grand London house complete with a dog washing room, a sun bed room and – according to some reports - a Christmas present wrapping room.

The one asset missing from her estate is any landed property. She never bought a country house and her grace-and-favour apartment at 1A Clock Court in Kensington Palace was rent-free. The only house that was ever owned in her own name was overseas - Les Jolies Eaux on Mustique. Princess Margaret first visited the small Caribbean island in 1960 while on a honeymoon cruise with Lord Snowdon. She arrived on the invitation of an old friend and suitor, Colin Tennant (the future Lord Glenconner) who had bought the island for a mere £45,000 in 1959 after selling a property in Florida (his wife thought he was crazy to acquire this barren patch of wilderness). Later - when he was Lord Glenconner - he sold the island at enormous profit. Some more cynical observers have suggested that he used his royal friends and other famous acquaintances to get publicity for the island in order to boost land values.

Colin Tennant who died in 2010 told a different story: "When I learnt of her engagement I asked her if she would like something wrapped in a box from Asprey's or a lot of land on Mustique. She was obviously submerged by little wrapped boxes from Asprey's. So she chose the land."[12] Although it was a wedding present, it was given to Princess Margaret alone rather than the couple together. When Lord Snowdon was later asked to comment on this, all he would say was reportedly "odd, don't you think?"[13]

A few years later Princess Margaret asked Tennant to build a house on the land. Designed by Oliver

Messel, Snowdon's uncle, and financed by the princess and probably Tennant as well, Les Jolies Eaux was not completed until November 1972. It soon became her private playground - off limits to Lord Snowdon who according to some reports never returned after the honeymoon visit.

This story of the Mustique property took a surprising turn on 3 November 1988 when she transferred it to Lord Linley on his birthday. Why would a fifty-seven-year-old princess dispose of her most prized possession to her twenty-seven-year-old son? When in 1999 he sold the house to James Murray, an American telecommunications tycoon, for a reported sum of £1.5m and bought a cheaper villa in the south of France, she was according to some reports plunged into depression. Although it could not have come as too much of a surprise as the property had been on the market for over a year.

The transfer of the Mustique villa provides a clue to the mystery of what happened to her missing millions. Princess Margaret was known for her forward thinking (her friend Jocelyn Stevens remarked on how she even planned ever last detail of her holiday itinerary)[14] and more than likely she applied this planning habit to preparing for her death and the effects of inheritance tax. As someone who was also financially astute, she must have been well aware that if she waited until within seven years of her death, any transfer of her assets would have been subject to inheritance tax as a chargeable lifetime transfer.

So by transferring the property in 1988 rather than 1999, she would have saved her estate a large tax bill.

Although she was denied the full constitutional education granted to her sister (an error, incidentally, not repeated by the Queen who pays for special tuition for Prince William) Margaret was without doubt very clever. Gore Vidal, the author and a friend for forty years, recognised a kindred spirit in his memoirs - "she is far too intelligent for her station in life. She often had a bad press, the usual fate of wits in society...but one can note her kindness to friends, to those employees whose pensions she paid out of fairly meagre resources."[15] When it came to her own personal finances, she had shown an interest in prudence from an early age. When on her ninth birthday she received some little notebooks she decided to keep one especially for money since her father was going to give her sixpence a week.[16] Later in life she was notoriously careful ensuring wherever possible that her expenses were met by other means. She reportedly once admitted to an acquaintance "we never pay the full retail price of anything."[17] One anonymous former member of staff was quoted as saying "she was the embodiment of the old maxim 'take care of the pennies and the pounds will take care of themselves'. She was not mean exactly but she was certainly very careful."

She would undoubtedly have taken advice on inheritance planning. If she gifted her Mustique property to her son on his 27th birthday, then presumably for reasons of family fairness she would have made some similar transfer to her daughter. Lady Sarah Chatto studied at the Camberwell School of Art and as a professional painter she may possibly have received some of the art work that her mother bequeathed from Queen Mary but which was noticeably absent from the Christie's sale. According to Leslie Field in her study of royal jewellery, she received from her mother a string of turquoise and pearl beads that she had been given as child.[18]

If Margaret had indeed done this then she would only have been following a pattern of behaviour established by her own parents and grandparents. It soon becomes apparent that the master planners of the House of Windsor like to transfer wealth not on their deathbed but much earlier during their lifetime when it is not be subject to death duties. If you examine closely the Christie's catalogue, you can see how birthday, Christmas and even confirmation presents were used as a transmission belt for wealth transfer. The benefit of the auction list is that not only does it identify what Margaret owned but it also gives a monetary value to those possessions and in many cases a clear line of provenance. If you limit the analysis to just birthday, Christmas and confirmation presents in the first twenty-one years of her life and further restrict it to a single donor - her grandmother, Queen Mary - the inventory provides a fascinating insight into how the wealth was passed from generation to generation by stealth.

The cornucopia of presents began on her first birthday when she received the first of twelve George V, Edward VIII and George VI candle holders dated 21 August 1931 and so on that were given each year until she reached the age of twelve. Although not the most practical present for a newborn, they brought in £18,000 at auction for her own children. Her second birthday present was no more suitable for a toddler - a ruby cultured pearl necklace (worth £27,600), nor was the additional gift of a French painted fan (£28,800) with the accompanying note explaining that the fan had been given to her in 1932 by Queen Mary having previously belonged to Queen Alexandra.

On her ninth birthday she received another chain gift that continued over several years - an Edward VIII and George V silver nine piece tea and coffee service worth £28,800 with the note from her grandmother explaining that she was giving her parts of a tea service by degrees for birthdays and Christmas.

The idea of "giving by degrees" is a perfect description of Queen Mary's method of transferring her wealth. Sometime around Margaret's ninth birthday, the old queen also gave her a Honiton lace fan (worth £14,400). For her fifteenth birthday, her grandmother gave her furniture in the form of a French walnut and gilt brass mounted miniature vitrine (worth £20,400). In the same year the Archbishop of Canterbury confirmed her into the Church of England which triggered more gifts from grandmama - including a set of George V silver-gilt mounted mother-of-pearl fruit knives and forks (£312,000) and an art deco sapphire brooch (£66,000). On her eighteenth birthday, she received from Mary an art deco pearl and diamond necklace (£276,800) that became one of her favourite pieces of jewellery. In the same year for Christmas she received a mahogany fire screen (£18,000).

In total Princess Margaret received by the age of twenty-one around £800,000 worth of gifts from her grandmother from birthday, Christmas and confirmation presents. This total at 2006 prices represents only the gifts we know about from the Christie's sale and the real figure is likely to be much larger. The total does not include the Fabergé clock worth £1m that was gifted at some unknown date. One might ask what the hurry was as the twenty-one-year-old had another half century of life ahead of her. But the donor - then eighty-four - must have felt that time was running out and indeed she would be dead within two years of her granddaughter's birthday party. Although it was normal practice for members of the royal family or peerage to pass on family heirlooms at important rites of passage, the sheer scale of the transfers went beyond normal aristocratic practice and suggests the possibility of some element of inheritance planning at work.

In planning her own estate, Princess Margaret would in all likelihood have consulted Lord (Nigel) Napier, her private secretary and comptroller between

1973 and 1998 and her treasurer from 1992 until her death. A friend of the royal family and a quintessential safe pair of hands, Napier was appointed co-executor of her estate along with William Sackville, the Earl of de La Warr, who had a background of stockbroking in the City. The third executor was Sir John Grenfell Nutting QC, a barrister and deputy high court judge who married one of the princess's friends (later in 2002 he would also advise the executors of Princess Diana's estate during the trial of Paul Burrell). If Sir John provided the legal expertise, Earl de la Warr the financial nous and Lord Napier the personal connections, what united the three was that they were all products of Eton.

The last mystery surrounding Margaret's estate is who were the beneficiaries of her secret will. In her heyday in the sixties and seventies, she had a wide circle of show business friends and her active social life - including the well-publicized affair with Roddy Llewellyn as well as her earlier aborted engagement to Group Captain Peter Townsend prompted gossip of illegitimate offspring. Would she have left any mementos to Roddy who was present at the funeral along with Lord Snowdon who after the divorce remained on friendly terms with her and might have been remembered in her will (his biographer revealed that his valuable collection of cufflinks for some reason remained in her safe which was not cleared out until her death)? Presumably there would have been some bequests to her three executors in recognition of their past friendship and future work for the estate.

Immediately after her death, it was widely rumoured in the press that she left everything to her children. The picture became slightly clearer when following the grant of probate in June 2002 a spokesman for Viscount Linley briefed the media. He confirmed that the bulk of the estate went to Lord Linley and Lady Sarah, apart from personal bequests (these, according to Buckingham Palace, were to friends and former members of staff). No further details of the will would be made public although it was made clear that the Queen was not a beneficiary.

Chapter Twelve
From Queen Mother
To Daughter – 2002

"A marsh-mallow made on a welding machine"
Cecil Beaton on the Queen Mother

The Queen Mother's appearance at the funeral of Princess Margaret on 15 February 2002 would be her final public engagement. The centenarian consort retreated to the Royal Lodge at Windsor where her increasing frailty raised doubts about whether she would be able to take part in the Golden Jubilee celebration in June. She suffered a number of falls injuring her arm and ultimately making her bedbound. She was able to make a few farewell telephone calls - including one to Princess Anne and another to her racing manager, Michael Oswald. By Good Friday, March 29, she was so frail she could barely lift her head from the pillow.[1] The next day her condition took a turn for the worse. The Queen, Lord Linley and Lady Sarah Chatto were called to her bedside and she died at 3.15 pm.

The Palace announced the news two and half hours later and by 5.50 pm it was across all the television channels. This time it was not the colourful flashing graphics of Sky News that grabbed the attention but one BBC newsreader's purple tie. As BBC-1 cleared the schedules for the breaking news, it was noted that despite the decades of preparation for this event its veteran newsreader Peter Sissons was not wearing a black tie. The tabloid newspapers led by the Sun accused him of being insensitive and the story rumbled on for days before the palace issued a statement that they had had no complaints about the BBC's coverage. In fact, ITN's newsreader at the time, Nicholas Owen, had also forsworn a black tie for a dark blue one which unlike Sissons's burgundy item appeared black on TV screens. But regardless of the real colour the hue and cry in the popular press illustrated how volatile was the public mood.

Her death may not have come as a surprise but the public outpouring of grief and affection did. At first it was rather muted as the crowds failed to materialize for the lying-in-state in Westminster Hall. But over the week as the weather turned unseasonably chilly the mood changed and by Monday evening one hundred and seventy thousand people had braved the plummeting temperatures to file past her coffin. The interest was now so great that the hall had to remain open until 6 am the next morning – an echo of Edward VII's lying-in-state. One of the officers standing guard during the week of mourning was Captain

James Blunt of the Life Guards, who three years later would find worldwide fame as the singer/songwriter of the smash hit "You're Beautiful."

The funeral was held on the morning of Tuesday 9 April in nearby Westminster Abbey. Among the two thousand and one hundred mourners - well away from the heads of state, prime minister Tony Blair and all the senior members of the royal family assembled in the front row - at the back sat William ("Backstairs Billie") Tallon who had served as the Queen Mother's valet for forty years. The former equerry Colin Burgess lamented how sad it was to see people like Tallon who had devoted his life to the Queen Mother being left out of the main proceedings.[2] Some people - among them, according to Burgess, the Duke of Edinburgh - thought he should have been accorded a more prominent place, but he was hidden at the back, obviously distraught.

After a flyover down the Mall by two Spitfires and a Lancaster bomber, the hearse containing her coffin arrived late that afternoon at Windsor for its final resting place. The delay was caused not just because it avoided the M4 as the Queen Mother had always insisted in her lifetime but also because it had to slow down to accommodate the crowds of up to one million people who lined the route. Once the corpse had been embalmed, the coffin was taken into the King George VI Memorial Chapel and laid to rest next to the old king. Later, a casket containing the ashes of

Princess Margaret was deposited in the tomb so that mother, father and daughter were united at death.

As we have seen in the case of Princess Margaret's death, lawyers for the Queen Mother had already begun the process to seal her will either before or at the time she passed away. Consequently when some time after March 30 an application to seal her will and grant probate was put before the president of the Family Division he could refer to the blanket direction on royal wills rather than assess the matter purely on its own merits as would be the case with any ordinary citizen. This would clearly expedite the process. But when one looks closely at the timeline of events following the death, it is evident that the process was completed with unprecedented speed. On April 10 - just sixteen days after her death - the application to seal her will was granted. Then on April 15 probate was granted. We know from a later appeal court judgment that the Attorney General – possibly acting in his capacity as representative of the public interest - "was joined as defendant to each application."

Normally, once the application has been lodged, it takes a few months for probate to be granted. In the case of Princess Margaret there was a gap of eighteen weeks between her death and probate being granted. Even allowing for the fact that there was no tax to pay which might have excused her executors from doing a detailed inventory of her assets, she still had an estimated £7 million worth of debts to deduct from the gross value of her assets. So, how could all this have been accomplished within nine working days of her death?

The most likely explanation is that probate went through almost automatically and that the whole process at the Family Division may have been little more than a legal rubber stamp or a formality. Indeed, it is rather surprising that probate was even applied for since it is customary for probate not to be required for sovereigns - although whether this applied to *consorts* of sovereigns is unclear. In the case of the last consort to die - Queen Mary in 1953 - probate was granted and her estate openly valued at £406,407 9s 8d. When it came to the Queen Mother no probate figure was recorded. So there appears to be little consistency in this area. Presumably the granting of probate amounted to no more than proving the will and giving authority to her executors to dispose of her assets, rather than the normal process of making an inventory of all the assets and liabilities (and if necessary, paying any inheritance tax). In practical terms there is little way that the Queen Mother's vast estate could have been valued in under a fortnight.

Princess Margaret died seven weeks *before* her mother and yet her probate was granted almost eleven weeks *after* her mother's (June 24 compared to April 15). Why did it take four months longer to complete her probate? A clue to solving the mystery may lie in tax. Princess Margaret's estate was liable to inheritance tax at 40% (after the first £250,000 tax-free allowance) and as such a detailed inventory of all her assets and liabilities had to be drawn up. Since there was no tax to pay on the Queen Mother's estate, one can assume that it was deemed unnecessary to draw up a list.

But why was the Queen Mother's estate exempted from inheritance tax in the first place? The convention dated back a mere decade to an agreement between Queen Elizabeth and her prime minister John Major reached at Balmoral in September 1992. In the early 1990s - when the country braved the worst recession since the thirties - the palace had faced a storm of criticism about its privileged financial situation. The Queen's tax exemption on private income was singled out for attack in Phillip Hall's influential 1992 book "Royal Fortune: Tax, Money and the Monarchy" which formed the basis for a subsequent television investigation by the ITV "World in Action" programme. Hall uncovered that earlier monarchs including George V had actually paid income tax. Editorials in the Sunday Times censored younger royals for using their Civil List payments to finance their lavish lifestyles and an opinion poll in 1991 revealed that 90% of the population thought the Queen should pay tax. The time was thus ripe to clean out the royal stables. On the urging of Prince Charles who had begun to style himself as a moderniser of the monarchy, Michael Peat, the royal household's director of finance and a former partner of a leading accountancy firm Peat Marwick McLintock (today KPMG), was enlisted to devise a new fiscal framework.

The royal finances were part of KPMG's DNA. Peat's great-grandfather had founded the firm that audited the sovereign's Privy Purse and as a young man he had helped his father in going through the books of the Queen's private funds.

Over the course of the year Peat's team of advisors were in discussions with the Treasury about whether the Queen should pay tax. The earlier reorganisation of the royal household expenditure by Peat's accountants had taken away one of the traditional objections – the Queen could not afford to pay tax. Thanks to the palace cost-cutting, Her Majesty's finances were now on a much firmer footing. Ironically the one person who had serious doubts over the tax reform was the prime minister himself. John Major later told the Queen's biographer Robert Hardman that he did not require the Queen to pay tax.[3] A palace official told another royal biographer that John Major's team were not at all keen about the measure since it would give the impression that they had all turned republican.[4] But the palace took the view – helped by private polling evidence - that there was genuine public hostility to the tax exemption and that the only way to dampen the media firestorm would be to agree to pay tax.[5]

On 11 February 1993 - following a brief statement to parliament by the prime minister - the new arrangement was announced in full at a press briefing by the Lord Chamberlain, Lord Airlie, and later on live television news by Michael Peat. The headline story was that the Queen and the Prince of Wales had agreed to pay income tax and capital gains tax on their private income, although this would be done on a voluntary basis. The Civil List was also reduced to just two royals (the Queen Mother and the Duke of Edinburgh) while the previous recipients (Prince Andrew, Prince Edward, Princess Anne, Princess Margaret and Princess Alice) would have their annuity paid by the Queen.

When the Queen Mother was told of this major tax reform, she was far from pleased. After Sir Robert Fellowes, the Queen's private secretary, had spelt out all the details, she paused to consider their significance and then declared that she thought this might be a good moment to have a drink.[6] She ordered a Martini. What worried her most - according to members of the royal family - was that the new agreement amounted to a tacit acceptance that the Queen and more particularly George VI should have paid tax earlier. Although the Queen Mother took a carefree attitude to her personal finances, she was remarkably sensitive to general questions of taxation.

The deal, however, included one key tax advantage for the royal family: there would be an exemption on inheritance tax on any bequest from the sovereign to sovereign. This major concession - which according to Prince Charles's biographer caused "a serious difficulty" in the negotiations between the palace and the Treasury[7] - received relatively little publicity, although the Queen's own biographer described it as "crucial" to the survival of the royal family's way of life.[8]

Earlier, in the House of Commons John Major had explained that the exemption was to stop royal assets from being "salami-sliced away by capital taxation through generations, thus changing the nature of the institution in a way that few people in this country would welcome." There was a real danger in his opinion that the wealth of the monarchy could be decimated by a succession of premature deaths.

In the view of the royal family this could also undermine their political independence since in order to be constitutionally impartial, the monarch needed to be financially independent. At one stage, Prince Charles even floated the idea of doing away with the Civil List altogether in return for allowing the royals to keep all the revenue from the Crown estates - by his rough calculation, the sums of money were almost the same. In this way the monarchy would be self-financing and autonomous.

This was never acceptable to MPs who jealously guarded their control over the royal purse strings. When the agreement was laid before parliament it included a clause to ensure that any sovereign did not abuse the arrangement as a tax shelter ("the provisions included in this memorandum will not be used to reduce tax payments by themselves [the Queen and the Prince of Wales] or other members of the Royal Family in circumstances which the provisions were not supposed to cover").[9]

Although not referred to by name, the agreement was clearly designed to protect the private residences of Balmoral and Sandringham, but some MPs were worried that it might be used as a blanket tax exemption for all private property. In the parliamentary debate in February 1993 John Smith, the leader of the Labour opposition, asked pertinently: "Will the prime minister explain why all private assets passing from one sovereign to the next should also be exempt? Although private assets such as Sandringham and Balmoral could well be regarded as having at least partial official use, which could be recognized, why is it necessary to exempt all other private wealth?" John Major did not comment directly on the two private residences but argued that "the Rt Hon. and Learned gentleman will accept there is a unique circumstance in a hereditary monarchy, and it is right therefore that there should be specific exemptions for assets passing from one sovereign to his or her successor."

It should be noted in passing that although he could not be certain what would be in the Queen's last will and testament Prince Charles clearly regarded himself as the future steward of Balmoral and Sandringham having told his biographer Jonathan Dimbleby that he wanted to look after Balmoral so that it could be passed on to future generations in the best state possible.[10] By all accounts, he felt a similar sense of responsibility for Sandringham but of the two he held a special affection for what he often described as "the best place in the world – Balmoral." Elsewhere he recorded his support for Sandringham and parts of Balmoral being open to the public - which some cynical voices might interpret, having seen what has happened to the opening up of Highgrove House to general visitors, as a way of enhancing their status as part of the royal heritage and downplaying their role as a purely private residence.

The new arrangement was set out in the palace's official guide to its revenues "Royal Finances." It justified the inheritance tax privileges on the grounds that "a sovereign who does not retire is unable to mitigate inheritance tax by passing on assets at an early stage to his or her successor." Curiously, the term sovereign was widened to embrace not just the reigning monarch but also his or her consort. As such, the Queen Mother as queen consort of George VI was included. It should be said that not everyone was happy with this addition to the exemption rule. When in 2003 a Fabian commission into the future of the monarchy looked into the matter, it recommended that "special exemptions, such as those made for the Queen Mother, are not appropriate and should not be made in the future."[11]

What worried the Fabians is that while it might be legitimate to exempt public assets - such as the crown properties and the royal collections - from inheritance tax, private property might also slip through the net. It has been estimated that the queen consort exemption may have cost the Exchequer £20m-£30 million in lost tax on the Queen Mother's estate.

At the time of her death, estimates of the Queen Mother's financial worth varied between £50 million and £70 million. The Royal Rich Report which came up with a figure of £53.4 million calculated that her art collection alone was worth £36 million.[12] From her early days as a child visiting the Uffizi gallery with her Florence-based grandmother, the Queen Mother had harboured a deep passion for paintings. Encouraged to explore contemporary art by Sir Kenneth Clark, the surveyor of the king's pictures between 1934 and 1945 and later a director of the National Gallery, she built up a valuable collection of the works of modern British artists. She bought an Augustus John portrait of Bernard Shaw for £750 and Wilson Steer's Chepstow Castle for just over £1,000. Many of these purchases were handled by her other artistic mentor, Sir Jasper Ridley, a trustee of the National Gallery and a chairman of the Tate Gallery as well as Coutts Bank. He helped to arrange the acquisition of her most impressive work - Landscape of the Vernal Equinox by Paul Nash. It was not to the taste of her twelve-year-old daughter Margaret who reportedly thought that her mother was mad to buy it.[13] We do not know how much the Queen Mother paid for the visionary painting of a Thames Valley landscape but today Nash's pre-war work regularly commands hundreds of thousands of pounds and one abstract piece from 1936 recently fetched £937,250 at auction.

The Nash landscape was bought in 1942 and World War Two proved a beneficial period for picking up valuable paintings at knock down prices. In 1939 she bought Alfred Sisley's La Seine sur St Cloud and William Sickert's Ennui and in November 1940 two works by Duncan Grant - Newhaven Pier and St Paul's. Around 1940-41 when London (and the royal palaces) were under constant bombardment she commissioned a series of water colours of Windsor Castle from the renowned landscape artist John Piper who later became an official war artist and designed the stained windows for the war-damaged Coventry Cathedral. Again she was guided by Kenneth Clark who told Piper he would be paid £150 (including expenses) for fifteen paintings - in retrospect, a bargain for the palace. The Queen Mother later displayed them prominently in Clarence House and today they are recognised not just as a faithful invocation of London under the Blitz but as a work of considerable artistic significance. At the end of the war in 1945 the Queen Mother picked up her greatest bargain - paying Gallerie Wildenstein £2,000 for Claude Monet's Study of Rocks: Creuse, Fresseline.

Clarence House soon became her own private gallery. On one side of the hallway was a fine sketch by Simon Elwes of the Queen Mother that was the basis for a major magisterial portrait of her for Windsor Castle. Also in the hallway was a group portrait by James Gunn entitled "Field Marshall Montgomery in his mess tent in Belgium in 1944" which she snapped up in 1945 at a Royal Academy exhibition before Monty could buy it himself (when she later refused to let him have it Gunn had to paint another version). Over the fireplace in an adjoining room hung an unfinished portrait begun in 1939 by Augustus John. In the end she apparently got it for free as in 1961 it was presented to her as a gift. Edward Seago also gave her many paintings for her birthday and at Christmas, and her portrait by John Singer Sargent was a wedding gift. The house contains other important paintings by Singer Sargent as well as works by Graham Sutherland and Philip de Laszlo. Interestingly for two such dissimilar royals her penchant for Laszlo, Seago and Nash would closely mirror Prince Philip's choice of favourite painters.

Although it is notoriously difficult to track down the exact provenance of all of the Queen Mother's gems, we do know for sure the source of one of the most valuable additions to her jewellery collection. Ironically this is due to a publicly available will and the generosity of a society hostess who did not allow her own mortality to get in the way of social climbing. When Dame Margaret Greville died in September 1942 she left behind an estate worth £1,505,120 and a will running to fourteen pages. In the schedule devoted to bequests, she left £20,000 in cash to Princess Margaret, £12,500 to Queen Eugenie of Spain, £10,000 to Sir Osbert Sitwell, £10,000 to the national anti-vivisection society and £500 to her goddaughter Rosalind Cobitt. In the schedule devoted to her jewels, once again she gave preferential treatment to royalty: to Queen Elizabeth she gave all her jewels but to her friend Marie Adeline Liron just small items of jewellery and personal possessions valued at less than £100.

Her gem box contained one of the finest private collections of jewellery in London. The most valuable items included Marie Antoinette's diamond necklace and Catherine the Great's diamond ring as well as an openwork diamond tiara designed by Lucien Hirst and various emeralds and diamonds owned by Empress Josephine. Not a bad haul for an illegitimate daughter of a housekeeper and a self-made brewer. When her father, William McEwan, died she inherited the famous brewing business and used the wealth - as her obiturist put it - "for the purpose of a wide but discriminating hospitality." Being childless she had no one to leave her money to and so she gave it to her surrogate children - the Duke and Duchess of York. When the future duchess began making arrangements for her wedding in April 1923, Mrs. Greville even offered to buy the linen for the new household as a wedding present. But as the price tag was in the region of £1,500, the over-generous offer had to be declined.

She cultivated the Windsors with the passion of a royal horticulturist. As an alternative wedding gift, she invited the couple to spend their honeymoon at her country mansion near Dorking, Polseden Lacey. At one stage, she wanted to bequeath them the whole house but as soon as it became clear that Bertie would be king and have no shortage of country houses, she had to restrict herself to just offering them hospitality. As the visitors' book ostentatiously shows, they became frequent dinner guests in the years before the abdication. Life was never dull with Maggie Greville and her smart set. The Queen Mother later wrote to Osbert Sitwell saying how she found Mrs Greville such good fun and quite a character.[14] She was, however, a Nazi sympathiser and in the early thirties was "delighted" to meet with Chancellor Hitler in Nuremburg. The diarist MP Harold Nicolson recognised her at the time as a pernicious influence on society, describing her as a "virulent little bitch."[15]

But the inheritance brought some embarrassment to the queen consort. When after weeks of society gossip about the estate Mrs Greville's solicitor came to the palace to hand over some of the jewellery, she asked him what was the point of pretending she knew nothing about the will, when everyone told her that the property was left to the National Trust.[16] To clear up the matter, the executors were forced to issue a public statement immediately. In private, however, she was as pleased as punch with the bequest, acknowledging to Queen Mary that like most women she had a soft spot for beautiful stones.[17] In the event, the jewellery was kept locked away in the jewel box during much of the war and the Bucheron tiara only appeared in 1947 during a state visit to South Africa.

The king, according to her official biographer, may have had reservations about the bequest. It was widely believed at the time that the reason why Mrs

Greville had given her jewels to royalty was to ensure that they would be displayed in the most public arena. In other words, they would become part of the royal collection. Even today the precise ownership of the jewels is in doubt. The constitutional historian Michael Nash summed up the dilemma: "there has been speculation as to which of her jewels belonged to the state as official gifts and which were personal property."[18] Of course, if the will were open to public inspection, the provenance of the jewels would be much clearer.[19]

In truth the Queen Mother - unlike Queen Mary - was never a great hoarder of jewels. She tended to wear the same favourite pieces of jewellery: a brooch inherited from Queen Victoria, a necklace inherited from Queen Alexandra and a diamond brooch passed on by husband at their wedding. This is just some of the jewels she received from the royal family. She must have been left many jewels from her own family - bearing in mind that her mother and her father the Earl of Strathmore were both dead before her forty-fifth birthday and she outlived her six brothers and three sisters (not to mention fifteen of her twenty-two nieces and nephews). We know for certain that her father gave her as a wedding present a diamond tiara which has been valued at around £400,000.

Her horses are easier to track. She grew up in a world of equestrianism finding delight in hanging around the stables of the family's country home in Hertfordshire. Her love of the turf - and particularly steeple chasing which drew a wider social spectrum than the more upper crust flat racing - became a driving passion of her life after the death of George VI. In an echo of her profligate grandfather-in-law, Edward VII, she began to acquire bloodstock. Her first big buy was Double Star in 1956 which at £4,000 was a major outlay even for a dowager queen consort. She went on to purchase a string of sixteen jumpers under the trainership of her friend Peter Cazalet and was famous for never selling a horse, however lame or old. Eventually costs caught up with her. After one disastrous year, the Queen had to step in to pay Cazalet's bill on behalf of her mother who scribbled under the total her apologies for the high figure.[20] She also spent much on gambling both on course and at Clarence House where she could listen to the commentaries and latest odds thanks to the "Blower" - her own loudspeaker system similar to that used at a betting shop. The settlement of bets was handled by others, most notably her personal treasurer.[21] At the time of her death - according to her biographer, Hugo Vickers - she had eleven horses in training, most with Nicky Henderson at his Lambourn stables.[22] Even though some of these were homebred or bought as inexpensive one- or two-year-olds, they each would have been of value - perhaps up to £100,000.

The Queen Mother's other great passion was entertaining and to that end she possessed a valuable wine cellar, the worth of which was once estimated at over £100,000. Unfortunately there is no known inventory of her stock of fine wines and spirits - although reportedly it included a rare vintage of Veuve Cliquot champagne called Rich England. All we have to go by is the record of dinner guests at Clarence House and her other residences who complimented her on both the quality and quantity of the alcohol on offer. The interior designer Nicky Haslam in his memoirs recalls a working visit to the castle of Mey where on arrival at midday her valet William Tallon offered him a choice from the drinks tray - "the bottles, many less than half full, contained every single aperitif known to man. Dubonnet naturally [her favourite tipple] but also red and white Martini, Punt e Mes, Fernet-Branca, Amer Pico, Cinzano, Crodo, Campari, Ricard...with much Alsatian wine."[23]

The expenditure on her public duties - although some critics have suggested that it leaked into her private life too - was met by a generous annuity from the Treasury. Over the decades her Civil List payments were the source of much friction between government, parliament and the palace. When George VI died in 1952, the Queen Mother was granted the same annuity that the Dowager Queen Mary received in 1936 - £70,000. This remained unchanged until the 1971 Select Committee inquiry into the Civil List which raised the payment to £95,000. In defence of this increase for a seventy-year-old who was performing fewer official engagements, the Lord Chamberlain, Lord Cobbold, stated that in his personal view any pay rise should be considered "as something of the nature of the payment for services rendered over years of peace and war."

The uplift seemed very generous, but we now know that the Queen Mother (via representations by her own mother) in fact wanted more. The released cabinet papers from the National Archives disclose how the Heath government had to veto the palace's proposal for a 100% pay rise to £140,000 saying that "it might well lead to embarrassing criticism of the royal family." Senior ministers suggested that the amount must be kept under £100,000 and recommended £90,000 instead.[24]

The Queen Mother's response to scrutiny of her Civil List expenditure was that the public expected her to maintain a lifestyle appropriate to the mother of the sovereign and this inevitably involved special transport and other privileges.[25] In the long run she got her way: her annuity was raised to £493,000 in 1991 and by the time of her death it was £643,000.

This amount was insufficient, however, to pay for her lavish lifestyle maintained by a staff of over fifty. When she died, she is believed to have left debts of £5m-£7m. Thanks to a leak from a bank employee, we know that in 1996 her overdraft with Coutts stood at £4m. Her official biographer does not dispute this figure, conceding that there was a widely held perception that she was extravagant and lived beyond her means.[26] He also discloses how every three months someone would deliver in person from Coutts her passbook which in longhand gave details of all her personal cheques.

Over the decades, treasurer after treasurer in the royal household grappled manfully with her chaotic finances. In the fifties, Arthur Penn tried to remind her of the need for prudence through a series of polite letters, although as a friend as well as a courtier it was hard for him to put his foot down - or even resign as he wanted to as he reached seventy. In 1961 the poisoned chalice passed to Sir Ralph Anstruther, an old Etonian "martinet" who had served in the Coldstream Guards and been awarded the Military Cross in 1943. It was his responsibility to sign a lot of the Queen Mother's cheques and oversee her expenditure. Since she never carried cash, he had to discreetly arrange payment for purchases when she was out of earshot. Although he had an almost unsurpassed knowledge of royal protocol and an impressive network of international contacts that smoothed the way for the Queen Mother's many foreign trips, he knew very little about finance. Eventually the pressure of dealing with a spendthrift dowager queen and the onset of age took its toll: he would according to legend turn up for work on a Sunday unaware that it was not a weekday and he would be found wandering round Clarence House not wearing any trousers. In 1999 he was replaced by someone with a real financial background, Sir Nicholas Assheton who had just retired as deputy chairman of Coutts (or as an annoyed Anstruther called him "a little clerk from Coutts").

Even his financial skills and inside knowledge of the ways of the bank did not stem the overdraft. The Queen who probably subsidised her racing costs is thought to have funded the shortfall (reportedly contributing as much as £2 million a year) and it is believed that Prince Charles may have also made an annual contribution of £80,000.

Another reason why the Queen Mother was short of cash is that she is thought to have placed £19 million into a trust fund for her great-grandchildren. Some people have disputed that figure but according to a well-sourced report in The Times, Princes William and Harry would share a £4.9 million payday on their 21st birthday.[27] The financial benefit of the trust was that if the Queen Mother survived for seven years, her great-grandsons would receive the money tax free. The trust was set up in 1994; she died in 2002.

Although the Queen Mother is often portrayed as a spendthrift who had but the haziest notion of organising her finances, as a scion of one of wealthiest aristocratic family in the country, she could not have been unaware of the effect of death duties and the need for inheritance tax planning. Before she reached the age of fifty she had lost her father (the 14th Earl of Strathmore), her mother (the countess of Strathmore) as well as four brothers (including Patrick, the 15th Earl of Strathmore) and one sister.

David, the surviving brother whom she was most close to and who happened to be managing director of the investment bank Lazard Brothers, regularly gave her financial advice. Without trusts and other conduits of inheritance tax planning, the Bowes Lyon estate - including the Castle of Glamis in Scotland, the family seat for nearly seven hundred years, and the St Paul's Walden Bury, the country home in Hertfordshire - could have been decimated by death duties. In a letter to her friend Osbert Sitwell, she let slip her interest in such matters when she gave as one of the main reasons why she loved Rhodesia was the absence of any inheritance tax.[28]

Her concern about high taxes was part and parcel of her wider political outlook which her friend Woodrow Wyatt once described as "much more pro-Conservative than the Queen or the Prince of Wales." According to her official biographer, she was annoyed with some aspects of the taxation policy of the Labour government of Harold Wilson and particularly disliked its new selective employment tax. There were Labour politicians with whom she got on well - James Callaghan and also Ernest Bevin - but as an aristocratic Edwardian lady who was bought up in a traditionally Conservative family, she could never escape her ideological inheritance. When the first Labour government came to power in 1924, she wrote privately about how their values were so diametrically opposed to her own.[29]

What she liked was not tax and spend but rather spend and not worry about the tax. This approach to life was best illustrated in the purchase of the one house she ever owned - the castle of Mey. She would never have bought it but for the premature death of George VI which left a void in her life. Although her role in giving him the confidence to be king throughout the trauma of the abdication has been widely acknowledged, it is often forgotten how much she relied on *him* to be taught the protocol of royal life and metamorphose from being a commoner to a queen-empress. She saw him as her mainspring, once writing to her brother David that she could not envisage life without the king. In her deep grief she needed a place with no association with her husband where she could be alone.

She found it in one of the most remote parts of Scotland - the Pentland Firth, six miles west of John O'Groats and fourteen miles south of the Orkney Islands. Her friends Clare and Doris Vyner owned a house there and on a visit a few months after the death of her husband, she discovered a romantic-looking castle by the sea. It stood in a wonderful location overlooking the Orkneys but it was near derelict after years without maintenance and a roof that had not survived a recent storm. On learning that it might soon be demolished, she became determined to save it. The owner, Captain Imbert Terry, offered it for free but since it was considered improper for a member of the royal family to accept such a gift they agreed on a nominal sum of £100. Later she bought some more land along the coast for £300.

The real cost of the property was not the land but its restoration. A decrepit, 16th century Z-plan castle had to be turned into a habitable dwelling for a fifty-two-year-old dowager queen consort. This would require considerable capital. At first she kept her costly plans under wraps. She did not break the news to her treasurer Arthur Penn until early August and disguised the purchase to Queen Mary as an act of heritage preservation.[30]

Such was the scale of the restoration work - involving a new dining room and bathrooms and the installation of electricity - that it would be another three years before she spent her first night in the castle. From 1955 until the summer of 2001 she visited the castle every August entertaining her friends and courtiers - some of whom got up to spirited activity in the isolated castle. Mey became her Mustique. One of the rooms was even called Princess Margaret's Bedroom, although her daughter never set foot in the place, reportedly calling it "Mummy's draughty castle."

To ward off the draught and add a bit of warmth, she commissioned a spectacular tapestry with her coat of arms for the dining room and hung on the drawing room wall a 16th century Flemish wool tapestry. As she got frailer, she had to rebuild the lift in the turret leading to her master bedroom with it panoramic view of the Pentland Firth. No one knows exactly how much money was spent on all the restoration and refurbishment but over five decades it must have approached seven figures. Another burden was the never-ending maintenance costs. Damp was a constant headache since the castle was built on porous sandstone and the roof continued to leak despite new leadwork.

In 1996 she found a solution to the rising maintenance costs by setting up the Castle of Mey Trust to look after the house. In return for handing over the deeds to a 1,800 acre estate complete with a prize herd of Aberdeen Angus cattle, she was spared all the running costs and allowed to stay for a small rent in the castle every summer. In June 1996 she appointed her friend and former equerry, Ashe Windham, chairman of the trustees who also included her grandson Prince Charles. The charitable trust is designed to benefit the local community and economy.

The other advantage of the trust is that it may have saved her estate a fortune in tax. If she had still owned the castle at her death it would not just have been liable to inheritance tax at 40% (provided it was not left to the Queen) but it would have been subject to capital gains tax at a similar rate. Considering the gain in the property from a base figure of £400 to a final value well into the millions, the tax would have been several hundred thousand pounds. So, it was from a tax perspective an astute move to put the castle into a trust, although in fairness it also benefited the nation in that she took steps for the castle to be opened to the public – which it is today.

All we know for certain about her final will and testament are the names of its three executors: Nicholas Assheton, her last Treasurer, David Cospatrick, the Earl of Home and scion of the a family with long links to the Queen Mother, and Marshom Boyd Carpenter, another member of a family with close ties to the Windsors. Their main task was to distribute the contents of her estate although the Queen Mother had actually begun the process on her deathbed. On Good Friday 2002 - a day before she passed away - she gave to her page Leslie Chapell, a pair of cuff links and to her dresser and carer Jacqui Meakin, a brooch with her "ER" emblem on it. A Buckingham Palace spokesman later confirmed that she made "certain bequests to members of her staff." William Tallon, her faithful valet over many decades, would almost certainly have been among the other staff beneficiaries.

Before her death she also gave instructions for the distribution of her stable of horses. In the last week of her life she telephoned her racing manager, Michael Oswald, to say goodbye and give him a list of things to do. A little later she rang Princess Anne asking her to take some of her horses.

A clue to what might have happened to her jewellery is given in a remarkable wartime letter she wrote to the then Princess Elizabeth. In June 1944 - when London was under daily V1 bombardment and

Buckingham Palace had narrowly missed an attack that hit the nearby Guards Chapel - Queen Elizabeth specified that in the event of her death all her possessions should be divided between her two daughters in a right and proper manner.[31] Of course, by the time of the Queen Mother's passing, Princess Margaret was already dead and so all the jewellery would have reverted to Elizabeth.

It was also widely rumoured at the time that the Queen had decided that the most important of her mother's paintings and works of art should be transferred to the Royal Collection. After much speculation about the fate of the Queen Mother's estate, Buckingham Palace felt obliged in May 2002 to issue a short statement:

"Queen Elizabeth the Queen Mother has bequeathed her entire estate (which mainly comprises the contents of her houses) to the Queen. In her will, she asked the Queen to make certain bequests to members of her staff and these will be subject to Inheritance Tax in the normal way."

This statement glossed over the fact that under the sovereign to sovereign exemption almost all of the multi-million pound estate passed to the Queen tax free. But it confirmed that:

"The Queen has decided that the most important of Queen Elizabeth's pictures and works of art should be transferred to the Royal Collection. Some of these items, including works by Monet, Nash and Carl Faberge, from Queen Elizabeth's collection will be on display in the 'Royal Treasures' exhibition, which is due to open at the new Queen's Gallery, Buckingham Palace, on 22 May [2002]."

At the time, it was far from clear how many of the art works were actually transferred to the Royal Collection and put on permanent display to the public. When a search was made on their publicly available on-line catalogue, there was no record, for instance, of the Monet painting "Study of Rocks". The complicated situation was later clarified by the Senior Curator of Paintings who explained that Royal Collection On-line is based on a wider database of the comprehensive computerised inventory of the contents of the royal palaces, although she did acknowledge that there is "no single comprehensive catalogue...Collection on-line is not a comprehensive inventory of the Royal Collection but every year we [are] adding more entries to the website."[32] In the eyes of some more sceptical palace critics, a certain ambiguity about the contents of the Royal Collection might actually suit members of the royal family. According to Jon Temple in his book "Living off the State": "even the Palace may not know or at least would probably find it convenient not to know."[33]

Some credence to the suspicion that some of the more valuable items were retained away from public view was given by the former Labour MP and government minister Chris Mullin. In his diaries he records a visit to Clarence House in November 17, 2005 for a private reception with Prince Charles who took over the Queen Mother's residence after her death. At the end of the two hour meeting he was allowed a glimpse of the dining room where he discovered that the walls were "crammed" with paintings:

"A veritable art gallery. A Sickert of George V at the races, an unusual Monet depicting a stark granite mountainside, various portraits of the Queen Mother, a large one of her as a young woman hangs over the fireplace, a series of bleak paintings of Windsor commissioned at the outbreak of war because the King and Queen feared that the castle would be destroyed and wanted to preserve the memory."[34]

At first sight it seemed likely that these items were part of the Royal Collection but not on permanent public show. But there seemed little point in donating the items to the Royal Collection if they remain in the royal residence of the Prince of Wales and the public is unable to see them. Three and half years after the Queen Mother's death, it would have been expected that some attempt would be made to put such an important works as Monet's "Study of Rocks" on permanent display.

After further inquiries were made to Royal Collection Trust, the Senior Curator of Paintings confirmed that the Monet painting and indeed the whole of the Queen Mother's collection belonged to the Queen – "Her Majesty The Queen inherited the collection which belonged to Her Majesty Queen Elizabeth the Queen Mother and as such it *is* the private property of Her Majesty [author's italics]. The Royal Collection Trust cares for the Collection on behalf of the Queen. The painting by Monet is on display at Clarence House."[35]

Limited public access to Clarence House is now available. Between August 1 and 31 the public can enjoy a sixty-minute tour of the rooms – including according to its website "outstanding 20th century paintings such as important works by John Piper, Graham Sutherland, WS Sickert and Augustus John" - for the cost of a £9.50 entrance ticket or £35 if they want a private guide.

Chapter Thirteen
A Royal Car Boot Sale – 2006

"David sells everything"
Lord Snowdon's reported comment on his son's penchant for selling

In June 2006, a full four years after probate had been granted to Princess Margaret's executors, the saga of her estate took an unexpected turn. The £7.6 million legacy was liable to inheritance tax at 40% which meant a £3 million bill for its two main beneficiaries, Lord Linley and Lady Sarah Chatto. To pay it, they said they needed to sell off their mother's most valuable possessions, including the tiara she wore on her wedding day and the silver Fabergé clock that sat on her bedroom table. The auction was set for June 13 and 14 at Christie's central London salesroom.

The renowned auction house whose first sale took place during the reign of King George III stood in the heart of St James's at 8 King Street - barely a stone's throw from Margaret's childhood home at 145

Piccadilly. With its long pedigree in organising royal auctions (including the sale six months earlier of the Duke of Gloucester's personal artefacts), Christie's was delighted to host another prestigious - and no doubt highly profitable - sale. "It was the first time in history that the private jewellery collection of the sister of a reigning sovereign is offered for sale" trumpeted their press office although they were quick to emphasise that "the jewellery offered is neither part of the Crown Jewels nor part of the Royal Collection."

So, when it came to promoting the sale and creating that vital buzz that elevates prices, they really pushed the boat out. An exhibition of ninety items of jewellery - whose highlights featured the famed wedding tiara and the Queen Mother's diamond brooch - was put on the road being shown first at Balmoral Hotel, Edinburgh in early May and soon after at the Earl of Harewood's ancestral pile Harewood House, Yorkshire and Wilton House, near Salisbury before going on a world tour to Geneva, Moscow, Hong Kong and New York. Rich overseas buyers were clearly in their sights.

When the full collection of over eight hundred items was put on show at the London auction rooms on the weekend before the sale, it drew huge crowds, the like of which had not been seen at Christie's since the Queen's diamonds were put on display before the coronation. The press and television cameras were allowed in too prompting even Channel 4 News to run several reports on the sale of the century. It was also announced that the auctioneer would be Francois Curiel, chairman of Christie's Europe, who promised that "we will stage an auction that pays tribute to Princess Margaret's glamorous style and beauty."

Not everyone, however, was happy about the auction. A day before Curiel opened the bidding, Kenneth Rose, the historian and friend of Margaret, wrote in The Daily Telegraph "there is something melancholy - isn't there? - about turning over the possessions of the well-remembered dead" before suggesting that some of the wedding gifts should not have been included and that the bridegroom might also share this view.[1] In fact, Lord Snowdon - according to his biographer - was "furious" about the sale of some of the wedding presents which he regarded as much his as hers. He even wrote to the chairman of Christie's UK, Dermot Chichester, querying the right of his son to sell some items. He was later quoted as saying in an apparent reference to his son's penchant to monetise property: "David sells everything."[2] By all accounts, Snowdon's disapproval was not to the sale itself but rather its extent - but in the fullness of time any family tensions were soon amicably reconciled.

The Queen also reportedly intervened to register her concern but in this case it related to the grey area between public and private gifts. She is said to have asked Lord Linley to make a clear distinction between goods his mother had received in an official capacity and those that had been personal gifts from family and friends. One senior royal official told the Sunday Telegraph: "The Queen has made sure that the sellers are aware of the issue and the various implications involved...It is up to Princess Margaret's beneficiaries what they do with her estate. However, the Queen made it clear from early on that, if there were any items given to Princess Margaret in an official capacity, and then any proceeds should go to charity."[3]

Prompted in part by this intervention, it was decided that the revenue from the sale of forty-seven lots should go to charitable causes. The two catalogues had to be altered so that the titles of the charitable items were highlighted in blue and Lord Linley felt obliged to issue a statement saying how pleased he was to be able to support such worthy causes as the Stroke Association and SOS Children's Villages UK. (His mother had died following a stroke.) This gesture helped to dampen some of the press criticism but apart from a few passing references to "a silver water jug donated by Bolton Borough Council" or "a cigar box from the King of Cambodia" no journalist made a detailed study of the items allocated to charity.

When it comes to considering the forty or so charity items and distinguishing personal gifts from official ones, it is useful to refer to the palace's Guidelines and Procedures Relating to Gifts issued in March 2003. It states that gifts are classed as personal when "they are: given by people whom the Member of the Royal Family knows privately and not during or in connection with an official engagement or duty; given by public bodies, businesses or private individuals with whom the Member of The Royal Family has an established relationship, such as Warrant Holders, on the occasion of a marriage, birth, birthday or other notable personal occasion (including Christmas), and where the value of the gift is less than £150 (if a gift is given where there is no established relationship, other than on a notable personal occasion or is over £150 in value, the gift should be classified as official)."

Let's consider first the status of lot number twenty-eight. In 1947 on her first solo engagement at the Harland and Wolff shipyard in Belfast the seventeen-year-old princess was given by the builders of the new royal mail ship a diamond and emerald heather brooch housed in a case engraved "RMS Edinburgh Castle Oct.16th 1947". It was the first of her many ship-launchings. Another apparently unambiguous item was a West Indian gilt cigarette box which bore a plaque reading: "presented to Her Royal Highness the Princess Margaret by the Government and People of the West Indies as a token of their abiding loyalty and affection on the occasion of her visit to Port of Spain in April 1958 when on behalf of Her Majesty the Queen she graciously inaugurated the Parliament of the West Indies." Then there was the Canadian salver which bore the equally unequivocal inscription "presented to HRH the Princess Margaret Rose by the Government of Canada May 1939."

Perhaps the most clear cut public gift was given by President Tito during a state visit to the United Kingdom in March 1953. Not previously noted as a close friend of the royal princess, the Yugoslav communist leader gave her a filigrée cigarette case and cigarette holder. Inside was a note in an unknown hand: "From Tito 1952 or 3." Its sale brought in £6,600.

The other striking feature is the apparently arbitrary way in which items were designated public or private. Take two wedding gifts from two Commonwealth countries. A pair of silver model kiwis from the government of New Zealand was deemed public and consequently the proceeds from the sale were given to charity - a move diplomatically welcomed by a spokesman from its London High Commission: "we are pleased that the proceeds from our gift are going to a good cause".[4] Yet a set of four gold candlesticks given by the government of South Africa (then still a member of the Commonwealth) was not granted charitable status. It was sold for £31,200.

In some cases it was a close judgement call as to whether a gift was given in an official capacity or not. A set of Iranian cups and saucers - which bore the crown and arms of the Shah of Iran who had "presented" the gift in some unrecorded capacity - was according to the official catalogue re-designated a charitable item with a blue title, although curiously after it was sold for £5,400 the Christie's website of auction results omitted to classify it a charitable item. This might of course have been just a clerical mistake. A more ambiguous case was a present from the Pope which fetched £14,400. A travelling icon depicting the Virgin and Child mounted in a gem-set frame and presented to the princess by Pius XII in May 1949 was not granted charitable status. At first sight, this was surprising since it appeared on a state-like engagement on a par with President Tito's cigarette case or the Canadian government's silver salver. A possible explanation why this gift slipped through the net was that the princess received it during a private audience with the pontiff, although one wonders whether she would have been given a papal audience and a gift if she had not been a member of the royal family. After visiting the Pope, the princess lunched with the Italian head of state, President Einaudi, and the leaders of the Chamber of Deputies and the Senate.

If there was a whiff of arbitrariness about how the choice was made, then one might also wonder whether there was a tendency to choose less valuable items for charitable status. When you analyse the lots as a whole it is obvious that the more valuable items were not given charitable status. The top priced non-charitable items hit seven figures with the Fabergé clock realising £1.24m and the Poltimore tiara just falling short on £926,400, while the bulk of the other lots went for five figures. The top priced item among the charitable lots was the £36,000 pair of silver kiwis followed closely by the Harland and Wolff brooch at

£31,200 but two thirds of all the items went for four figures. At the low end, the cigar case from the King of Cambodia was sold for £1,560 and the silver water jug from Bolton Borough Council realised £4,200, while at the top end the army's wedding present of a dining table sold for £18,000 and an Irish oak linen chest from the women of Belfast went for as much as £26,400.

At the time of the sale, Christie's declared that the proceeds from forty-seven lots would be donated to charity and it was also reported that the actual amount was around £410,000. But if you examine Christie's auction results with the final list of realised prices, you can find recorded – and again this might be just an innocent clerical error - only *forty-one* charitable lots and a final total of £314,700 - a sizable amount by anyone's standards but still less than 3% of the total receipts from the sale.

In fairness to the sellers, the charitable status of items was established before the start of the auction and at that stage no one could have predicted how much would be realised. In the case of the two Commonwealth wedding gifts, the non-charitable South African gift had an estimated price of £10,000-£15,000 and realised £31,200, while the charitable New Zealand gift had an estimate of just £600-£900 but fetched £36,000. So, there was a strong element of lottery in how much each lot realised at auction. It should also be pointed out that one reason why the charitable items were relatively low priced is that they tended to come from public bodies whereas many of the other non charitable items came from wealthy friends and relatives.

The grey area of what is public property and what is private was dramatically put under the spotlight by lot number seven hundred and ninety-three - Pietro Annigoni's portrait of Princess Margaret. Painted in 1957 and hung in the National Museum of Wales and then at the entrance to the Kensington Palace apartment, it was a companion piece to his more famous portrait of the young Queen Elizabeth II in a deep blue cloak that hung in the National Portrait Gallery. In the view of several commentators, such an iconic image should have been presented to the National Portrait Gallery or at least retained in the family.

When Christie's released details of the number of foreign buyers on the first day of the auction, there seemed a real danger that the painting might be lost to the nation the following day. The auction house revealed that while 58% of sales came from the UK (many of whom were private bidders), 15% resulted from the rest of Europe, 16% from the Americas, 10% from Asia and 1% from the Middle East. But the crucial figures concerned the top selling five items - two of which went to Asia and one to continental Europe.[5] When twenty-four hours later they gave a similar breakdown for the concluding day of the auction, the top selling item was the Annigoni portrait whose buyer was listed as "anonymous". It transpired that the mystery buyer was Lord Linley himself

- paying £680,000, three times the original estimate and a world auction record for the artist.

Another item that many thought should never have been offered for auction was a ten inch high glass crucifix. Made by the renowned French glass maker René Lalique, it was given to the princess by the Queen Mother almost exactly a year before her death with a note saying that the crucifix was given to her early on in her marriage by Princess Beatrice, Queen Victoria's youngest daughter. The shaky handwriting of her dying mother on the letter paper is testament to the highly personal nature of the gift. It was rumoured that the Queen was concerned about the sale of such an intimate family heirloom and at the last moment, Lord Linley withdrew it from the auction. In the end its sentimental value outstripped its reserve price of £500-£800.

The crucifix was not the only item that many wanted withdrawn. At the end of the first day a storm of controversy suddenly blew up over a set of cast iron railings called the Royal Ascot Balustrading. After the Duke of Norfolk decided in 1963 to build a new stand at the race course, the old ironwork dating back to 1929 was "presented" to Princess Margaret who duly put it in her rose garden at Kensington Palace. Under Lord Snowdon's supervision, it was reassembled to create a shadowed arbour replete with climbing plants and later - as the catalogue highlights - it became a backdrop for some of Cecil Beaton's My Fair Lady-like portraits of the princess. Christie's put a reserve price on the lot of £8,000-£15,000 warning bidders that it had to be "removed from Kensington Palace London at the purchaser's risk and expense."

At the last moment, the Historic Royal Palaces - the agency in charge of running the princess's Kensington Palace apartment - expressed their fear that the ancient balustrade might fall to pieces if removed and questioned whether it was permissible for such "a fixture and fitting" to be put up for sale in the first place. According to advice received from English Heritage, as a Grade I listed building the Wren-designed Kensington Palace was covered by Scheduled Monument Consent and so dismantling the balustrading would have required special permission. In practice, the purchaser would have to convince English Heritage that the railing could be removed without detriment to the palace. Unlawful removal of a fixture from an historic site was punishable by a prison sentence of up to seven years.

Faced with another banana skin, Lord Linley this time deftly sidestepped the danger, leaving it to a Christie's spokeswoman to announce: "the client has decided to give it to the nation. After the success of yesterday, we were told to withdraw the lot so that it could remain in situ at Kensington Palace." He could afford to be generous because on the first day, the auction realised £9,597,680. The staggering prices reportedly left him and his sister "hoarse" with disbelief. By the close of day two, the total figure had risen to £13,658,728 - £10 million more than the original estimate and significantly £6 million more than the probate value of the estate.

Given that most or possibly all of the sale items apparently came from their mother's estate, how can one reconcile the auction figure of £13.6 million with the probate figure of £7.6 million? Does it suggest that the estate was undervalued and if so was the apparent undervaluation aided by the fact that the contents of the will were kept secret?

An interesting parallel to the sale of Margaret's possessions is the auction of the property of Prince Henry, the Duke of Gloucester, which took place at Christie's six months earlier on January 26 and 27, 2006. Again it was undertaken to pay a large inheritance bill, again controversy surrounded the sale of personal items and again the sale realised many times the value of the estate. As we shall see in more detail in Chapter Sixteen, the probate value was set at £734,262 while the auction realised £5,063,362 (although in this case there was a gap of 32 years between the two events).

But by 2006 the heirs of the estates of both the Duke of Gloucester and Princess Margaret benefited from extremely favourable market conditions. It should be remembered that Margaret's auction took place in June 2006 at the height of an unprecedented arts bubble when many foreign buyers were paying outrageous sums for paintings and other precious objects. As the novelist and columnist Frederick Forsyth wrote at the time: "what happened was that the bidders went bananas...there are a lot of people around with more money than sense."[6] If the sellers had waited until the crash of 2008/9 the prices would have been much lower. It should also be pointed out that even without the art market bubble normal price inflation between the probate valuation and the auction four years later would also have pushed prices up a few percentage points.

The other factor inflating prices was of course the cachet of a royal name. "Her glamour and aura were such that collectors flew especially from Asia and America for just one day to participate in this landmark auction," cooed the auctioneer Francois Curiel in his own inflationary rhetoric.[7] But he was not exaggerating when he added - "pieces fetched...up to one hundred and fifty times their original estimates, which is unprecedented, as the market decided the added value of the royal provenance."

So when it came to putting a price tag on the assets should the executors have taken into account their added royal value? According to Her Majesty's Revenue and Customs, the responsibility for correctly valuing the property lies with the executors and if there are any special items with an extra value brought on by celebrity status or some other exceptional factors then they should be factored in too and assessed if necessary by a professional valuer. The value is based on the price an asset would command if passed between a willing seller and buyer immediately before the owner's death. At a later stage, the tax office may reassess the valuation if they consider it too low or high.

But even if the celebrity premium was taken into account, was the estate still undervalued? This is a trickier issue. It should be emphasised that the total value of the estate is based on its worth at the time of death and it is possible that the celebrity cachet and the arts bubble pushed the "fair price" of the princess's possessions up several million pounds, but whether it could explain a difference of £6 million is open to debate. Another complicating factor is whether the sale might have included items outside of Princess Margaret's estate – in other words, property that she may have passed on as non-chargeable lifetime gifts more than seven years before her death. But on the other side of the ledger, it could be pointed out that not everything in her formal estate was put up for sale.

Perhaps the fairest judgement one can make about the way the estate was valued is similar to the one made by a royal biographer about how Christie's went about their own valuation: they were "conservative with their estimates."[8]

The extra profit from the auction inevitably meant that there was more tax to pay. But this time it was capital gains rather than inheritance tax. The children were liable to CGT at 40% on the increase in the value of the princess's possessions between when they inherited them and when they were sold. The tax bill on the gain was estimated at £2.1 million.

From a tax perspective, it could be argued all the children succeeded in doing by putting their mother's possessions up for sale was to swap inheritance tax at 40% for capital gains tax at 40%. So, was the whole exercise tax neutral? Did the Revenue get the same yield but under a different tax regime?

Although it is indisputable that the heirs were landed with a large tax liability, the CGT bill would have been lower than the IHT one. Under the CGT regime they would have benefited not just from taper relief but also from certain exemptions. For instance, chattels (tangible and moveable private property) worth less than £6,000 were exempt from CGT. But even if the children had saved a few thousand pounds or even ten thousand pounds, the difference between the two regimes was at best marginal - as they would have still had an additional tax bill of anywhere between £2m and £3m.

But few tears were shed on their behalf. Assuming that the tax calculations above are broadly accurate, the children were still left with a net profit of a few million pounds. The popular press saw this as pure greed. The Daily Mail called the auction a "vulgar royal car boot sale" and Lord Linley was branded "the Del Boy at the palace."

In a later interview with the Sunday Telegraph in January 2007 Lord Linley offered a robust defence of his actions - "I had the sale for a very simple reason, which was an inheritance tax situation, and wanting to build for my family's future and my children's education – normal family requirements." He went on to point out that: "We are a modern family who need to live in a certain way. The sale rationalised the collection. We still have some of the best pieces, which we will always treasure, but it was an opportunity to put everything on an even keel." When it came to the contentious sale of the Poltimore Tiara, he insisted that: "We looked very long and hard about whether to include it or not, but I think that my mother would have felt it was a good idea. It was an iconic piece, but who in the family would be in a position to wear that very often, versus the opportunity it gave? So it was a very rational decision." He also rejected rumours of any family splits and said he still remained "very close" to his father and his sister.[9]

Ironically up until the auction, Lord Linley had generally received a good press. He was praised as one of the better behaved royals who was not snobbish, kept out of the limelight and earned a living from his furniture business. His parents had sent him to Bedales in Hampshire - a progressive boarding school that encouraged his passion for carpentry. He went on to study at the Parnham House School for Craftsmen in Wood before setting up his own workshop in Dorking. When the business began to take off and furniture shops were opened in the King's Road and then Albemarle Street, he took the decision at the age of twenty-two to stop doing the carpentry himself and concentrate on being a businessman. The Queen Mother was one of the first shareholders in the enterprise. He once said of his shop that "he was in it for the money." He also set up a chain of restaurants called Deals with his relative Lord Lichfield. Some believe that he had long harboured grander entrepreneurial ambitions. Before the auction, he had already been a non-executive director of Christie's for two years and later he was also made Chairman of Christie's (UK). Past chairmen had numbered Lord Hindlip and Lord Carrington and no doubt when Christie's made the decision they took into account both his business skills and the cachet of his royal name. Foreign clients could not fail to be impressed by a call from the Queen's nephew.

A few years before the auction, the Royal Rich Report had valued his wealth at £20.7m.[10] This included £10m from trust funds, £4.3m from property, £7m from art and furniture and £4.4m from business assets. This might be a slight exaggeration - especially when it came to business assets as his furniture company had not made enormous profits but the Royal Rich Report included assets from his immediate family. In 1993 he wed the Hon. Serena Stanhope, daughter of the Earl of Harrington who had a vast property portfolio valued at one point at £250m. Serena is believed to benefit from a generous trust fund, but the family wealth is shared around a large tribe of siblings.

Linley's younger sister Lady Sarah was also not short of money. Thanks to a trust fund and two London properties, her wealth was put at £4.7m by the Royal

Rich Report.[11] A professional painter who trained at the Camberwell School of Art, she married fellow artist and erstwhile actor Daniel Chatto in 1994. His mother is the successful theatrical agent Ros Chatto who represents among others Alan Bennett. Both Lady Sarah and Lord Linley would benefit from her father's £4 million town house in South Kensington that as part of the divorce settlement with Margaret had been purchased by the Queen for his lifetime use although, according to Land Registry documents, the freehold was now in their joint names. She is also thought to have been gifted some jewellery by the Queen as well as a diamond pendant once owned by her grandmother, Queen Mary.

Given such family wealth, some people wondered whether the children could have afforded to pay the inheritance tax out of their own pocket without selling their mother's possessions. This is perhaps unfair. The two heirs had every right to sell off their bequest to pay a large tax bill since finding £3m in cash - even for a junior royal - is a tall order. Finding space for all the property was another problem. "What were he (David) and Sarah going to do with all the stuff?" asked Ingrid Seward, the royal watcher and editor in chief of Majesty magazine. "You've got to store it somewhere; you've got to insure it."[12]

Other critics thought the Queen might have advanced the money to save for the nation her late sister's possessions. She almost certainly came to the aid of Prince Charles in funding his multi-million pound alimony payment to Princess Diana and as we have seen she in all likelihood part-financed Margaret's divorce settlement. But when it came to the Christie's auction, Buckingham Palace on the whole took the view that it was "a private matter for Margaret's children."

In the end, many items did go abroad. A private Italian buyer paid £60,000 for a silver dressing table service, while a £42,000 four poster bed and a £276,000 jewelled clock both went to private Asian buyers. Overall, Christie's recorded registered buyer activity as 30% from the UK, 44% for the rest of Europe, 17% from the Americas, 9% from Asia and the Middle East.[13]

Historic Royal Palaces who were left in charge of an empty Kensington Palace apartment were unhappy about having to compete in an open auction for items such as the dining room table - which they hoped to put on show for the general public. The agency was able to afford the pair of regency blackamoors holding their torches aloft that used to adorn the entrance to the dining room. They also picked up for a reasonable price the turquoise glassware that she was fond of collecting, as well as three bottles of Kensington white wine made in 1976 from her own grapes in the garden and a set of menu cards. The daily menu gave a choice of three dishes per course and reveal how the princess indicated choice with written annotations.

Until recently, any member of the public could go on a tour of Kensington Palace including apartment 1A where the blackamoors were on display in the drawing room and bespoke bottles of wine in the kitchen. But access has now been denied to Margaret's home due to the arrival of new tenants – the Duke and Duchess of Cambridge who have totally refurbished the interiors. It is assumed that the Ascot Balustrade remained unaffected by the major refit, although at the time of writing the palace could not confirm one way or another whether it was still in situ.

Chapter Fourteen
The Princess's "Love Child" – 2006-2008

"I was...opposed to monarchy, believing with Tom Paine that a hereditary head of state is as sensible as a hereditary poet"
Geoffrey Robertson QC, barrister representing Robert Brown

In the summer of 2006 as Princess Margaret's two children were busy auctioning her personal chattels, a fifty-one-year-old accountant who claimed to be her illegitimate child began a legal challenge to open up her will and find out what if anything she had left him. Its ultimate significance would lie not in the individual merits of his case but in what it revealed about the history - and even legality - of the sealing of royal wills. By chance it would also establish an important legal connection between Princess Margaret and her great uncle, Prince Francis of Teck.

In May of that year Robert Brown drafted a fifty-six page summons setting out the background to his claim. The documents included his birth certificate recording that he was born on 3 January 1955 in Nairobi, Kenya, the son of Cynthia Joan Brown (née Lyall) and Douglas Richard Brown. She was a society model who worked for Hardy Amies, the Queen's dressmaker; he was an army officer posted during the Second World War to Kenya who stayed on to become a successful building contractor. It was Robert Brown's contention that this birth certificate signed by Cynthia was inaccurate. The date was inconsistent with the one listed in the births section of the Times of 7 January 1955 which gave his birthday as the 6th and not the 5th of January. To add to the confusion, his birth was not registered until February 2 and the certificate recording it was dated as late as June 4.

Although Cynthia brought him up as her own she was not according to the affidavit his true mother: "[My] conclusion that I am the illegitimate child of Princess Margaret is based upon a jigsaw of personal recollections, events, circumstantial evidence, conversations, reactions and extensive research."[1] The pieces began to fall into a pattern at a cousin's wedding in Wales. It was a high class occasion overflowing with titled guests who made Brown acutely aware that he was one of the few commoners present: "When I mentioned this to my uncle he gave an embarrassed half-laugh and said 'wrong side of the sheets'."[2] This off-the-cuff comment triggered a hunt for his true mother.

By this time both his "adopted" parents were dead. Cynthia had died aged forty-nine in 1980 when he was twenty-five. Douglas had earlier separated from her and moved to Jersey before his own death. They were survived by one son who was born after Robert and whom he believed was their clear favourite. The key indicator pointing Robert in the direction of Princess Margaret as his true mother was a photograph dated October 1956 at the time of a visit to Kenya by Princess Margaret. The image shows a child peering through the closed front window of a car with the reflection in the rear window of the photographer who according to Brown bears a resemblance to the princess. He also records as a five-year-old being taken by Cynthia to Nairobi town hall to see the Queen Mother. His supposed "grandmother" visited Kenya in February 1959. Piecing together these items of evidence and inchoate recollections, he came to the conclusion that Princess Margaret had had a concealed pregnancy and that to avoid a scandal he had been adopted by Cynthia and Douglas Brown. As to who is his true father, Robert suggested it could be either Group Captain Peter Townsend or Robin Douglas-Home, both of whom had well-publicised affairs with the princess.

Robert Brown hardly fitted the mould of a fantasist or fortune hunter. Trained as an accountant, he worked for eight years for an Irish bank in the offshore tax haven of Jersey. He had moved there in the footsteps of his legal father and settled in St

Lawrence outside of St Helier where unmarried he lived a life of relative tranquillity. Using his financial skills, he did well out of the island's booming property market helped by the absence of capital gains tax and the low rate of income tax.

Rakishly thin with piercing blue eyes and a balding pate, he came across as an articulate, well-mannered and likable figure. He spoke in public meetings of the need for the Jersey government to show greater openness and accountability in their handling of a controversial reform to the island's tax regime and in March 2004 he stood unsuccessfully as a senatorial candidate for the parliament - "the states" - on a platform opposing some of the fiscal changes. The only hint of a more rebellious side came when he challenged his bank over the nature of some of its offshore products and ultimately parted company with the bank, although he felt vindicated by a later investigation into its investments. Passionate about dietary matters, he also found time to research a book about the harmful effects of Omega 6 oils.

⚜ ⚜ ⚜

He was also minded to investigate the legal rights of illegitimate children of the royal family. In the last century there has been no shortage of conjecture and rumour surrounding the offspring of British royals born on the wrong side of the sheets, but hard facts are thin on the ground. As we saw with the story of

Lady Kilmorey and the Cambridge emeralds, Edward VII had a string of mistresses (one royal researcher put the figure as high as fifty-five) and hence it was thought more than possible that he might have fathered a love child (the most commonly proposed mother being his mistress Lady Sarah Vane-Tempest who reportedly gave birth to a child in 1871, although it may have died soon after or been offered over for adoption).[3] Yet he never acknowledged any illegitimate children and despite detailed studies of his love life no definite proof has emerged. Since as sovereign his will was automatically sealed there is no clear testamentary evidence to prove bequests to any illegitimate issue.

We heard earlier the story of how Edward's best friend Lord Louis of Battenberg may have fathered a love child by Lillie Langtry - although doubts persist about its true paternity. However, we do know for certain of one modern royal who famously had a child "out of wedlock" – or rather when he was still married to his first wife. George Henry Lascelles, the 7th Earl of Harewood and first cousin to the Queen, married the operatic singer/pianist Marion Stein in 1949 and then in 1964 had a child by the violinist Patricia Tucker. Two years later the Queen gave her permission under the Royal Marriages Act, 1772 for him to marry his second wife and mother of the child. At the age of eighty-eight, Lord Harwood died in July 2011 and the precise details of his will and the size of his estate remain unclear.

Royal Legacy

⚜ ⚜ ⚜

So when Robert Brown embarked on his legal challenge to open Princess Margaret's will, he was entering a world of whispers, half-truths and secrets. In this topsy turvy realm, some royals who had no illegitimate offspring kept their wills sealed, while others who had love children preferred them open. In order to help him through the legal labyrinth, Brown engaged another Brown as his solicitor. Her full name was Amber Melville Brown. No relation to Robert, Amber had cut her teeth in the chambers of a well-know media specialist Finers Stephens Innocent rising to become the head of their defamation department. She went on to become a partner of Schillings which had a reputation for tenacious litigating. Later she would work as counsel to Withers, one of Britain's largest law firms which, as we shall see in Chapter 16, has had several members of the royal family among its clients.

After Melville Brown applied to the family court to open up the wills of Princess Margaret and the Queen Mother, on 5 December 2006 she wrote to the palace's lawyers Farrer and Co. requesting copies of the orders to seal the two royal wills and the applications that accompanied those orders. This was the opening shot in a battle over disclosure of evidence which would dominate legal discussions for the next three years. To Brown's camp, the best way to unlock the wills was to find fault with the original order to seal them and the only way to do that was to pick holes in the arguments employed in the application. But without access to the documentation, they had nothing to dispute.

On 7 December Farrers wrote back refusing the request. Brown would have to produce the evidence of his parentage before they would even consider whether to supply the documentation. The executors' lawyers apparently wanted to move the legal battleground from Brown's *public* interest to view the will - which formed part of the basis of his initial application - to a purely *private* interest one. The reason for this is that the burden of proof in a private interest approach is much higher - in that he has to establish a clear, personal interest - or "standing" - for wanting to see the will. In other words, he had to supply concrete evidence that he was the child of Princess Margaret - which as Farrers pointed out he had patently failed to do up to then.

Farrers must have been well aware that Brown did not have bottomless pockets and the longer the case dragged on with disputes over disclosure, the higher his legal bill would climb and the more likely it would be that he would throw in the towel. Equally, Brown's lawyers as specialists in media matters would have been well aware that the last thing the palace wanted was for the legal battle to be played out in open court before the press and that the prospect of negative publicity could not fail to boost their case.

On 31 January Farrers launched a counter-attack by issuing a summons to strike out Brown's claim. It was supported by a sworn affidavit arguing that Brown had no public interest justification to see the will and he had yet to establish a private interest claim. As evidence it laid out a series of photographs of Princess Margaret around the time of Brown's birth which apparently showed no hint of a pregnancy and which supported the conclusion that his claim was "frivolous, vexatious and an abuse of procedure" and should be struck out.[4]

The affidavit was signed by the Hon. Mark Bridges, the Queen's solicitor. Amber Melville Brown's opposite number had taken the old school route into the legal profession. The product of Eton and Corpus Christi College, Cambridge, he joined Farrers as an assistant solicitor in 1980 and became a partner five years later. In 1998 he was appointed solicitor to the Duchy of Lancaster before graduating in 2002 to the post of the Queen's solicitor (later he would be rewarded with her personal honour of Commander of the Victorian Order). As the son of Thomas (Baron) Bridges KG - a much distinguished diplomat who served as ambassador to Italy and undersecretary of state in the Foreign Office - he is heir to the title of third Baron Bridges of Headley. On his mother's side, he is also related to Baron Farrer, a scion of the law firm's family.

Melville Brown responded to Bridges's strike out application by seeking his agreement that should it fail the original hearing would go ahead as planned and by repeating the request for copies of all the documentation that supported the 2002 application. Brown's solicitor also made it plain that they would apply for the hearing to take place in open court.

The Royal Courts of Justice where the President of the Family Division is based is an imposing, gothic building which was opened by Queen Victoria in 1882. It was designed by George Edmund Street, a lawyer turned architect, and financed by £70,000 in cash left over from intestate estates. On entering through the main gates in the Strand, any plaintiff is immediately made to feel small by the Great Hall - a judicial cathedral two hundred and forty feet long, forty-eight feet wide and eighty feet high, lined with cloister-like alcoves and recesses. The building as a whole contains over one thousand rooms and three and a half miles of corridors - as well as one hundred and fifty judges, registrars and masters.

Behind court thirty-three are located the spacious chambers of the President of the Family Division. When in April 2005 Sir Mark Potter was appointed President in succession to Dame Elizabeth Butler Sloss, the tightly-knit world of family law was reportedly left "reeling." He was a commercial court judge with relatively little direct experience of the workings of the Family Division. But he was seen by others as the new broom who would sweep away the cobwebs in the family courts. One of his old pupils at Fountain Court, Charlie Falconer, was now Lord Falconer, the

Secretary of State for Constitutional Affairs. The government was reportedly keen to change the public perception that the courts operated in unnecessarily secretive way.

When the public hearing opened on 27 March 2007, the sixty-nine-year-old President would have been wearing the traditional black silk gown and short wig. Before him sat Geoffrey Robertson QC and Anthony Hudson representing Brown, and Frank Hinks QC and Jonathan Adkin representing the executors. Although both colourful figures, the two QCs could hardly have been more different in background and outlook.

A bouffant-haired Australian who had studied law in Sydney and only come to the United Kingdom as a Rhodes Scholar, Robertson had little atavistic deference to the royal family. He supported the anti-monarchist pressure group Republic which campaigned for an elected head of state and was himself the author of "The Tyrannicide Brief," a sympathetic portrait of the lawyer who prosecuted King Charles I in the trial that led to his execution and ultimately to the establishment of a republic in England. In another work - "The Justice Game" - he spelt out the reasons for his aversion to royalty: "I was...opposed to monarchy, believing with Tom Paine that a hereditary head of state is as sensible as a hereditary poet."[5]

Robertson's court room manner owes a debt to John Mortimer QC who was his senior counsel in many cases and taught him by example that "the art of cross examination is not to examine crossly." Today he acknowledges the creator of Rumpole of the Bailey as the most influential person in his life, calling him "his forensic father." It is ironic that John Mortimer's own father, Clifford, was the author of the standard work on probate that would be quoted in arguments opposing Robertson in the case.

Given that his mentor was John Mortimer, one might have thought Geoffrey Robertson would have had a natural sympathy with his opposing barrister since he too enjoyed a second string to his bow as a writer. Frank Hinks QC was the author of The Dim Daft Dwarves (2004), the Magic Magpie (2004) and Gary and the Frog Prince (2005). Hinks got into creative writing as a teenager - penning his first children's adventure as early as 1966 but it was not until he had children himself that he began to write professionally in the down time between court assignments.

Hinks's speciality lay in land law and property work. In 1990 he acted for the Duke of Westminster in the celebrated "working class case" which provoked leaders in the Times and Guardian about whether Westminster Council should honour an historic contract to use leased land exclusively for housing for low income groups. He began to attract high profile clients such as earls, marquesses and other members of the aristocracy. In one celebrated property dispute, he even established the Queen's title to the bed of the river Severn.

As soon as court proceedings got under way, Hinks argued that the claimant had produced no evidence to support his application: having failed to establish any *private* right to unseal the wills, he now claimed a *public* right. But he had no legal status to do so. The rights of the public were protected by the Attorney General alone. If individuals in general were allowed to claim the right to represent the public and seek judicial review, there would be "anarchy," according to the QC: "This week Mr Brown; next week Mr White, Mr Pink, Mr Green." The principle was laid down to avoid "busybodies, cranks and mischief-makers... With all due respect, this applies to Mr Brown. He is suffering from a delusion."[6]

The court also heard that a total of twenty-seven people had claimed to be the illegitimate relations of the royals in 2005. "This appears to be part of a wider phenomenon," submitted Mark Bridges, "whereby people become psychologically obsessed and fixated with the affairs of the royal family."

The Queen's solicitor might also have mentioned that Brown was not the first person to claim to be Princess Margaret's love child. Around January 1992 Peter Townsend was approached at his home outside Paris by a well spoken man with a Welsh accent called Philip Thomas who claimed to be the son of the princess and Townsend. The former Group Captain reported the "bizarre visitor" to the Queen Mother's private secretary hoping the matter would all blow over. But a year later he received a letter from Thomas requesting his support in getting Buckingham Palace to respond to his claim to royal blood. This time, Townsend was obliged to engage a solicitor and after considering all the options - including sectioning the claimant - it was decided that the best course of action would be to avoid any unpleasant publicity and a short letter was duly dispatched asking Thomas not to communicate with Townsend again. This appeared to do the trick in the short term but Thomas did occasionally emerge in the media repeating his claims. Townsend died of stomach cancer in June 1995.[7]

Back in the High Court, Frank Hinks told the judges that Robert Brown's claim was both "frivolous" and "vexatious." Geoffrey Robertson responded by arguing that Brown was "a perfectly rational man who seeks peace of mind." His client was simply exercising his right as a member of the public to inspection as provided for in sections 124 and 125 of the 1981 Supreme Court Act. Neither section 124 nor rule 58 of the non-contentious probate rules made an exception for royalty and the fact that the royal family might occupy a special status in society should not be a reason why public inspection should be undesirable. Indeed, he argued, the status of the royal family made it more - not less - legitimate that the public should be able to inspect their wills.

He offered a number of reasons for this - which in terms of our wider story might be seen as providing a key insight into why the royal family have traditionally been so secretive about inheritance. In the first place, royal wills should be open in the interest of history: historians should be allowed access to such an important royal archive in order to record the nation's narrative. Linked to this argument was the interest of the media who performed a watchdog role in reporting on the workings of the tax arrangements for senior royals. Another consideration, argued Robertson, was what he called the "transparency interest:" anyone should be able to see that "nothing is being done improperly or unlawfully, that appropriate procedures have been followed and that there is nothing in the bequests or signatures of those witnessing the will from which an inference could be drawn of undue influence or foul play." This of course is the principal justification for why all wills are open to public inspection.

Robertson went on to argue that there is a public interest in verifying the probate figures in the cases of royal wills where a court has ordered that no figures should appear on the grant of probate document or no copies of the grant should be made public. The reason for this is "to ensure that those who are given charge of national assets should not mix them up with their disposal of personal property." He did not mention her by name but Queen Mary was an obvious example of a royal whose estate was never given a clear net probate value and who appeared to "shapeshift" public and private jewellery.

He also submitted that there is a public interest in checking whether a will indicates the existence of unrecognised offspring who might have a hereditary claim to some form of royal provision. In a separate point, he argued that Lady Butler Sloss, the former President of the Family Court, might have been misled in deciding to seal the wills if she did so merely on the basis of convention. He told the court that there was no proper basis for this practice and it amounted to nothing more than a smokescreen: "A secret, unconstitutional and unlawful practice has grown up of the attorney general going to the court and asking to put royal wills outside the law." He added that parliament had never legislated to grant secrecy to royal relations and that this practice had been invented in 1911 to conceal the will of Prince Francis, George V's brother-in-law, who had given family jewels to a mistress.[8] This was a reference, of course, to Prince Francis of Teck, the black sheep of the family whom we met in Chapter Three.

The final outcome was long coming. Amber Melville Brown and Mark Bridges had to wait another three months before on 5 July 2007 Sir Mark Potter delivered his judgement: "[while] the Plaintiff's claim is made in good faith in the sense and to the extent that he has a genuine belief that he is or may be the offspring of Princess Margaret, I am equally satisfied that there is no rational basis whatever for such belief, as his own evidence clearly demonstrates." After weighing up all these arguments in a sixty-nine paragraph-long judgement, Sir Mark concluded that Robert Brown's claim should be struck out as "vexatious and an abuse of process, made as it is solely for the purpose of seeking to establish an imaginary and baseless claim."[9]

Following the hearing, a disappointed Robert Brown addressed the throng of media on the steps of the Royal Courts of Justice. Despite the reversal he remained defiant: "It is deeply worrying, but I have a need to resolve this. It is simply a matter of identity. It is not an attempt to embarrass the royal family." But would he appeal the decision? Indeed could he afford to?

In deciding whether to go the Appeal Court, Brown would have had to weigh up a number of competing considerations. On the one hand, he would have realised by now that the only way to unlock his supposed mother's will was to get hold of the documentation behind the sealing orders and having unsuccessfully tried various freedom of information requests, the only realistic way to obtain this core evidence (and thereby challenge the former president's decision) was through an order from the appeal court. On the other hand, there were costs. Engaging high profile solicitors and counsel did not come cheap and even if he was cushioned to some degree by his remaining private savings in Jersey and by the possibility of a conditional fee arrangement ("a no win, no fee deal") with his solicitors, going to the appeal court remained a perilous business.

In the end, he decided to take the risk. After a preliminary hearing on 17 October, the panel of three appeal judges met again on December 17 to resolve among other matters the key issue of the disclosure of the evidence surrounding the original sealing orders. The appellant wished to see it but the respondents were reluctant to release it.

The most senior of the three judges, Lord Phillips, took pride of place on the bench as presiding judge sitting on a pointed, high-backed chair in front of the royal crest in the middle of the raised dais. He had precedence over the other two by virtue of his status as Lord Chief Justice - in effect, the most senior judge in the land. He had gained that position in 2005 after five years as Master of the Rolls and head of civil justice where he had won a reputation as a reformer and moderniser. He implemented a raft of reforms first outlined by his predecessor Lord Woolf designed to make civil justice quicker and cheaper. He took the unusual step of going on BBC television to lobby for more money for the courts and later put the case for the modernisation of court dress, arguing that wigs should be scrapped in civil cases and that judges should wear French-style robes.

Sitting to his right on the panel of judges was the fully robed Lord Justice Dyson, an experienced former Queen's Bench judge who would later be appointed Master of the Rolls, and on his left Lord Justice Thorpe, an expert in family law from his many years sitting as a judge in the Family Division.

Once the hearing got under way, the thorny issue of disclosure soon dominated the proceedings. Hinks began by repeating the executors' standard argument: since Lady Butler Sloss had made her original ruling on the basis of the private interest (or *locus standi*) to see the will, then no disclosure should be made until that issue was resolved. If Brown's appeal succeeded, then the executors would "put in detailed evidence of the history and justification" but to require this before the issue of *locus standi* had been settled would run the risk of the case being "seriously derailed."[10]

But in the course of making this dry legalistic point, Hinks disclosed one new piece of information. Around the time of the death of Princess Margaret, the Senior District Judge in the Family Division had drawn up a lengthy document that reviewed the practice of sealing royal wills. This involved a system of checks and balances that was highly confidential. "The primary reason and purpose of the sealing royal wills," Hinks stated, was "to protect the privacy of the sovereign." This special procedure was discussed by the Attorney General, solicitors for the Treasury and lawyers for Buckingham Palace before the President of the Family Division finally approved it. The conclusions of the written document were kept secret and Lady Butler Sloss's successor, Sir Mark Potter, was not told of their existence.

In response Geoffrey Robertson told the court that the decisions to seal the two wills "were made without jurisdiction, according to a practice direction that does not exist as far as the law is concerned." He went on to argue that they were taken "in utter secrecy" and were "quite plainly unlawful and unconstitutional."[11]

It is interesting to note that this revelation went unreported at the time, most probably because the press tends to follow just the opening and closing stages of long trials. The news was only picked up a month later on 23 January 2008 when the Daily Telegraph ran a piece headlined "Queen had her mother's will sealed in secret'" which quoted from a transcript of the December 17 hearing.

The three judges met for the final time on 8 February 2008 and the secrecy surrounding the original orders to seal the wills featured prominently in their closely-argued judgment:

"The problem is, however, that the process under which the late President [Lady Butler Sloss] made the orders was not transparent, nor the criteria applied by the former President plain." Robert Brown's appeal, according to the judgment, raised two important issues about the royal family:

"iv) Was it appropriate to have a special practice in relation to royal wills? If so:

v) What, if any, information about that practice should be made public?"

The judges concluded that if Robert Brown was not allowed to challenge the 2002 orders, then it was hard to see how anyone else could do so:

"If Sir Mark Potter is right," as Judge Dyson had stated in his earlier ruling giving permission to appeal, "it follows that the President's application of

Rule 58 to members of the Royal Family will never be capable of being considered by a higher court."

The key question was whether Sir Mark Potter was right to strike out Brown's claim (thereby blocking him from raising the issues listed above). The panel of judges decided he was not right. Until those issues had been resolved it was impossible to say that Brown's claim was doomed to failure. In a final paragraph, the judges came to the following decision:

"It is unfortunate that the important issues to which we have drawn attention should be raised by an application made by a person motivated by a belief that is both irrational and scandalous. We have, however, concluded that the appellant was and is entitled to have a substantive hearing of his claim to inspect the wills. For these reasons this appeal is allowed."

Robert Brown was in court with his solicitor Amber Melville Brown to hear the judgement. When the happy couple left through the iron gates of the Royal Courts of Justice – he wheeling his heavy trolley full of document boxes, she carrying a copy of the judgment and other court paperwork - they were immediately engulfed by the waiting reporters, photographers and cameramen. Brown was naturally overjoyed at the ruling: "I am delighted we have won this case. It is a victory for openness and justice. I continue to seek the truth." But in a later separate interview with ITN, he gave a hint of his conflicted feelings: "I don't want to embarrass the royal family...It is not easy. I would just put a plea to Her Majesty that if I am wrong, please get someone to tell me authoritatively and if I am right please tell me because I do not want to live with this for the next 20 years as it is not good for my CV and it's not good for anything."

Standing at his side Amber Melville Brown cut a striking figure for the photographers in her stylish black suit, knee-length boots and blonde bobbed hair. Her comment on the judgement went to the central tenet of their case: "[there is] a statutory presumption in favour of the openness of wills in the UK and a constitutional principle of open justice... Yet there is nothing open about these wills, whether it's what's in them, why they were closed and under what procedure this was done. They are quite simply shrouded in mystery. By winning this appeal, Robert Brown may be able to peel away some of the layers of secrecy and put himself, and the public, a step closer to the truth." She added: "Robert Brown's success on this appeal means that the court will be asked to consider whether it is desirable and appropriate in this day and age that mystery should give way to transparency and that conventions that belong in the dark ages should be brought into the light."[12]

Now that the case was over and the court reporting restrictions lifted the media were able to comment freely on what the judgement had revealed. They went to town on Frank Hinks's bombshell that there had been a secret agreement to keep the royal wills under wraps with the headlines thundering

Queen 'had her mother's will sealed in secret: Are the secrets of the Royal Family wills about to be revealed?" (the Daily Telegraph) and "Accountant lifts veil from royal wills" (the Guardian). On the whole the coverage was sympathetic to Robert Brown although the Express On Sunday branded him a "royal fantasist" while acknowledging that he had "struck a blow for equality and an equally powerful one against secrecy."[13] The Guardian went so far as to publish a leader entitled "In Praise of Robert Brown" which argued that "In a monarchy operating under the law, the wealth of the royal family is a very proper subject for public transparency. Mr Brown may or may not be who he claims to be, but he has stood up bravely for a principle that matters."[14]

In all this extensive coverage and comment, one significant revelation slipped under the radar. In resisting pressure to release all the documentation Hinks had disclosed that the Attorney General was consulted in the run up to the sealing of the wills when the "special procedure" document was drawn up. Why was "the crown's solicitor" involved? Was he just there – as Sir Mark Potter stated in his original 2007 ruling - to safeguard the public interest in a case of sealing two royal wills where otherwise there would be no public representation? If so, then it seems odd that his role in the "special procedure" was kept hidden from the public until the appeal hearing.

Chapter Fifteen
The Storming of the Palace – 2008

"There must be a suspicion that the reason that the royal family has been so determined to keep the wills secret is that, if the public realised how much money is being passed from generation to generation, they might question how much is being handed to them from the public purse"
Norman Baker MP[1]

When Robert Brown won his appeal in February 2008 to make an application to unseal Princess Margaret's will the only prominent MP to comment on the judgement was Norman Baker. In a typically forthright interview on the day of the ruling, the member for Lewes told ITN:

"Every other will is public. Why should the royal family be any different? This particular case here involving Robert Brown - I have no idea whatsoever if his claim is justified or not and frankly I'm not interested. What I am interested in is his right to inspect that will in the same way as he would have a right to inspect any other will of any other person in the country".[2]

Norman Baker was no newcomer to the cause of unsealing royal wills - or indeed to investigating wider succession matters and the royal finances. As a committed republican, he had followed Brown's campaign closely and raised the matter in the Commons as early as 2006. His office had even been in contact with Brown over the wording of questions.

Shortly after the appeal court judgment on 8 February 2008, Baker tabled a written question to the cabinet minister Jack Straw: "To ask the Secretary of State for Justice what representations he has received from lawyers acting for the royal family on publication practice on royal wills in the last ten years."[3]

Given the revelations in the Brown case about the secret agreement between the government, the High Court and palace lawyers, Baker was no doubt fishing for evidence of special privileges being granted to the royal family. Sidestepping this potential elephant trap the Justice Secretary delivered a carefully worded response:

"Neither my predecessors, nor I have received any representations from lawyers acting for the royal family on publication practice on royal wills in the last ten years. An application to seal a royal will is made to the Principal Registry of the Family Division and is decided by the President. In the last ten years there have been two such applications; namely those in respect of Her Royal Highness

Princess Margaret, Countess of Snowdon, and Her Majesty Queen Elizabeth, the Queen Mother."

It is worth noting that Jack Straw referred only to his "predecessors" as Justice Secretary (formerly the post of Lord Chancellor) rather than the Attorney General who we now know was involved in the 2002 procedure to seal the royal wills. Baker was well acquainted with the cat and mouse game of parliamentary questions and the less than candid responses. He has been described as "one of the most prolific questioners in British parliamentary history."[4] In his first three months as an MP he asked more written questions to ministers than his Conservative predecessor had in twenty-three years and after a decade in the house, his tally of PQs had risen to eight thousand. In 2001 the Spectator magazine awarded him the title of Inquisitor of the Year.

His critics have suggested that "Stormin' Norman's" inquisitorial technique owed too much to the scatter gun. In 2006-07 he asked fifty-four written parliamentary questions about the death of David Kelly, the inspector of Iraqi weapons who died in mysterious circumstances after he was outed leaking information to a BBC reporter. Unhappy with the Hutton inquiry which concluded that Kelly had committed suicide he wrote his own investigation into the affair - "The Strange Death of David Kelly" - arguing that Kelly was the victim of a conspiracy and could possibly have been murdered. Some members of Kelly's family disagreed with his findings and one recent author who picked over the case accused him of slipping into a conspiracy theory mind-set.[5]

One of his long-standing crusades has been to modernise the royal family, famously declaring in 2000: "it's odd - being the 21st century at a time of fundamental constitutional reform to be saddled with a 19th century monarchy."[6] In the past he has supported the pressure group Republic in its campaign for an elected head of state and as a backbencher in the Commons asked many pointed questions about the royal finances - whether it was the cost of the sovereign's travel arrangements or what happened to gifts to the royal family. His ire was particularly directed at the Queen's many financial privileges:

> "Why should the one of us who happens to be monarch benefit from a highly advantageous tax position - exempt from inheritance tax and capital gains tax, able to determine what level, if any, of income tax is paid, exempt from the requirement to publish details of what is bequeathed, and so on."[7]

In early 2009 came a further bombardment of critical questions aimed at Jack Straw. First on January 12 he asked the Secretary of State for Justice:

> "what discussions his Department and its predecessors have had with *(a)* Buckingham Palace and *(b)* lawyers acting for the Royal Family on the publication practice on Royal Wills in the last 10 years; and if he will make a statement?"[8]

But the Justice Secretary explained that such matters were the responsibility of the Family Division and denied any direct involvement - although it was slightly qualified with this rider:

"*So far as I am aware,* [author's italics] there have not been any discussions between my Department and its predecessors with Buckingham Palace or lawyers acting for the Royal Family in relation to the policy or practice on the publication of royal wills."

Then on January 22 the member for Lewes tried a different tack:

"To ask the Secretary of State for Justice:

(1) If he will publish sealed Royal Wills in cases where such Wills were sealed prior to 1990.

(2) If he will review his policy on the practice of allowing Royal Wills to be sealed."[9]

Jack Straw responded with the normal straight bat to the first part of his question:

"The power to seal and unseal all wills is exercised by the court. The decision whether or not to permit inspection of a will of a senior member of the Royal Family that has been sealed by the court is a matter for the President of the Family Division upon application."

But the second part elicited a significant new piece of information:

"The President is currently considering setting up a committee to review the Non-Contentious Probate Rules 1987, which will include consideration of the current rules relating to the inspection and/or publication of Wills. The power to make new rules is vested in the President with the concurrence of the Lord Chancellor."

Some media commentators took this surprise announcement to mean that that in the future the wills of senior royals – including Prince Charles and the Queen - could be made public. Baker very much welcomed the news. "There should be one rule that is the same for everyone," he told the Times. "If other people's wills have to be published so should those of the royal family who are in receipt of large amounts of public money."[10] He assumed that the Ministry of Justice had found that there was no constitutional justification for sealing wills - and the Brown case might have prompted this realisation. "It is a matter of equity and transparency that people are able to see wills and it is quite wrong that the Royal Family is treated differently," he informed the Express on Sunday. "They pass on gigantic sums of money without paying death duties. If we had the wills made public there might be fresh questions about whether they need quite so much money from the Civil List."[11]

Nothing happened about the review for five months and then out of the blue on July 24 the Judicial Communications Office issued a news release entitled "Working Group set up to revise non-contentious probate rules." Included in its remit was the issue of sealed wills.

The announcement was a masterpiece in news management. By July 24 parliament had long since risen for the summer recess and so there were no danger of embarrassing questions from the backbenches. It was slipped out late on a Friday and so it was missed by all of the national newspapers.

The only story in the lengthy press release on the reform of non-contentious probate rules was the commitment to review royal wills but this was hidden in the body of the text and couched in the most round-about language:

"The President of the Family Division, Sir Mark Potter, announced today that he will be establishing a working group to consider the revision of the Non-Contentious Probate Rules 1987...The publication and disclosure of wills, including those of the Royal Family, has on occasion been a subject of some interest, and the Committee's remit will extend to consideration of this topic."

Although the committee was expected by some to report within a couple of years, more than four years went by without a word appearing. We now know from court records that as early as November 2010 a copy of the so-called "practice direction" on the sealing of royal wills (the "quite lengthy document" referred to in the 2008 appeal ruling) was supplied by the Attorney General's office to the Ministry of Justice "in connection with the review the MoJ is carrying out on probate procedure."[12] Then in June 2013 a consultation document was slipped out without much publicity. Under the draft probate rules, the general public would not be able to see the will of the consort of the sovereign (or former sovereign), the child of a sovereign (or former sovereign) or a member of the royal family who is first or second in line to the throne (or the spouse or child of such a person). Although the exemption does not cover the entire royal family, it is still a long list running to over half a dozen people. At the time of writing, the draft rules had been sent to the Ministry of Justice for further consideration and there was no indication of how they might be revised or implemented.

For his part Robert Brown had never been optimistic about the chances of the inquiry producing anything that would advance his case. By now, his main advocate in parliament, Norman Baker, had been effectively muzzled when he was made transport minister (later home office minister) in the Conservative-led coalition government and thus subject to the rules of collective responsibility and not speaking out of line. Brown's judicial challenge in the High Court had also become becalmed due in part no doubt to the prohibitive legal costs involved. A more economical route was available through the Freedom of Information Act. Now that it had been established in court that there existed a written protocol of some sort for the sealing of the wills of Princess Margaret and other senior royals, all he needed to do was to put in a FOI request to obtain the document. At first the court service said the Ministry of Justice/ HMCS did not possess the document as specified by Brown – although they later acknowledged that the

Attorney General's office had a copy as did the lawyers Farrers (although it might have been classified not as a formal practice direction but as some form of a "quite lengthy document" dated 2002.) Then in June 2009 came another blow when the Ministry of Justice announced plans to restrict access to royal documents. Under a new set of rules designed to protect particularly sensitive material, royal papers would be subject to an absolute exemption from FOI requests for twenty years.

When he persisted with his request it was ruled invalid as the disputed information fell into the category of "royal correspondence" and was thus exempt from inspection. Challenging the decision, he found himself back at the High Court where again he won a minor victory. In December 2013 Mr Justice Philips granted him permission to seek judicial review of the refusal to allow him access under the Freedom of Information Act to documents he claims show that there was a secret judicial process for sealing royal wills. "It's an important day for open justice," declared Brown outside the court before adding an aside on his parentage - "Hopefully I am not a nutcase. I am either right or wrong."[13]

At the time of writing, it is unclear how long his case will run.

Chapter Sixteen
The Best-Laid Plans of Alice and Men –
2008-2010

"She was the oldest ever member of the royal family"
Obituary of Princess Alice, Dowager Duchess of Gloucester

When Norman Baker asked his original parliamentary question in February 2008 about the sealing of royal wills, the Justice Secretary Jack Straw replied that in the last ten years there had been only *two* such applications - for the estates of Princess Margaret and the Queen Mother in 2002. Yet a cursory glance of the Times' Court Circular – or indeed its obituary page - showed that in the previous decade a *third* royal death had occurred - that of Princess Alice, the Duchess of Gloucester, in 2004. Although relatively little known, Alice was no minor royal. The Dowager Duchess was the Queen's aunt and died aged one hundred and two, the oldest ever member of the British royal family. Curiously, her name did not feature on the list of sealed royal wills in the probate registry. When inquiries were made at their London office as to why it was absent, a clerk explained that that their list was not necessarily comprehensive and assumed that Princess Alice's will had been sealed like those of all other senior royals.

To confirm this assumption, the author made a request for a copy of the will in the manner of any member of the public. On payment of the customary £5 it should take less than an hour to receive a photocopy of the will that is stored in the Birmingham repository, yet when more than two hours had elapsed with no sign of a response, it seemed that the official's assumption was correct. The royal will was unavailable for public inspection. But as registry staff prepared to close down the search room for the day and the last members of the public had departed, much to the surprise of the remaining clerk at the desk a copy of the royal will miraculously arrived in his in-tray. It ran to thirty pages (thirty-two if you include the codicil) and was signed simply Alice. But there was no doubting its royal authenticity from the opening sentence that referred to Her Royal Highness Princess Alice Christabel, Dowager Duchess of Gloucester.

Its royal provenance was further confirmed by the accompanying grant of probate document that recorded that "HRH Princess Alice" left a net estate of £569,849. Although her will was open to the public (unlike the will of her husband, Prince Henry), its very transparency raised more questions than answers. Why was the probate figure so low when she came from one the wealthiest families in Britain which possessed a jewellery collection valued at £8m? And what happened to the million-pound manor she had lived in? Seemingly by definition, it could not have been fully included in her £569,849 estate or (even allowing for the then lower property prices) the estate of her husband that was valued at £734,262. Why was her will open and his sealed? What had happened to their joint wealth?

When Alice wed Prince Henry, the Duke of Gloucester and the third son of King George V, her parents worried whether she might be marrying beneath herself. Lady Alice Montagu-Douglas-Scott hailed from one of the grandest aristocratic families in Britain. Her father was Earl of Dalkeith, later the 7th Duke of Buccleuch and 9th Duke of Queensbury; her mother, Lady Margaret, a daughter of the 4th Earl of Bradford. She was born on Christmas Day 1901 in the family's London town house, Montagu House. Standing opposite the entrance to Horse Guards Parade, the 19th century mansion built from Portland stone and staffed by up to fifty servants was one of the very few private residences on Whitehall and it was not until after the First World War that it was pulled down to make way for the government building that eventually became the Ministry of Defence. She spent much of her childhood peregrinating between the family's many residences: Eildon Hall, in the Scottish borders; Drumlanrig Castle,

Dumfriesshire; Dalkeith House, near Edinburgh; Bowhill, outside Selkirk. Her favourite was the magnificent Boughton House, an English Versailles set in the middle of the Northamptonshire countryside, which had been first built in the late 17th century and which she once described as part palace, part village.[1] The constant disruption caused by the migrations from Scotland to southern England was eased by the fact that - like the royal family - Buccleuchs had their own special train which transported not just their boisterous family of three boys and five girls but also the servants, carriages, horses and eight tonnes of luggage.

After an unconventional early adulthood travelling the world like some Jazz Age gap year student and experiencing all the thrills of climbing Mount Kenya, illegally visiting Afghanistan dressed as a man and working her way round the Indian subcontinent from Peshawar to Lucknow, in 1935 on the urging of her father she decided it was time to settle down. Prince Henry, who was the son of her father's close comrade in the navy (George V) and the best friend of her brother in the army (Lord William Scott), proved a good match. They shared a love of the countryside, a diffident manner and a dislike of pomposity. Portly, balding and sporting a Lord Lucan-like clipped moustache Prince Harry possessed little of the good looks and charisma of his eldest brother, David, the future Edward VIII, being closer to his middle and more reserved brother Bertie, the future George VI.

His bluff manner was the source of much merriment in official circles. After attending an apparently interminable performance of Tosca at the Royal Opera House, he – as the story has it - could not disguise his glee when Maria Callas at last disappeared over the ramparts: "well if she is really dead, we can all go home."[2] At home, he was known to watch children's television programmes, Popeye the Sailor, according to his butler, being a favourite.[3]

It suited both their natures that their wedding was a private, low key affair - the original public ceremony having being cancelled after the sudden death of Alice's father. In a revealing passage in her memoirs, she describes how her father battled heroically against cancer, mindful that if he survived to a certain date, the family's inheritance tax bill would be mitigated. In the event, he did not quite make it and they had to pay the full whack.[4]

She does not say what property she inherited from her father's estate, but it is clear that her wealth was greatly boosted by various presents received on her later wedding. In the same memoirs she records how she received many gifts of jewellery and silver from King George and Queen Mary,[5] omitting to mention that many of them - especially the silver items - were worth hundreds of thousands of pounds, as we saw in Chapter Six, when they were put up for auction. As was mentioned in the same chapter Alice was also a beneficiary of Queen Mary's largesse when it came to jewellery. As soon as the engagement was announced,

Prince Henry was told by his mother not to buy a lot of jewellery as she had already selected many items for the bride from her own collection.[6] On the wedding day Alice duly received a magnificent seven-piece suite of emerald, pearl and diamond jewellery which included a brooch that had once belonged to Queen Alexandra. There were also two pearl and emerald necklaces made from an ornate collar that had originally been the property of Queen Victoria. Clearly, the royal collection was being passed down the generations.

After the marriage in November 1935 Prince Henry resumed his life as a soldier with the 10th Royal Hussars but the death of George V two months later and the subsequent abdication crisis dramatically reoriented his career path. With his brother George VI now on the throne and his eleven-year-old niece Princess Elizabeth still under age to be next in line, Henry was promoted to the position of Regent Designate which much to his disappointment meant retirement from active military service. This was the legal consequence of the 1937 Regency Act which laid down that if the monarch is under eighteen when he or she succeeds to the throne, a regent is automatically appointed. That person who would be named Prince of Wales must be over twenty-one and next in line to the throne.

Thus, if the German bomb that hit Buckingham Palace in September 1940 had landed a few feet closer to the office of the king then Prince Henry would have found himself Prince Regent. The 1937 Act also provided for the incapacity of a monarch through ill health or old age. If ever a nonagenarian Queen lost her mental faculties and was deemed incapable of carrying out her responsibilities, Prince Charles as heir apparent (and over twenty-one) would be regent.

Prince Henry's changed professional circumstances did at least give him time to resume one of his great passions. Encouraged by his father who amassed an invaluable collection of stamps and his mother who put together the richest assortment of jewels of any British queen, Henry threw himself into collecting books. Since his other great passion was outdoor pursuits, the books not unsurprisingly concerned horses and country sports. He had begun collecting as a schoolboy at Eton and his library started to take shape in the 1920s as he scoured bookshops and auction houses for rare editions. After his marriage Alice often accompanied him on the trawl and tried with limited success to protect him from being ripped off by overzealous booksellers.[7]

In 1937 he paid top dollar at the New York sale of the Dixon collection, a highly sought after American sport and hunting library, but uppermost in his sights was the famous Schwerdt collection of sporting books. Later in the year he attempted to acquire the entire library but his offer was rejected. But little by little - as some of the more important works were put up for auction during the war years - he managed to buy around five hundred books which became the backbone of his own highly valuable library.

Now discharged from the army, the newly-married Prince Henry was able to set up home in the country and begin a new life as a gentleman farmer. Alice, who as a child had spent many a happy summer in Boughton House in Northamptonshire and still retained many friends in the locality, had her eye on a nearby property - Barnwell, an Elizabethan manor house built in 1586 and later re-enlarged in the 19th century. The estate included farmland, a spacious garden and a ruined castle that had been a Buccleuch property from the 16th century until 1912 when it passed out of the family's possession. In 1938 the Gloucesters bought it back, paying £37,000 (£1.2m at today's values) for the buildings and the four tenanted farms. The bulk of the money apparently came from Henry's £750,000 inheritance from George V.[8]

The £37,000 outlay on Barnwell soon proved a shrewd investment. When in December 1944 Prince Henry was sent to Australia for two years to be Governor General, he was obliged to sell the tenanted parts of the estate (to among others the magnificently named Augusta de Cock-Brogniaux) which brought in £47,000. On his return he could afford to buy up more arable land so that the total size of the farm was close its pre-war level of 5,000 acres. The farm, however, was never run as a modern agribusiness and in Alice's view probably never paid for itself.[9]

Surprisingly Alice's exile in Australia as the Governor General's wife cemented her relationship with her mother-in-law. Queen Mary had originally been delighted with the marriage as it brought her a much sought after second daughter and during the war she invited her to stay at Badminton where they went antique hunting together. But it was during the Australian sojourn that they grew close through a lengthy correspondence. With Henry not being a natural letter writer and often away from the Governor General's residence on tours of the country, Mary found it easier to keep in touch with her son through her daughter-in-law. Their correspondence contained intimate and witty exchanges and helped forge a bond of affection between two women who were both naturally shy and reserved.[10]

By this time Queen Mary also had two grandchildren. Both wartime babies, Prince William was born in December 1941 and Prince Richard in August 1944. Their godparents were the two spinster-sister princesses described in Chapter Five. Princess Marie Louise was named Richard's godmother at his baptism at the private chapel at Windsor and later left him a stunning Russian-style diamond tiara, while Princess Helena Victoria became William's "sponsor" or godparent in the same Windsor chapel where she gave him a silver tankard as a christening present. William's other godmother was Queen Mary who true to her generous nature showered him with a rich spray of christening and confirmation presents (see Chapter Six). This was the start of a cascade of valuables that passed from the septuagenarian Mary not just to her two grandchildren but also to her daughter-in-law. By the time of her death in 1953, she had left Alice two diamond tiaras, three diamond brooches and a pearl choker lined with diamonds.[11]

Queen Mary survived to the ripe old age of eighty-five but it soon became apparent that her son Henry was unlikely to make old bones. The first inkling that something might be seriously amiss occurred on the day of Winston Churchill's funeral in January 1965 when the duke was driving back to Barnwell Manor with the duchess at his side. Just before he reached home, his Rolls-Royce swerved, left the road and turned over. Fortunately he was thrown free and escaped with a few scratches, but his wife was not so lucky. She broke her arm and nose, cracked her knee and suffered deep facial injuries which required fifty-five stitches and a two week stay in hospital. In her memoirs, she seems to blame herself for not being sufficiently alert and not steadying the wheel when her husband lost control of the vehicle. But Henry's biographer suggests that the duke might have suffered the first trace of a stroke.[12] His doctors had earlier told him to give up driving but he had refused. Less than eight weeks after the accident the duke suffered an unequivocal - albeit mild - stroke. He was in Canberra to take part in the commemorations for the 50th anniversary of the Anzac landing at Gallipoli when just before the opening ceremony he tried to get up. His legs gave way and seemed to lose all awareness. He managed to complete his official functions but the big blow came in the summer of 1968 when he suffered two more serious strokes that left him in a wheelchair and virtually deprived of speech.

At this point Alice could not have failed to realise that her sixty-eight-year-old husband's days might be numbered. She acknowledges in her book that he was now a complete invalid and she could not even be certain that he could understand what anyone said to him.[13] In the light of her own personal experience witnessing her father unable to survive long enough to avoid crippling death duties it is reasonable to assume that she would have discussed with her husband or his financial advisors how to pass on his wealth to his family in the most tax efficient manner. The traditional device to avoid estate duty was either a discretionary trust or a lifetime gift. Although in the sixties, the transfer could be made one year before death to escape all tax, by 1972 the period had been extended to seven years with a sliding scale determining the liability to be paid if the death occurred during that period. So, if he gifted assets in 1968 after his serious stroke, he would probably have needed to survive until 1975 to escape the full force of death duties.

Apart from the family silver (in the shape of the Gloucesters' valuable collection of jewellery, furniture and other heirlooms), the duke's most important asset was Barnwell Manor and its surrounding farmlands. Here he would have been faced with the dilemma of whether to transfer title to his wife who loved the manor and its gardens but who was like him in her late sixties, or to his two sons - with the elder Prince William the more likely recipient since he would inherit the title Duke of Gloucester and would need a country seat. After Henry's stroke, William retired from the diplomatic service so that he could spend more time managing the Barnwell estate. Between 1970 and 1972 the heir to the Gloucester title worked closely with the farm manager Mr Vinson learning the intricacies of livestock breeding and trying to introduce more modern farming methods.

Regardless of whether some lifetime transfer took place in the years after Henry's major stroke, any significant long term estate planning would have been dramatically cut short by a second transport accident. Prince William had a reputation as a "wild boy" - not just in his pursuit of older, divorced women (such as his long-time lover the Hungarian-born Szuzui Starkloff) but also in his outdoor pursuits. He was a brave polo player, a fearless skier and a dare-devil pilot. He had first started flying when he left Eton and fully got the bug during his diplomatic postings in Nigeria and Japan, on one occasion completing a two thousand mile flight to Tokyo. After stepping down from the Foreign Office, he took out a competition flying licence and began to enter rallies.

On 28 August 1972 he enrolled for the Goodyear International Trophy at the Half Penny Green Airfield near Wolverhampton. In the first paired race his yellow and white Piper Cherokee Arrow was trying to catch up with the aircraft in front piloted by his Irish friend, Tim Phillips, when it took a steep bend at too low an altitude. It managed to pass over some houses but the left wing glanced the branches of a large tree and the impact broke off part of the wing. The aircraft rolled over, dived inverted into the ground and burst into flames. The crash was witnessed by a crowd of thirty thousand people but the heat of the blaze prevented onlookers and firemen alike from rescuing him and his co-pilot Vyrell Mitchell. A later investigation found no fault with the aircraft. Both pilots were fit and fully qualified to fly the aircraft. The final word was left to one pilot friend who concluded that "there are risks in all competitive flying."

By her own admission Princess Alice was never quite the same again after the death of her eldest son. It is not clear what long term effect the news had on the ailing Prince Henry who saw the crash on that evening's television news bulletin but within two years he too was dead. In the early hours of 9 June 1974 he passed away at Barnwell Manor. In an ironic twist, the estates of father and son would be united in death by death duties.

Prince William's gross estate was valued at £416,001 61s, but it had massive debts and other liabilities in the region of £100,000 and the net figure was reduced to £318,378. He may have been eleventh in line to the throne but this was still a substantial sum for a thirty-year-old farmer. Over the years William must have benefited from royal bequests: we know his grandfather, George V, set up a trust for his grandchildren and we know that Princess Helena Victoria left him a small cash sum in her will (although somewhat typically he spent some of the money to buy a racehorse) and of course there was all the silverware and furniture from his grandmother, Mary. The bulk of his wealth is likely to have come from his father who is believed to have passed on many family heirlooms to him. But it seems unlikely that Barnwell Manor was included. With an estimated price tag over £500,000, it would have pushed his estate well beyond its probate value of £318,378. Even without the heavy tax burden of the manor house, some reports suggest that he left to his brother Richard "crippling death duties" of over £70,000. Under the 1972 Finance Act, there was no tax to pay on the first £15,000 but the rates climbed from 25% to a staggering 75% on the slice above £500,000. It seems likely that despite Henry's possible attempt to mitigate inheritance tax by gifting assets to his son, the family was hit by a double whammy of paying tax first on William's estate and soon after on Henry's. It is possible that Henry left his elder son some possessions that in the space of a couple of years would have been subject to two lots of estate duty.

What was apparently happening was the nightmare scenario for the Windsors of their wealth being decimated by a succession of premature deaths. John Major as prime minister had raised this possibility when he warned against royal assets being "salami-sliced" away as he argued the case in the Commons for the 1992 exemption on inheritance tax for the sovereign on transfers to the heir to the throne. A double death can kill even the best-laid schemes of estate planning.

If press reports are true that Richard was left a crippling tax liability, this would suggest that he was the main beneficiary of his brother's will.[14] But William's will - unlike his mother's - was sealed. It seems odd that a mere thirty-year-old would have written a will but given his taste for dangerous sports and the fact according to several reports he had been diagnosed with the serious skin disease porphyries, he may have harboured thoughts of dying young – an opinion subscribed to by his mother in her memoirs.[15]

We know from the probate records that Prince Henry died in June 1974 leaving an estate worth £734,262 19s before tax. Since his will was sealed we cannot be sure whether he left his landed property to his surviving son or his widow. But one clue to its ultimate fate lies in the name of his estate's executor. He was Arthur Collins and his name would reappear in many documents relating to ownership of Barnwell Manor, even though he was in no way related to the Gloucester family. For sixty-five of his eighty-nine years Collins was a solicitor with the London law firm of Withers. By the time of Henry's death in 1974 he had been a senior partner for over a decade and his speciality was looking after some of the great noble estates of England for whom he often acted as a trustee or guardian. He served as trustee for the Duke of Manchester and in one high profile case was also a trustee for the estate of the Duke of Marlborough which included Blenheim Palace and a £100 million inheritance. When its heir James Blandford, the Marquess of Blandford, began to squander the family fortune on his drug habit, the family instructed Withers to go to the High Court to limit his inheritance and set up a new trust in which Blenheim Palace and the bulk of the estate was then placed outside of his control. Collins had a personal interest in the marquess's affairs as he was distantly related to the family through his mother, Lady Evelyn Innes-Ker, a first cousin of Sir Winston Churchill.

Collins often became friends with his clients and his professional and social life tended to overlap. An old Etonian who served in the Royal Horse Guards before marrying the widow of the 6th Lord Sudeley, he moved effortlessly in the upper echelons of society. He owned a country estate in North Yorkshire and loved fox hunting, shooting and racing. As the advisor to the body that ran Royal Ascot, he regularly came into professional contact with the Queen's representative at the race course, the Duke of Norfolk, and during Ascot week would inevitably rub shoulders with senior members of the royal family. When Lord Mountbatten heard that the Duchess of Windsor needed an executor for her and the duke's estate, Collins was immediately recommended as a man who could be relied upon to be tactful.[16] In 1980 he was appointed KCVO in recognition of his services to the royal family.

It is not known when he first met the Gloucesters but some relationship of trust must have developed since he was made with Princess Alice co-executor of Prince Henry's estate in 1974 and in the 1990s his name regularly appears in the title documents to Barnwell Manor and the surrounding estate. It would be a mistake to assume from the title documents that Sir Arthur was actually the joint owner of Barnwell Manor and its surrounding land. If the estate had been transferred into a trust then the trust could either be registered at the Land Registry under the name of that trust or the name of the trustees (without mentioning the fact that they were indeed trustees and not private individuals). Given that Collins had previously acted as a trustee for at least two other great aristocratic families and given that he was named executor of Henry's estate, the most likely explanation for his name appearing on the Land Registry documents is that he was co-trustee of the trust that controlled Barnwell Manor and surrounding lands. This trust could have been set up after Henry's death, but since any transfer to Alice on death would have been subject to high death duties, it would have been prudent to do it during his lifetime. At this time of rising tax rates, trusts were all the rage with the landed rich. As one leading historian of the British aristocracy observed, "the sixties saw the widespread proliferation of elaborate discretionary trusts among landowning families which were a more effective means of tax avoidance."[17] A Buckingham Palace spokesman later confirmed that Barnwell Manor had indeed been placed in a family trust, although it was not made clear when this transfer took place..[18]

Following her husband's death, Alice lived happily in Barnwell Manor for the next twenty-one years. It was a tranquil, almost idyllic location, overlooking the gently rolling fields of the east Northamptonshire where ponies and shire horses grazed and nestling beside the picture postcard village of Barnwell with its babbling brook, thatched cottages, medieval church, cricket pitch and one inn – the Montagu Arms. In fact, all of Barnwell seemed branded with the red and gold coat of arms of Alice's family.

Barnwell Manor had something of the flavour of a Northamptonshire Balmoral – but with a slightly warmer hue due to the cream-coloured brickwork, neat hedgerows and lush greenery. No stately home, the manor was less than luxurious but certainly more than comfortable. Set back from the road on a piece of high ground near a derelict castle, the two-storey building contained eight bedrooms and four reception rooms with a cottage, a coach house, swimming pool and tennis courts. But her pride and joy - as was shown by the many photographs in her memoirs - was her garden which she cultivated with a Panglossian passion. The lawns were beautifully manicured and the hedges trimmed with a maze-like precision. She liked to tell visitors that few people were lucky enough to have a castle in their garden inside which was a tennis court.[19]

But the Barnwell estate was becoming a drain on the family's finances, its upkeep costing an estimated £35,000 a year. Prince Richard, who had tried to run the farm in a business-like fashion but without making much money, reportedly decided in the spring of 1995 that the only way to break even was to rent out the manor house and move his mother into his grace-and-favour apartment in Kensington Palace. This prompted some press reports suggesting that what he really wanted to do was to put the property up for sale rather than for rental. Shortly after on January 4 1996 a letter appeared in the Times from Paul Howell of Berengar Antiques denying that that Barnwell had been put on the market. In fact, "the duke has leased the manor and the medieval castle," he wrote "…to me for a period of ten years, and I understand that there is every probability that the Gloucesters will return to Barnwell when the lease expires." The rental arrangement reportedly brought the duke £60,000 a year – and with it, more bad publicity.[20]

Although Prince Richard did his best to ease the transition for his mother by recreating the Barnwell drawing room for her and letting her enjoy a walled garden at Kensington Palace, it must have been an enormous wrench for a ninety-three-year-old to decamp to the capital. The Duke of Edinburgh reportedly gave the Duke of Gloucester a severe dressing-down, arguing that his mother should be permitted to see out her last years in her old home regardless of the cost.[21] It was unjust, he is reported to have said, to uproot an old lady who lived only for her garden and dog. Prince Richard's apparent response was the matter was out of his hands since the family's coffers had been drained by the crippling death duties on the estates of his brother and father. But others might have wondered why the duchess could not have sold off some of the family heirlooms - such as the valuable collection of antique books - to pay for the upkeep of Barnwell.

The fact that Princess Alice was not sufficiently cash rich to find another £35,000 a year to run her home strongly suggests that some of her assets might have already been transferred out of her estate to mitigate inheritance tax. We know for certain that she gave a magnificent turquoise suite of tiara, necklace, earrings and bracelets to the present duchess on her wedding to Prince Richard and at some stage this was supplemented by a valuable pearl and diamond dog collar originally owned by Queen Mary. In 1995 she was well into her nineties and so with prudent planning would have handed over her possessions at least seven years before to escape any death duties.

We know that she wrote her last will in November 1988 and amended it with a codicil in April 1993. We also know from the Land Registry records that she was still in control of the Barnwell Manor and the farmlands as late as July 1996 but since Sir Arthur Collins' name was also attached to the documentation then it is likely that it was still in a trust and technically outside of her estate. Around this time, she was beginning to lose control of her own faculties. In July 2000 Prince Richard announced that his mother had decided to step down from public life since she had become "increasingly forgetful" and no longer felt "confident in carrying out official engagements away from Kensington Palace or in coping with the clamour of social gatherings." Princess Alice died in her sleep at her London home on 29 October 2004, aged one hundred and two.

By this time Sir Arthur Collins and his replacement as executor of the estate Edward Ram had both died. This left as executors, Prince Richard and Roger Wellesley Smith, a family friend and stockbroker, although in the event it appears that Withers was put in charge of the probate process and permitted an important role in the general management of her estate. When probate was granted in May 2005 the estate was valued at £817,146 gross and £569,849 net. As was the case with Princes Henry and William, the executors were able to deduct several hundred thousand pounds of debts and other liabilities which reduced the chargeable amount of the estate by almost a third. There was nevertheless a considerable tax bill to pay. This might in part have been a legacy of Henry's estate which may have been subject to a peculiar feature of death duties in the seventies – something that might explain the mystery of what happened to Barnwell Manor.

Prince Henry's death in June 1974 straddled two inheritance tax regimes. The previous regime of estate duty was considered by the new Labour government as almost a discretionary tax because it could easily be avoided by giving away property and living for seven years. One socialist Chancellor of the Exchequer famously joked that estate duty was a voluntary levy paid by those who distrust their heirs more than they dislike the Inland Revenue.

So, in 1975 Harold Wilson replaced estate duty with capital transfer tax which was based on the principle that all gifts of property - whether made at death or during one's lifetime - should be added together and a progressive rate of tax applied to the total. In order to protect a surviving spouse, who might need to stay in the family home, a special exemption was now allowed. This applied to all transfers on *death* from 3 March 1975 but it did retrospectively cover *lifetime* transfers from 26 March 1974 to 12 November 1974 (with a slightly different hybrid regime from then until March 3 1975). So, if Prince Henry had gifted members of his family property between March 26 and his death on June 10, 1974 they might have been taxed under the new regime although any transfers on death would have been covered by the old one.

Because the spouse exemption did not operate in June 1974, the estate duty regime allowed some latitude to a surviving spouse so that he or she might not be charged for use of their house. For example, if a husband dies and leaves property to his wife for life, with the remainder to their children and assuming that his wife has no power to use the capital of the trust fund, it will normally be left out of the account in determining the estate chargeable to inheritance tax on her death. In plain language, a widow could receive her husband's property tax free as long as she did not later sell it.

Some press reports suggest that Princess Alice might have benefited from an arrangement of that sort. A well-sourced article in the Sunday Times in January 2006 stated that "when the Duke died, his will left the use of the family's home, Barnwell Manor in Northamptonshire, and his possessions for her lifetime."[22] The only problem with this argument is that again the official stated value of his estate - £734,262 - does not appear large enough to include the £500,000 plus Barnwell Manor. Moreover, for the exemption to be available some tax has to be paid on the estate of the first to die. But in the same article Prince Richard is quoted as saying in reference to the estate duty liability: "I couldn't have afforded to pay it in 1974." Speaking in January 2006 he defended his decision to auction off family heirlooms at Christie's to pay the delayed tax bill: "With the sale, the more that is made, the more goes to the government. There can't be many people left for whom those tax rates apply."[23]

At the time of writing, a spokesman for the Duke of Gloucester via the palace press office was unable to clarify the exact details of the inheritance process. But from the evidence available what seems to have happened is that when Henry died in 1974, the Gloucesters having already paid hefty death duties on William's estate accepted a heritage property election whereby they elected to postpone payment on all or parts of the duke's estate until his wife died. It seems highly likely that Barnwell was not part of his estate having been put into a trust at some unspecified time but the contents of the house might have been in the estate and when you include the interest on the outstanding liability there was still an enormous tax bill to pay. Since Princess Alice survived for another 30 years, yearly interest would have been charged on the remaining taxable amount. So, even if one averaged up the annual interest rate to a figure of 5% (a relatively conservative number given inflation rates in the seventies and eighties), the Gloucesters might have faced a total tax bill on Prince Henry's estate of over half a million pounds. In addition they would have had to pay tax on Alice's £817,146 estate which might have added another £240,000. When you also include the professional fees of Withers - both solicitors and tax consultants as well as possibly valuers

- Prince Richard could easily have been saddled with a bill of one million pounds or more.

No wonder in January 2006 he decided to auction his father's movable property. The press release from Christie's stated that the sale was taking place to "settle the deferred capital transfer tax liability on the estate of HRH the late Prince Henry." The disposal of over seven hundred family heirlooms ranging from the rare 15th century hawking manuscript The Master of the Game to a collection of the duke's sporrans was expected to raise £1 million but in fact realised £5,063,362. The Master of the Game alone fetched £198,000 and two silver George III wedding tureens brought in another £142,000. Intriguingly, two items were removed from the sale at the last moment: lot 502 a medieval manuscript called The Kerdeston Hawking Book and the lot 503 leaves from The Kerdeston Hunting Book. These were offered to the nation in lieu of inheritance tax with the family expressing a wish that they should be housed in the British Library. Given that Henry possessed one of the finest private collections of field sport books in the country, one wonders why other items of national heritage value were not left to the state, although it is possible that the rest of the collection had insufficient heritage appeal.

The reason why Prince Richard was able to put the family silver up for auction is that he had been given control over his mother's chattels and property by her will. Due to the fact that it was not sealed, for once we know what her wishes were. According to clause four, she agreed to give all her chattels free of inheritance tax to her trustees and clause five allowed them to sell all the property and convert it if necessary into cash. An earlier clause had already appointed Prince Richard and Roger Wellesley Smith her trustees - a term that presumably included both being executor and being in charge of any trusts in the estate. Clause four then established that the trustees should dispose of her chattels according to any memorandum or note that she might leave behind. So, rather like Diana, another princess who lived at Kensington Palace, it is possible that she left a letter of wishes to govern her estate.

Jewellery does not appear to feature prominently in her chattels. Given that her jewel box was once valued in millions and her net estate was only worth £570,000 it is likely that she would have already transferred some of it as lifetime gifts - probably to her daughter-in-law, Birgitte, but possibly to her grandchildren. Jewellery was noticeably absent from the Christie's auction in January 2006 - although when six months later Princess Margaret's heir chose the same auction house to sell his family heirlooms the catalogue was overflowing with stunning jewels.

Princess Alice's will reveals how she was determined to provide not just for her family but also her wider household. She was an old-school royal for whom loyalty to staff - and vice versa - was paramount. The Gloucesters kept a big household of servants comprising, according to Peter Russell, their butler in the early sixties: one valet, two chauffeurs for the two Rolls-Royces, three footmen, a lady's maid, cook, housekeeper, housemaids and an odd job man.[24] The butler's duties extended to unscrewing the top of Prince Henry's tube of toothpaste and ensuring that next to every ashtray there was a matchbox with a match jutting out so that he did not have to open it. Another of his special requirements was that all his butter and cheese came fresh from the Barnwell farm – either by train to King's Cross or in the back of the Rolls-Royce. When one morning in the early sixties a rail strike halted the dairy delivery, the bereft duke complained to his staff that management should pay off the strikers immediately so that normal service could be resumed.[25]

Despite this privileged lifestyle, the Gloucesters were kind to their staff and the duchess was generous in her Christmas gifts, albeit a little misguided (the same butler records: "One year, the Duchess presented me with a pair of beautiful, old fashioned fire bellows. It would have been a marvellous present had my wife and I not lived in a centrally heated flat.")[26]

Peter Russell is not mentioned in her will - the fact that he wrote an indiscreet book about his service with the Gloucesters might have excluded him from their Christmas card (and cash gift) list but another former butler is remembered. He was Alfred Amos who began service in the thirties as Prince Henry's valet, acted as his bat-man in the army, accompanied him and his family to Australia after the war and helped him recover from his first stoke before becoming Princess Alice's butler at Kensington Palace. He was left £1,000, as was the butler at Barnwell Manor, D. Warner, who died too early to enjoy his bequest.

The amount bequeathed to different staff speaks volumes about the social stratification within the Gloucester household. Princess Alice's lady-in-waiting, Lady Jean Maxwell Scott, was allocated £5,000 as was Lieutenant-Colonel Sir Simon Bland who over four decades had served as comptroller to the duke, private secretary to Prince William and finally extra equerry to the duchess. A step or two down the pecking order, the head gardener at Barnwell, Nicholas Walliker, received £3,000 and the farm worker Ian Hamilton just £1,000 - although in fairness it could be argued that Alice was under no obligation to leave them anything and she did go out of her way to specify in her will that these individual legacies be free of inheritance tax.

The division of these cash gifts take up the first two pages of the will - the remaining twenty-eight deal with a trust. The will names the primary beneficiaries of the trust as her grandchildren and the other beneficiaries are listed as the issue of the grandchildren, their spouses and finally Prince Richard. So why would Princess Alice leave her will trust primarily to her grandchildren rather than her son?

Having lost her husband and her eldest son, she derived immeasurable joy from her three surviving grandchildren.[27] The eldest Alexander, the Earl of Ulster, was born in 1974 and then followed by Lady Davina in 1977 and Lady Rose in 1980. Being merely great-grandchildren of the sovereign, they did not possess royal titles nor did they later carry out official royal duties and as such received no Civil List payments or annuities from the Queen.

All three appeared on a Christmas card marking Alice's 80th birthday on 25 December 1981. Around about this time she also agreed to accompany the two eldest grandchildren on an exhausting flight to join up with their parents in Australia. But she was too frail to attend the wedding of Lady Davina to Gary Lewis, in July 2004, just three months before her death. Present at the ceremony was the bride's godfather, Roger Wellesley Smith who had been named along with Prince Richard as executor of Alice's estate and trustee of her grandchildren's trust. He was no doubt chosen partly on account of his financial expertise gained in the City as an executive director of the bank Société Generale.

One reason presumably why Alice left her trust fund to her grandchildren rather than her son is that he was already well provided for. Shortly before Alice's death the Royal Rich Report estimated his wealth at £19.5m.[28] In hindsight this appears an inflated figure, although he would have undoubtedly been wealthy in the light of his grace-and-favour apartment at Kensington Palace, the £175,000 annuity he received from the Queen to fulfil royal duties and everything he would have inherited from his grandfather, George V, his brother and his father - not to mention any lifetime gifts from his mother. Then, of course, there was also Barnwell Manor and the rental income of up of £60,000 a year. When the original tenant Paul Howell vacated the property around 2002 he did not apparently return to the family home.

Prince Richard's name, however, does not appear on the Land Registry documents for either Barnwell Manor or the many other units of the larger estate including Armston Grove. Instead one finds three non-titled names: Roger Wellesely Smith, James Palmer-Tomkinson and Murray Hallam. Wellesely Smith, a City financier, we know from his trusteeship of the Alice's estate and trust and Palmer Tomkinson was another family friend, probably best known as the brother of the socialite Tara, and son of Charles, the Olympic skier (who skied regularly with Prince Charles whom he first met through the old Duke of Gloucester) although he had carved out a career in his own right as a fund manager in the City. He worked as head of portfolio management with the private bank, the Torquil Clark Group, after having cut his teeth in financial services with Kleinwort Benson.

But the most intriguing name on the documentation is that of Murray Hallam. His address is given as care of Withers LLP, 16 Old Bailey, London EC4. Withers is today not just a leading City firm of solicitors but one the largest law firms in the world with offices in Europe, the United States and Asia. They also have a specialist probate and trust department where Hallam worked and which offers among its services an in-house trust corporation WITCO to act as executor or trustee for UK wills and trusts. He joined the firm as long ago as 1970 qualifying in 1973 and becoming a partner in 1977. His stated speciality is probate, estate planning and trust law and he is the author of two books on trusts and one on wills.

Hallam - as we have also seen - is part of a long line of Withers lawyers who have handled the affairs of the Gloucesters - not to mention representing other members of the royal family including Lord Snowdon. Princess Alice's original choice of trustee/executor was Edward Abel Ram, an erstwhile consultant with Withers as well as a director of the Daily Mail and General Trust, but he predeceased her dying in November 1996 (Murray Hallam was part of a large delegation of Withers staff who attended his memorial service along with the present Duke and Duchess of Gloucester and Roger Wellesley Smith). In the end, as we saw earlier, Princess Alice was aided by another Withers solicitor - Sir Arthur Collins.

According to the land registry documents, the last recorded time when Sir Arthur and Princess Alice were in control of the property was 5 July 1996 when they issued a grant of access to East Midlands Electricity. Sir Arthur died in December 2000 and Alice in November 2004. At some time between 1996 and January 2007 ownership of the property would have changed hands - at least once. Obviously Alice's death might have triggered some form of transfer but it could have happened before her death or after if as is likely the house was already in a trust. It is even possible that the house stayed in the same trust and all that happened is that the names of the trustees changed for reasons of death or otherwise.

This leaves the question of why Princess Alice's executors did not seal her will. One explanation might be that there was nothing to hide in so far as both her estate and estate planning would have been watertight. Barnwell would have been transferred and the rest of her assets put in a trust for her grandchildren. Since she lived to the ripe old age of one hundred and two there was no shortage of time to put her affairs in order. But this argument could also apply to the Queen Mother who survived to one hundred and one, undertook considerable estate planning for her castle of Mey, but whose will was nevertheless sealed.

One other explanation for the openness is the outlook of her heir and executor whose responsibility it was at the end of the day to decide whether to keep her testamentary affairs under wraps or not. Alice and Henry were determined to give their children a relatively normal upbringing. She took immense pride in the fact that her boys were raised with the minimum of fuss and formality.[29] In fact, they both went to an elite prep school and Eton but the desire for normality was genuine as being the son of the George V and the brother of Edward VIII Henry must have known only too well the psychological damage that could be wrought by an overbearing parent with a Hanoverian bent ("the House of Hanover are like ducks," wrote George V's biographer, "they trample their young"). So, even though he would have liked Prince William to follow in his footsteps and pursue an army career, he did nothing to discourage him from reading history at Cambridge University and then completing his studies in business administration at Stanford University in California.

Prince Richard followed a similar academic path going to Magdalene College, Cambridge where he studied architecture. After completing a five year diploma, he did his practical work with the Ministry of Public Building, bought a property in Camden and became a partner in a nearby firm of London architects. But his professional career was cut short by the deaths in quick succession of his brother and father which required him to take on increased royal duties. Had he not succeeded to the title, his mother believed that he would have become well known in his own right as an architect but she once admitted that she could never quite decide whether her children should lead a formal royal lifestyle at the service of the sovereign or be allowed to pursue their own chosen career.[30]

But in his choice of bride he decided to go down a distinctly non-royal route. In July 1972 he married the daughter of a Danish lawyer Birgitte van Deurs, whom he first met at Cambridge and who was then working as a secretary in the Danish Embassy in London. The wedding took place not at Westminster Abbey or St Paul's, but the petite St Andrew's Church, Barnwell which found space for the Queen Mother, Princess Margaret and Prince William, his brother and best man. He would be dead less a month later and the church today contains a plaque and wooden bench commemorating his life.

By all accounts, the marriage proved a happy union - untarnished by any hint of marital scandal that beset other Windsors. Birgitte, modest and well liked, divided her time between her relatively light royal duties (a patron of the national asthma campaign and various military patron work) and raising her three children. When her daughter, Davina, married in July 2004 again it was to a commoner, Gary Lewis, a New Zealand former sheep shearer who achieved the distinction of becoming the first Maori to marry into the British royal family. After the wedding a traditional haka dance was reportedly performed in the gardens of Kensington Palace.[31]

To add to the unconventionality, he was also reportedly father of an eleven-year-old boy from a previous relationship. But according to the bride's godfather, Roger Wellesley Smith, the groom's background was of no concern to her parents: "The only question they have asked is will she be happy and they feel she will be...The Duke and Duchess are people of today's world and things are very different to the way they were two generations ago."[32] The groom is reported as saying of his new in-laws that they were "no different to anyone else's." Once more, the ceremony was a low key affair. A spokesman for the royal household explained that "the Queen will not be attending. They are having a quiet private wedding."

As "a person of today's world" the Duke of Gloucester could often be seen riding around central London on his Honda 600cc motorcycle.[33] As a car enthusiast too, he was president of the Institute of Advanced Motorists for many years until he was obliged to resign in 2005 after being banned from driving for six months for speeding

For the most part, the duke fulfils his royal duties quietly, efficiently and to use his mother's phrase with a minimum of fuss. On the official royal website he records a normal working day as catching a train out of town, being met by the Lord Lieutenant of a county or district and then opening a new building – it could be a large factory or simple village hall. Using his expertise in architecture he sat for many years on the Historic Buildings and Monument Commissions (today English Heritage) and he is now President of Cancer Research UK and St Bartholomew's Hospital as well as a patron of ASH (Action on Smoking and Health). A passionate anti-smoker he sets himself apart on this issue from the traditionally nicotine-addicted royal family. Both his uncles (George VI and Edward VIII) of course died of smoking related diseases.

This more modern approach to royal duties may supply an answer to the mystery of why Princess Alice's will was not sealed: the royal making the decision on this occasion was a person of today's world. No doubt he wondered why his mother's will should not be open to the public like everyone else's in Britain. There might also have been a changed class element - Alice's generation worried about finding staff but did not talk about money or inheritance while the thrifty Richard without a chauffeur got round town not in his father's Rolls-Royce but a modest moped.

In keeping with the spirit of a greener age, there have been plans to build a wind farm on his ancestral land not far from Barnwell Manor which could bring in £120,000 a year in rental fees.[34] But the prospect of unsightly giant turbines has caused consternation among more conservative residents in the locality. No one can be certain how Princess Alice would have responded to the plans, but she might well be now spinning in her grave.

Chapter Seventeen
Charles's Cash Cow – 2010-2014

"He loves spending money...God knows how much money he would spend if he ever got his hands on Sandringham"
Anonymous palace source on Prince Charles's lifestyle[1]

If an absence of cash has obliged Prince Richard to prune his property portfolio, an abundance of funds has encouraged his distant cousin Prince Charles to go in the opposite direction - for maximum growth. In the course of his six decades' wait to be crowned, the oldest Prince of Wales in history has been able to build up an extensive network of houses in all four corners of his future kingdom.

The jewel in the crown, Highgrove House, lies in the heart of middle England, just outside of Tetbury in Gloucestershire. The former home of Maurice Macmillan, MP, the son of the Conservative prime minister, was purchased for £865,000 in 1980 in preparation for Charles's marriage to Diana. The neo-Georgian house with its nine bedrooms, eight bathrooms and four reception rooms (as well as an outdoor swimming pool) was ideally suited to entertaining and inviting friends to stay.

It was also surrounded by three hundred and fifty acres of farmland including the Duchy Home Farm and thirty-seven acres of relatively uncultivated grounds which soon became the focus of Charles's zeal for gardening. With expert advice from his friend and horticulturalist Lady Salisbury, he laid out the garden with honeysuckle, jasmine and other scented plants and created an experimental flower meadow, a walled kitchen garden and an orchard of rare varieties of apples. This labour of love ("I have put my heart and soul into Highgrove," he once told a Telegraph reporter) has grown into a personal garden of Eden.[2] It became the place where he was most at home, an oasis away from the pressures of palace life.

"A combination of unlimited resources and exquisite taste" is how the Labour MP Chris Mullin described Highgrove after a parliamentary visit in June 2006. "Everywhere little memorials, busts of friends, of the Prince himself and in a glade among the trees a delicate sculpture of the murdered daughters of the Tsar, there is even a little memorial to a dead dog. There is only one glaring omission – Diana. Of her, no mention."[3]

During the many low points in his marriage to Diana, Charles found Highgrove conveniently close to his long term mistress and future second wife

Camilla Parker Bowles who lived a fifteen minute drive away at Bolehyde Manor. After her divorce from Andrew Parker Bowles in 1995, she reportedly sold this home and moved to nearby Ray Mill House in Laycock, Wiltshire where her father lived.[4]

If Highgrove in the heart of England is one of Charles's oldest properties, then the newest is located on one of the most westerly points of the British mainland. In March 2007 he paid £1.3m for a Carmarthenshire farm in Llwynywermod, near Anglesey and spent another £1m or so transforming the coach house into a three-bedroom farmhouse-like home and converting the adjoining farm building into a reception area and dining room. He even recruited his sister-in-law, Annabel Elliot, to help with the interior design and furnishing of his holiday accommodation with the Duchy of Cornwall accounts for 2008 recording that she was paid "the sum of £103,000 (2007: £182,000) in total for consultancy fees and the purchase of furniture and furnishings." The purchase of the property as a whole was justified on the grounds that the Prince of Wales should have a house within the principality given that there had been no permanent royal base in Wales for him since the 17th century.

Charles has also leased a property on the northern-most tip of Britain. Every year usually in August he paid a week's rent to use the Queen Mother's former country retreat, the Castle of Mey - Britain's most northerly inhabited castle - at Thurso on the

Pentland Firth – and attended the Mey Highland Games with its tug-of-war competition initiated by his grandmother between the castle staff and a team from the local British Legion. His charity, the Prince of Wales Foundation, encourages rich donors to contribute to its upkeep, with one Canadian heiress giving £1m in 2007 to build a new visitor centre.

Another of the Queen Mother's former Scottish properties, the fourteen-bedroom Birkhall lodge on the Balmoral estate, has been used in the summer by Charles who has paid rent to the Queen. Under the guidance of his second wife, Camilla, he also reportedly spent hundreds of thousands of pounds refurbishing the interiors.[5] It was here that he used to find a place of refuge during the worst days of his marriage to Diana.

When the Queen Mother died in 2002, he also moved into her St James's home Clarence House which became his official London residence. Being one of the royal palaces held in trust for the nation, the state paid £4.5m to modernise the house for the prince and he paid the remaining £1.6m. He has furnished the house with his personal artefacts and treasures from the Royal Collection – including the Monet and several paintings by Piper that once belonged to the Queen Mother.

To maintain this diverse portfolio of properties as well as to organise the prince's official duties, a large staff is required. Their numbers (and costs) have swollen considerably in the last two to three decades.

Eyebrows were raised in 1992 when Charles's biographer Jonathan Dimbleby revealed a staff of 84 people - a number incidentally that so enraged his then estranged wife Diana that sometime after 1992 she reportedly sent to The News of The World a copy of the royal phone directory listing all the staff and advisors who worked for Charles.[6] But that is nothing compared to the army of 148 who assist him today (including 20 who work solely on his charitable projects at Clarence House). The breakdown of personnel from the official report makes interesting reading, particularly his 60-strong private household who include: 1 equerry, 1.3 butlers, 2.5 valets and dressers, 3 chauffeurs, 4.6 travel coordinators, 5.3 chefs and kitchen porters, 3.7 orderlies, 10.8 house managers and housekeepers, and 21.3 gardeners and estate workers.

There were another 31.7 people working in his official office (private secretaries etc), 20.4 in the finance and personnel office, 3.8 in the charity office and significantly for someone whose public image had taken something of a battering since the Diana divorce 11.8 in the press office. Some are on generous salaries - particularly those based at Clarence House where the average pay is reportedly £40,000 per annum.[7] Part of this growth in staff numbers can be explained by the new responsibilities brought by the transition process, the extra needs of his two adult sons (after the marriage of William and Kate, an extra press team became a necessity) and his new wife as well as by the expansion of Highgrove and its gardens and farmlands.

Charles lives lavishly and to some people's eyes even more grandly than the Queen. Few would deny that he appreciates food far more than she does. While his mother famously eats her breakfast of Special K off Tupperware bowls, Charles is known to be to be very discerning when it comes to his boiled egg. According to a story told to Jeremy Paxman, his staff were so worried about ensuring that the food was of the correct hardness that they resorted to cooking a variety of eggs which they laid out in an ascending row of numbers beginning with the most runny.[8] Even if this tale might have grown taller in the telling and it was officially denied by a royal spokesman, there is no disputing that Charles likes the finer things in life. At one plush dinner attended by donors to the newly restored Scottish stately home, Dumfries House, he was observed by a Time Magazine reporter to enjoy along with the sea bass and risotto a fine Puligny-Montrachet, Chateau Sarget de Gruaud Larose and pink Champagne.[9]

He drives a £60,000 Aston-Martin, owns or leases a fleet of top of the range Audis and for official functions uses a Bentley or a Jaguar XJ diesel. All of his personal wear is of the highest quality. His bespoke suits have come from Anderson Sheppard of Savile Row, his shoes from Lobb and his guns from Purdey. Even when he had to splash through the sodden fields of the Somerset Levels on a visit to flood victims in February 2014, he still managed to look immaculately turned out in his Argyll Wellington Boots, Barbour-styled jacket and Windsor-knotted tie.

He also pushes the boat out when it comes to travel and holidays. He enjoys summer Mediterranean cruises on friends' luxury yachts, takes a regular skiing vacation in Klosters and often hires private jets for his journeys when he is not using the personal planes of billionaire friends. In 2010 Charles was reported to have run up a bill of £29,786 for a plane to take him to Balmoral for a four day holiday. In April 2009 he spent £14,756 taking the Royal Train from London to Cumbria to launch the Red Squirrel Survival Trust and in 2014 he had to take a £246,160 charter flight to South Africa to be in time to attend the funeral of Nelson Mandela. Overall in 2014 his spending on official travel went over the million pound mark to £1.235m.

So, how can he afford to live in such a luxurious manner? Admittedly, he does receive £2.1m in public funding from government departments and the Sovereign Grant to cover his travel and other official costs but that makes a relatively small dent in balancing the books. The real solution to the mystery, however, lies in his private milch cow - the Duchy of Cornwall - which is the official owner of Highgrove House and all of his other private properties. The lion's share of his personal wealth derives from the revenues from the duchy which in 2014 paid him an annual income of £19.5m. But if you trace the accounts back sixty years the duchy has not always been as high-yielding a cash cow as it is today.

The first trickle of the revenue came on stream when Charles was three. On the accession of the Queen in 1952, Charles became heir to the throne and 24th Duke of Cornwall thereby gaining access to the duchy income. Being a minor, he was allocated only one ninth of the profits with the rest going to the Treasury which offset it against Civil List spending. By the time he was eighteen he was receiving the relatively small sum of £21,000 a year. The big payday came on his 21st birthday as he gained access to the total annual income of £248,000 and then volunteered to pay income tax at 50% (a considerable saving since the top rate at the time was over 90%).

In 1969 the Duchy of Cornwall was hardly in the rudest of financial health. Failure to invest in modern farming machinery and new agricultural techniques had resulted in relatively low rents on long leases and to balance the books, the duchy was obliged to sell land on such a scale that when Charles took over the reins the duchy was actually contracting rather than growing.[10] Some hoped that the newly-invested Prince of Wales would take on the white knight role performed by Prince Albert a century earlier and restructure the duchy holdings. But despite some subtle hints, Charles was perfectly happy to take a backseat and delegate the decision making to senior executives while he formally chaired the non-executive board of the Prince's Council. Over time more skilful managers were recruited who addressed the problems of the high costs and the low yield from long term rural leases and then developed a new investment strategy of switching from residential and rural properties into more lucrative commercial property.

In the late seventies the prince became more closely involved in the running of the duchy. Its financial health had by now begun to improve as the new investment strategy bore fruit. By the time of Charles's marriage to Diana in 1981 its capital reserves were large enough to buy him Highgrove House for £865,000 and marriage gave him the extra benefit of a reduction in the voluntary income tax from 50% to 25% to take into account his additional costs of a larger household. By 1992 duchy revenues had climbed to £3.4m but when under a new tax regime announced in that year the Queen agreed to pay income tax, Charles was obliged to pay tax at 40% himself and since his free use of Highgrove could now be seen as a taxable benefit in kind, he agreed under the Memorandum of Understanding with the prime minister to pay rent on the property (by 2013 it had risen to £375,548). Although Charles had to pay rent at a market rate, it made little real difference to his net income as the rental money went straight into the duchy's revenue account. In effect, he was paying it back to himself.

In 1998 he undertook another circular transaction with the Duchy of Cornwall. In July he sold to the duchy timber for £2,300,000 which in an odd arrangement he had grown privately on duchy-owned land. Why was someone who was already in receipt of a yearly income of £7m so short of cash that he needed to sell a pile of wood? The stated explanation from the duchy was that the timber would by its nature require harvesting at some time and since he had to sell it to someone, why not use the duchy which was already building up a portfolio of forestry land. But another factor may well have been his recent divorce settlement. Although the Queen is widely reported to have paid for the bulk of the £17m settlement since Charles's wealth was not sufficiently liquid to finance it himself, it is not beyond the realms of possibility that some of the proceeds of the timber sale might have been used as repayment of the loan from his mother. Charles would already have had some private funds (to the value £2m in 1994 according to his biographer), but they would not have been enough to pay for the divorce settlement - whether directly or as a repayment of a loan to his mother. When questioned by a parliamentary committee in 2013 about the curious timber purchase, a duchy official said "it was a one-off" and "it certainly has not happened again."[11]

At the turn of the millennium the duchy was producing a surplus for Charles of £6.9m - a doubling in profits in ten years - but the big jump in profitability would come in the following decade or so when the surplus would almost treble. In 2000-01 the surplus was £7.5m but by 2010-11 it was £17.8m. In short,

Charles received an extra ten million pounds in ten years.

The remarkable financial growth can in part be explained by the property and stock market boom of the nineties and early 2000's. But skilful new management was no doubt also a key ingredient as the duchy's investment portfolio was further restructured into commercial properties (which today represents around 45% of all profits) and into financial products (which brings in around 5-10% of all profits, depending on whether you use gross or net figures). A number of successful rent reviews have also helped increase income from agricultural holdings. One of the most influential recent managers has been Sir Robert (Bertie) Ross, its Secretary and Keeper of the Records (effectively its chief executive) from 1997-2013 who brought with him a wealth of commercial experience from his twenty-five years as director and head of the agricultural division of the estate agents Savills. In 2014 he was rewarded for his successful financial stewardship of the duchy "an emolument" - as the annual report genteelly puts it – of £257,974 bringing his total remuneration (including bonuses) over the previous five years to over £1m.

But some responsibility for the transformation of the duchy's finances must go to the Prince of Wales himself. Unlike his mother who takes no part in the running of her duchy estate, Charles is an active player. Recent annual reports pay tribute to how he "is actively involved in running the duchy and his philosophy [is] to improve the estate and pass it onto future dukes in a stronger and better condition."[12] In the past he has appointed members to the non-executive board of the Prince's Council and chaired its twice yearly meetings.

Like all good chairman he also has a succession strategy up his sleeve. He is grooming his eldest son to take over. In much the same way as Prince William of Gloucester was taught how to run his family's farmlands at Barnwell, so another Prince William has been taught about the soil management, although in his case it was done not in the muddy fields of Northamptonshire but in the seminar rooms of St John's College, Cambridge University where a special course in agricultural administration was devised for him.

When it comes to determining investment decisions, Charles has been keen to promote one issue close to his heart - environmental building and sustainability. Nowhere is the footprint of the prince's green Wellies more visible than on the Poundbury estate in Dorset, in the heart of Thomas Hardy country, where the duchy has owned a large swathe of land since the 14th century. After a conventional plan for development was rejected by the prince in 1988, he turned to the free-thinking neo-classical designer Leon Krier to draw up a blueprint for an environmentally friendly model village on the outskirts of Dorchester. The result was an ambitious plan for four villages with three thousand homes for eight thousand people all working and playing together in self-contained communities complete with schools, shops and offices. Even Charles's biographer, Jonathan Dimbleby, acknowledged that the prince had sometimes shown "a certain insouciance" about the cost of the project and when it was properly costed at many tens of millions of pounds, few were left in any doubt that the project as it stood could bankrupt the duchy.[13] Something had to be done. In its place a scaled down version was put forward by another group of architects which prompted an angry Krier to take his story to the Sunday Telegraph where he threatened to resign complaining his role had been undermined and his master plan had been sabotaged. After a hasty exchange of clear-the-air letters, the prince persuaded him to stay on the project at least for the time being - and in 1993 phase one of the watered down development finally got under way.

Over the intervening two decades the project has encountered many other hazards along the route - most notably the major roadblock of planning permission delays. A member of Dorchester's Civic Society described it "a tasteless pastiche of what Dorchester once looked like...It is HRH's theme park."[14] Many local residents objected to living check by jowl with commercial properties. By 2014 Poundbury was celebrating its 21st birthday but there was still another eleven years of work ahead, including completing the Queen Mother Square and building five hundred new houses in the North East Quadrant. The latest duchy accounts for 2014 do not spell out how much has been spent on the project up to now and but in the course of two decades it must have eaten up a not inconsiderable slice of the duchy money.

Over the past decade successive parliamentary committees have questioned why the duchy accounts are not inspected by the National Audit Office. Duchy officials have always resisted such a move arguing that the duchy is the private estate of the Prince of Wales and thus falls outside of the purview of the NAO which monitors only public money. The difficulty with this line of argument is that while the *income* from the estate is generally accepted as private, the *capital* is not.[15] By tradition the Prince of Wales does not have access to the capital or the right to sell it because he is deemed custodian of the lands which must be retained for future Princes of Wales to live off.

The status of the duchy is further complicated by the way in recent years it has begun to appear to behave like a commercial business even though as a private estate it escapes any corporation tax or capital gains tax. In November 2011 the duchy reportedly paid £38,385,500 for a supermarket distribution centre in Milton Keynes[16] which it then leased to Waitrose for more than £2m a year.[17] It is the leaseholder of the Holiday Inn in Reading and reportedly owns several shops in the area, including a hair and beauty parlour.[18]

It has also set up two innovative joint ventures with private sector partners. It owns a 50% stake in QMS (Poundbury) LLP, a partnership with a developer to construct an office and retail building in Queen Mother Square in Poundbury. In addition, it possesses 54% of the shares in J.V. Energen LLP, a renewable energy enterprise with local farmers. After investing £6.6m in an anaerobic digestion plant, it made £1.5m in 2013 by selling renewal electricity to the grid.[19] By operating in this way the duchy's joint enterprise is bound to come into competition with other renewable companies and MPs have questioned whether its exemption from corporation tax gives it an unfair advantage. Not surprisingly Charles's principal private secretary rejected the charge. In 2013 the Public Accounts Committee recommended that "*the Treasury should examine the impact on the marketplace of the Duchy engaging in commercial transactions while exempt from tax.*"[20]

The duchy has also been using well its exemption from capital gains tax by selling agricultural land. Admittedly with the Treasury's permission, in 2012-13 it was able to sell two farms and make a gain of £4m tax free.[21] The duchy maintains that this is perfectly above board since the Prince of Wales is not entitled to benefit from the capital gains realised by the duchy which are all reinvested in the duchy for the benefit of future dukes.

"It is a medieval anomaly," is how the plain-speaking Labour MP Austin Mitchell dismissed such arguments when the Public Accounts Committee heard oral evidence from duchy officials in July 2013. The fine distinction they made between the duchy as a private estate and a commercial business was lost of him: "if something looks like a duck and quacks like a duck, it possibly is a duck…You are really dodging around, aren't you, because for tax purposes it is not a corporation, but for every other purpose it is a corporation?"[22]

The committee's probing threw up two other embarrassing issues: how well do the huge profits of the duchy correspond to the actual needs of the Prince of Wales and why there is a lack of clarity between the prince's spending on his public duties and his private life.[23]

Since 2007, the prince has published an annual review disclosing his income, expenditure and tax liability, although for reasons his officials could not fully explain VAT was lumped together with his income tax figure and in one section of the report his National Insurance contributions were included under "tax". In 2013–14, the Prince of Wales received an income of £19.5 million from the duchy, and £2.1 million income from public sources yet paid only £4.18 million in tax (at the rate of 45%). The reason for this discrepancy is that he was able to offset more than £10 million in expenses.

Much of these are indisputable public or official expenses (including the £9.9m cost of his public duties and charitable activities as well as the

£2.9m spent funding the official work of the Duke and Duchess of Cambridge and Prince Harry) but when it comes to the use of his private residence Highgrove House there is potentially a grey area - or rather a green one. Prince Charles is rightly proud of the gardens at Highgrove which are exquisitely maintained. His financial statement discloses that in 2014 £140,000 was spent on total gardening costs in addition to the salaries of 21.3 gardeners (indicating that the cost of maintaining the Highgrove gardens must be sizable – certainly of the order of one hundred thousand pounds and perhaps as high as a quarter of a million). The 2014 annual review states that the "official as well as personal costs [of maintaining the garden] are met from His Highness's private income" but acknowledges that "*the majority* of the costs of the garden is allocated to official expenditure" [author's italics]. In other words, the lion's share is a tax deductable expense. One of the stated justifications for this is that "the garden is mainly used for visits by members of the public," with visitor numbers reaching 38,000 in 2013. But in that year the garden was open only between April and October and confined mainly to organised groups, generally on weekdays and not Sundays or when Charles and Camilla were at home. So in practice, the public appeared to have equal or less possible access to the gardens than did the prince, even though the bulk of their costs were deemed official spending.

When this criticism was put to Clarence House, a spokesman replied that the prince and the duchess "spent a lot of time away from Highgrove, and therefore the amount of time Their Royal Highnesses have access to the gardens are in fact quite limited." He also maintained that the allocation of costs in relation to Highgrove "reflects the use of the garden and house for official engagements."[24]

Charles is indeed able to claim some of the costs of running the house itself as a business expense since he uses the Orchard Room for official engagements and entertaining ("it was used," according to the 2013-14 annual review, "for 15 receptions, seminars and briefings"). In one sense, he would appear to be doing no more than what any self-employed person with a large income would do in similar circumstances: maximising his business expenses to minimise his tax liability. But Highgrove illustrates the wider issue of how he decides the division of his spending between public and private matters - and indeed what his public duties should be. When his principal private secretary was pressed on this last point by the Public Accounts Committee, the response was suitably Delphic: "His business – if you like – is being Prince of Wales."[25]

In the end, it would be left to members on the floor of the House of Commons to attempt to get to grips with royal income and expenditure.

Chapter Eighteen
Sovereign Grant or Sovereign Greed?
– 2011-2013

"I missed all these wonderful contributions on the Queen's new allowance - her winter heating allowance, or whatever it is"
Dennis Skinner MP lamenting his absence from the debate on the Sovereign Grant bill

It was billed as the most radical shake up of the royal finances in two hundred and fifty years yet there was almost no mention of reforming the two royal duchies when the Chancellor of the Exchequer told parliament his detailed plans to replace the Civil List with the Sovereign Grant. The debate on the third reading took place on a hot July afternoon in 2011 and the chamber was thinly attended as demob-happy MPs prepared to depart for the summer recess. Only a few hours were allocated for the debate on a draft bill that had only recently been shown to MPs and

413

some older hands suspected that the government was once more trying to railroad through the Commons a potentially embarrassing royal bill. "We are rushing through today a fundamental change", objected the Labour backbencher Denis MacShane who, as it would later emerge in his conviction for fraud and false accounting, was not unaccustomed to financial *légerdemain*. "We are proposing in two hours, if that, to change what has been in place for more than two hundred years."[1]

As Chancellor of the Exchequer in David Cameron's deficit-cutting government, George Osborne might have been expected to wield the axe to the royal finances or at least demand the strictest of belt-tightening in palace expenditure. Earlier in his political career as a fresh-faced MP on the Public Accounts Committee he had gained a reputation for demanding value for money in all matters of public expenditure. But as the scion of an Anglo-Irish aristocratic family, he might have harboured some atavistic sympathy for another ancient family struggling with modern day costs.

Sweating slightly in the heat of the summer afternoon, the Chancellor dismissed backbencher objections about the lack of debating time and pressed ahead with introducing the bill. The reason for the need of a new Sovereign Grant, he explained, was that the old system was now unsustainable: "the system is broken and we need to fix it." It was inflexible in that funds allocated to one spending area could not be used for another. For example, money saved in travel could not be used for urgent repair work on the palaces. It was opaque in the sense that the National Audit Office was not allowed to audit the palace books. Limited scrutiny was undertaken by the Public Accounts Committee and the permanent secretary to the Treasury, but the arrangement was not very transparent. Crucially it had run out of money. The system relied on a reserve of public money that had been built up over twenty years and was now exhausted due to inflation and rising costs. In crude terms, the royal household was running on empty.

The new arrangement did away with the previous fragmented system whereby funding came from four separate sources: the Civil List from the Crown Estate profits to meet core head of state expenditure, a grant-in-aid from the Department of Transport to cover royal travel and two other grants from the Department for Culture, Media and Sport to pay for both the maintenance of the royal palaces and communication and information. In its place would be a single Sovereign Grant derived from the profits of the Crown Estate alone. It would be set at around £31m in its first year and thereafter it would be based on either the previous year's grant or 15% of the profits of the Crown Estate, whichever was the greater.

So, when it came to the size of income there would be a guaranteed floor but no ceiling. To prevent the Royal Household getting too much money in a good year for the Crown Estate, a reserve fund was to be set up with a cap. It would hold any surpluses over expenditure and if the reserve reached more than half of expenditure, then the extra amount would be transferred to fund existing expenditure with a matching reduction in the grant. As an additional check, there would be a review every five years by the Royal Trustees (the Prime Minister, the Chancellor of the Exchequer and the Keeper of the Privy Purse) to assess whether 15% was the right proportion of profits from the Crown Estate when calculating the grant. The other safeguard to insure that the palace was not overspending or abusing the system in any way was the audit of the royal household accounts by the National Audit Office.

The new arrangement met with remarkably little criticism from the official opposition. This might be in part because there were few votes to be won in knocking the royals at a time when the Queen's personal approval rating had never been higher. But it has now emerged that the genesis of the plan came under the previous administration. Well before the 2010 election, the Queen's Treasurer, Sir Alan Reid, discussed with the Labour Prime Minister, Gordon Brown, and the Chancellor of the Exchequer, Alastair Darling, his idea of simplifying the myriad of funding streams into a single source. Just as happened with Harold Wilson and the Civil List review in 1970, the Labour government preferred to wait until after the election to see which way the wind was blowing rather than make a decision immediately.[2]

The Shadow Chancellor Ed Balls - another Treasury old-hand who would have been expected to get heavy on any royal waste - generally supported his opposite number's proposals since they aimed "to strike a fair and workable balance between the legitimate needs of the household and the interests of the taxpayer." He thanked the Chancellor for agreeing to his amendment to reduce the frequency of the review process by the Royal Trustees from seven to five years but warned that the cash floor in the bill would mean in effect an end to the current process of efficiency savings and that the years ahead were likely to see a real term rise in palace expenditure.

What placated the Shadow Chancellor and backbench MPs was the concession by the palace to allow the National Audit Office (and by extension the Public Accounts Committee) to audit Royal Household expenditure - something that parliament had been demanding for many decades.

However, one veteran bruiser from the Public Accounts Committee was not so happy. Ian Davidson, the Labour MP for Glasgow South West, feared that the Sovereign Grant might be open to abuse in the same way as the Duchy of Cornwall: "Quite clearly, the Crown Estate could be leant on by the monarchy to make decisions on expenditure and income in the short term to affect the amount of grant that the royal family receive. The grant would then be on, as it were, a golden ratchet - a bit like EU expenditure, it would always go up, and never down."

He was also unconvinced with the Chancellor's arguments for linking the funding arrangement to the Crown Estate's profits rather than the Gross Domestic Product: "If GDP went down the Queen and the monarchy would suffer the same as the rest of us, and if it went up, they would benefit in line with the rest of us." As was pointed out later by Lord Turnbull, the former Treasury permanent secretary who was responsible for the previous funding arrangement and was not averse to much of the new arrangements, it was odd to use as a benchmark a property company whose revenue in the past two decades had increased by double the rate of inflation. If the true aim was to maintain the grant in roughly real terms, then it would have made more sense to link it to some index of inflation as happened with other public funding such as the BBC licence.

The other lone voice of opposition came from another Labour member of the awkward squad – Kevan Jones, MP for Durham North. Having served as a junior minister at the Ministry of Defence in Gordon Brown's government, he had inside knowledge of departmental profligacy and creative accountancy. His main concern was the way the reserve fund might be open to abuse:

"Will the Chancellor explain how the controls over the reserve will work? Who will take the decisions about how it is spent? It does not take a genius or a financial wizard to work out that, if we draw down the reserve, we can certainly keep up the annual income at 15%. Who will have a say over how the reserve is spent? Will the government of the day have any control over how it is spent?"

Putting his ministerial background to good use, he also asked some embarrassing questions about departmental cross-subsidising of the royal finances. The Ministry of Defence, he pointed out, provided vital military support to the Royal Household in terms of staff which comes out of their budget rather than the palace's. It had also been reported that under pressure from the Prince of Wales the MoD had increased their subsidy to the cost of the royal flight. He also revealed in an earlier debate on 30 June 2011 that the MoD rented certain properties from the Royal Household, including the Chief of the Defence Staff's apartments in Kensington Palace, which cost the MoD £108,000 a year:

"Unless we know the full amount of money that is being paid to the Royal Household by other Departments...how can we determine, first, that those efficiencies are real and this is not just about moving money across and, secondly, that 15% is the right level?"

It was predictably left to the Labour backbencher Dennis Skinner, who made his name in the house by lampooning among others the royal family, to introduce a note of levity into the proceedings. The seventy-nine-year-old Beast of Bolsover was in the Commons when the last major reform of the Civil List was debated:

"I remember well, way back in 1971, being joined by a lot of people in the House who were on the left wing at the time in voting against the Queen's money. Quite a number of them are now in the House of Lords—[Laughter]."

But what he could never have remembered – because it was unknown to all but a few who had access to the released Treasury documents - was that a remarkably similar scheme to the Sovereign Grant was dismissed in 1971. As we saw in Chapter Eight, the plan of John Boyd Carpenter to hand over all Crown Estate revenue to fund the Civil List was seriously considered by the government and palace. It was eventually rejected on the grounds that it would provide no incentive to the palace to economise and that because it gave the palace so much licence it might perversely lead to more work for the Treasury since it would be obliged to account to parliament how the money was spent.

So why was a scheme that was rejected in 1971 now acceptable in 2011? Could it be that the Chancellor was ignorant of the opposing arguments on account of the fact, as he mentioned in the debate, that he was only born in 1971? It should be admitted that the Boyd Carpenter plan was more far-reaching than the Sovereign Grant in that it proposed that *all* Crown Estate revenue as opposed to just 15% be handed over to the palace. But the effect might have been similar in so far as any surplus unused by the royals would revert to the Treasury.

It should also be remembered that the scheme was rejected by the palace as well. Even though the scheme was enormously attractive in terms of the size and independence of its income stream, palace officials were worried that if the hereditary income from the Crown Estates were thrown in the pot, then it would automatically lead to calls to include the lucrative revenues from the Duchies of Cornwall and Lancaster which were vital to the funding of the private lifestyle of the Queen and the Prince of Wales.

The most likely explanation why the scheme was acceptable to the government was that at a time of extreme cost cutting it got the departmental expenditure for grants-in-aid off the books – making an above the line saving of over £18m a year. By setting up a scheme that would be reviewed only every five years it avoided annual rows with parliament about "a pay rise for the Queen". The reason why the scheme was acceptable to parliament is that MPs were allowed for the first time to open up the palace books to ensure that public funds were being properly spent. The National Audit Office would perform their audit and the accounts would be laid before the house and scrutinised by the Public Accounts Committee.

But there was one significant exemption to the scrutiny from the National Audit Office. The Comptroller and Auditor General would not be allowed access to the accounts of the Duchies of Cornwall and Lancaster on the grounds that they were regarded as "private funds." This must have been greeted with a sigh of relief from the palace who had long defended the privacy of its two milk cows. The royal family would also have been pleased with the one important change to the rules over who receives the income from the Duchy of Cornwall which under the old system was paid to the male heir to the throne (the Duke of Cornwall). Under the new arrangement, the money would go to the sovereign's eldest child, regardless of gender, which would have had significance if the firstborn of the Duke and Duchess of Cambridge had been a girl.

In many people's eyes, the palace was the big winner in the Sovereign Grant reform. A government source admitted when the plan was first under review that "the royal family must have been getting the champagne out when we considered this."[3] There were whispers that some Lib-Dem members of the coalition government had reservations about the generous settlement.

The Financial Times was one of the few newspapers to scrutinise the new scheme in any depth. In a leader entitled "Casino Royale" it argued that the royal pay plan was "excessively discretionary" and bore a remarkable resemblance to the generous performance-related pay packages granted to business executives by their indulgent boards. The perverse incentives of the scheme were frightening: "When the Crown Estate does well, royals win; when it does not, taxpayers lose."[4]

Some saw the changes as a missed opportunity for a root and branch reform. Although it was billed as an historic change, it did not address some of the underlying problems of expenditure. "If there is to be a serious assessment of efficiency and economy and effectiveness [of the monarchy]" Margaret Hodge, the chair of the Public Accounts Committee, pointed out in an earlier debate, "one has to look at the *total* income and expenditure" [author's italics].[5]

When it came to hidden expenditure items, the elephant in the chamber was security. The Chancellor refused the opposition's request to give a clear figure for the costs of protecting the royal family arguing that the information might help terrorists, but some estimates put the figure as high as £100m a year with the Metropolitan Police's bill alone thought to be close to £30m. Such figures are never included when the palace claims that the royal family's annual cost is little more than £35m – or just 56p a year for each citizen – and come under the Home Office budget. Other hidden costs take the form of cross-subsidies by government departments. In one well-publicised instance the Ministry of Defence reportedly gave a generous deal to the royal family when after lobbying from Prince Charles it reduced the fees of some royal flights.[6] Under the new funding arrangement, it was agreed that the MoD would still pay for many palace equerries and orderlies.[7]

⚜ ⚜ ⚜

At the time of writing it is too early to say whether some of the backbench fears will prove justified, but some of the early signs are not encouraging. In the scheme's first year 2012-13 the palace overspent its £31m grant by £2.3m and had to make up the shortfall – as anticipated by Kevan Jones – by delving into the reserve fund, reducing it to the dangerously low level of £1m. The Royal Household could of course have simply drawn back on expenditure to live within its means but the palace thought it "not wise" to limit the activity of the monarchy in the Diamond Jubilee year.[8]

The new settlement was supposed to encourage greater efficiency savings. The Royal Household employs four hundred and thirty people, a headcount that has remained constant for six years and a labour cost that eats up almost two thirds of the budget. But despite a pay freeze for the general staff, in 2013 the palace still managed to reward three of its top five senior managers (all earning over £80,000 pa) with extra money. This was justified on the grounds of them taking on extra responsibilities but the Public Accounts Committee questioned whether this was unfair to the rest of the staff and sent the wrong signal at a time of a general squeeze on the public finances.[9]

In its second year, 2013-14, the grant rose by £3m to £36.1m and in 2014-15 it is expected to increase to £37.9m (a rise of more than 20% in just two years). The palace claims that half of this extra money will go on vital repair work on the crumbling royal palaces (Windsor Castle's leaking lead roof needs replacing and the antiquated boilers in Buckingham Palace have not been upgraded in sixty years) but those Jeremiahs in parliament who warned of "a golden ratchet" might be excused a wry smile.

The real test will come in 2016 with the first review by the Royal Trustees of the level of the Sovereign Grant. If the grant continues to rise at the same pace, will they be strong enough to kick up a fuss and demand a cap on spending? This might be political suicide if the royal family's popularity ratings were still very high or if it coincided with a mood of public sympathy after, say, a royal death. In such circumstances it might be easier to let sleeping corgis lie.

To its critics, the key weakness of the new settlement is the absence of any clear connection between the level of funding and the actual requirements of the palace. Just as the revenues from the Duchies of Lancaster and Cornwall are in no way directly linked to the needs of the Queen and the Prince of Wales, so the revenues of the Crown Estate seem to be divorced from the requirements of the Royal Household. To some, this amounts to an invitation to inefficiency. Why try to make economies when your income is on a golden escalator going up every year as the profits of the Crown Estate rise?

Chapter Nineteen
The Duke's Farewell – 2014

"It wasn't my ambition to be president of the Mint Advisory Committee. I didn't want to be president of the WWF. I was asked to do it. I'd much rather stayed in the Navy, frankly."
Prince Philip on having to give up his naval career[1]

It was typical of the man that he should want a simple, unostentatious ceremony. Around 2013 Prince Philip reportedly told palace officials that there was no need to go to all the "fuss" of a lying-in-state ahead of a full state funeral.[2] There should be no gun carriage or grand procession through the streets of Westminster. His preference was for a private service at St George's Chapel, Windsor before being interred in the mausoleum of Frogmore House.

At first sight this seemed at odds with all the elaborate procedures drawn up by the Lord Chamberlain, the Earl Marshal and other palace planners. If there is one aspect of succession planning that is never left to chance then it is royal funerals. They are all given codenames associated with famous bridges – the Duke of Edinburgh's is Forth Bridge, the Queen Mother's Tay Bridge and the Queen's London Bridge. Linked to each name is a D number, D+9 down to D+1 indicating the number of days between the death and the funeral and giving precise details of the procedures of the lying-in-state and the public processions. The start date and length of mourning would also be specified along with which public buildings would fly the union flag at half mast. The details are normally confirmed with the royal concerned, although in the case of Diana's funeral there was little preparation due to the suddenness of the death and the fact that it occurred on foreign soil. Lessons were learnt and there are now detailed plans for having an aircraft on standby to repatriate the body of the sovereign or senior royal who dies overseas.

In the end Prince Philip's arrangements were left "under review" with the most likely scenario being that prior to the funeral his body would be laid in state not at the customary Westminster Hall where in 2002 two hundred thousand mourners filed past the Queen Mother's coffin but at the more discreet St. James's Palace where Diana, Princess of Wales had laid for several days after her death in 1997. Hers was not a state funeral.

Some palace watchers believed that the longest serving royal consort in history merited a better send-off. "The British public will expect him to have a state funeral and will be disappointed if the commemoration of his life and death happens behind closed doors," observed his biographical chronicler Philip Dampier. "Many people regard him as the glue that keeps the royal family together."[3]

There was no denying that after six decades of dutifully standing two feet behind the Queen, Prince Philip, Duke of Edinburgh, Earl of Merioneth, Baron Greenwich, Member of the Order of Merit, had done well for himself. He first arrived in this country as an eighteen-month-old baby with the help of a Royal Navy frigate and fruit crate as a crib after a military coup had overthrown his uncle King Constantine I and the Greek royal family had been forced into exile. Most of their wealth was left behind in Greece. "Stateless, nameless and not far from penniless" was how one royal biographer summed up his status.[4] But in the ninth decade of his life, another royal commentator estimated his wealth at £28 million.[5]

It was a remarkable turn-around in fortunes. But what does Prince Philip's change in circumstances tell us about the House of Windsor's capacity to generate wealth? Can it really turn paupers into millionaires? And if Philip is as rich as is claimed what form does his wealth take? Can he really, as some say, have accumulated millions of pounds in gifts?

By royal standards, his childhood was poor but hardly impoverished. He told one biographer that he was not exactly well off but did not recall ever wanting for anything.[6] His father Prince Andrea of Greece decided to settle just outside of Paris at St Cloud where his aunt, Marie Bonaparte, owned a large estate. An interesting feature of his upbringing was how a succession of rich aunts – none of them blood relatives and all heiresses – came to his financial rescue. Marie Bonaparte, the granddaughter of the founder of the Monte Carlo casino, put the family up in one of her lodges. The wealth of aunt Nancy, the widower of the tin-plate magnate William B. Leeds who remarried Prince Christopher, the younger brother of Philip's father, paid for the fees at his progressive American school in St Cloud.

But by far the richest aunt was Edwina, wife of Lord Mountbatten, his mother's brother, who had inherited the banking fortune from her German-born grandfather, Sir Ernest Cassel. In 1924 she generously took out a life insurance policy for her nephew and allowed him to use their luxurious Park Lane mansion when he passed through London on his peregrinations between his boarding schools, guardians and absentee parents. He was also allowed to enjoy the facilities of her country retreat Adsdean in Hampshire which boasted a golf course, three tennis courts, a shooting range and a polo practice ground.[7] As we saw earlier, Philip was just following a well trodden family path, becoming the third generation of Windsors to benefit from the Cassel coffers.

While one German provided a taste of wealth another supplied a check on extravagance. Kurt Hahn, the Berlin-born educationalist, was probably the most important influence on the young Philip's attitude not just to expenditure but life in general (the prince later described him as a great if eccentric man).[8] The Jewish intellectual believed that society was suffering a malaise caused by a decay of fitness, self-discipline and initiative and when Nazi persecution forced him to flee his school at Salem on Lake Constance, he set up on the windy Moray Firth in Scotland a new spartan academy called Gordonstoun designed to drum into the pupils the virtues of hard work, thrift and self-reliance. After five years of bracing cold showers, early morning runs, sailing in the foulest of weathers and all manner of discomforting, character-forming outdoor pursuits, Philip ended up as head boy.[9]

Philip was soon left to his own devices when his parents separated and he was shuttled amongst relatives. From the age of eleven to twenty-six when he got married, he had no permanent address (he famously wrote on the Mountbattens' visitor's book "No fixed abode!")[10] In December 1944 his father died of a heart attack at the age of sixty-two. At the time the prince was serving on a Royal Navy destroyer in the Indian Ocean and there was no possibility of attending the funeral in the South of France. Although he was left seven tenths of the estate in the will, the inheritance proved meagre. It turned out that Prince Andrea had debts of more than £17,500, the result of living beyond his means in Monte Carlo with his long-term mistress Comtesse Andrée de la Bigne, granddaughter of the *chère amie* of Napoleon III, who according to some accounts frittered away much of his money.[11]

Royal Legacy

When after the war Philip managed to arrive in Monaco to pick up his personal effects, he got on surprisingly well with the elegantly-attired "Comtesse" who turned out to be a former actress. But all that was left of the chattels were some moth-eaten suits, a pair of monogrammed hairbrushes, an ivory-handled shaving brush, a small collection of books and a few paintings. The only item of real value was a gold signet ring which he wore for the rest of his life. There was also the bejewelled Star of the Order of the Redeemer which he planned to wear at his wedding until he discovered that his father had substituted the real diamonds for paste ones.[12]

When his engagement to Princess Elizabeth was announced in July 1947, a few court gossips wondered in an echo of the cynicism surrounding Prince Albert's nuptials whether Prince Philip might be a fortune hunter. As a first lieutenant in the Royal Navy on a salary of less than £350 a year, he was certainly not flush with cash. He travelled third class by train and often wore the most threadbare of clothes. According to the Mountbattens' butler who looked after the young prince when he stayed at their Chester Street townhouse, his wardrobe was "scantier than that of many a bank clerk."[13] He often turned up with nothing more than a razor and during the night his makeshift valet would have to darn his socks and wash and iron his one shirt.

As a counter to any spurious gold-digging charge, it should be pointed out that the marriage was clearly a love match and Prince Philip was later reluctant to accept a Civil List allowance from the state and had to be talked into it by his uncle Louis Mountbatten. After considerable horse-trading with Attlee's Labour government it was agreed that he should have an annual allowance of £10,000. After the coronation he had new duties as consort to the Queen and had to give up his naval career (and salary). He would later admit that his one big regret in life was having to leave the navy.[14]

Up until the coronation he had shown great promise – becoming one of the youngest first lieutenants in the Royal Navy at just twenty-one and taking command of his first ship HMS Magpie before he was thirty – and some thought he might have emulated his uncle and gone to the very top. "Prince Philip was a very talented seaman," commented Lord Lewin. "If he hadn't become what he did he would have been First Lord Sea Lord and not me."[15] For his part, Philip took a less sanguine view of his chances of advancement, suggesting to one interviewer that the British media would have viewed every promotion as a case of special treatment.[16]

In setting his Civil List annuity, the government had to take into account compensation for his potential loss of earnings. When the head of the Royal Household, Lord Cobbold, was questioned on this point by a parliamentary select committee in 1971, he referred to "the high salary which he would undoubtedly command in the outside world" and admitted that "the real remuneration amounted to £15,000-£20,000" (£180,000-£250,000 at today's prices).[17] He also let slip that some of the allowance was "to build up savings for the future", a surprising admission given that when the annuity was first established it was generally considered to cover only his official expenses and not to be set aside for his retirement or purposes of capital accumulation. Since 1992 his personal allowance has been £359,000 a year.

So – apart from his expenditure on official duties - how does Prince Philip actually spend his money? As a bachelor he famously owned a stylish black MG sports car but once he joined the royal family he preferred to drive a Land or Range Rover in the country and a converted London taxi in town – far less conspicuous than the flashy green Aston-Martin of his son, Charles. When it came to food and wine, he also had relatively modest tastes. Breakfast amounted to little more than a cup of coffee and toast, other meals were hardly lavish or overflowing with alcohol. Even in the navy he had never been much of a drinker. He did not smoke either, having on Princess Elizabeth's insistence given up the habit on marriage (one of the recurring threads of this history of inheritance is the number of royals who would die of smoking-related illnesses and the duke's longevity must owe a lot to his healthy lifestyle). Like his young wife, he developed a passion for horse-related sports. Encouraged by Louis Mountbatten, he took up polo and then later competitive carriage-racing for which he won a number of international trophies.[18] The cost of maintaining a stable of horses reportedly set him back £15,000 a year.[19]

Prince Philip would have been acutely aware of such high maintenance charges as he was responsible for managing the estates of Balmoral and Sandringham, both a big drain on resources. His only comment on the cost of this lifestyle came in November 1969 at the height of a crisis in royal funding when he was interviewed on the NBC programme "Meet the Press":

> "We go into the red next year...now inevitably if nothing happens, we shall either have to – I don't know, we may have to move into smaller premises, who knows? We've closed down, well for instance, we had a small yacht which we've had to sell and I shall probably have to give up polo fairly soon, things like that."

Although the remarks were delivered slightly tongue in cheek, they did highlight his other great sporting passion – yachting. He loved to sail – whether a small dinghy or a full-size ship. Up until its decommissioning in December 1997 he had always been a fervent defender of the royal yacht *Britannia* which he had helped design. In October 1956 he had taken it on a well-publicised sixteen-week tour of Commonwealth countries. At the time no one seemed concerned about the cost of such a marathon voyage which took him everywhere from the Seychelles to the Falkland Islands. When the yacht reached Australia for the opening of the Melbourne Olympics, he invited the painter Edward Seago to accompany him on the return voyage via Antarctica and the South Atlantic. It proved a fruitful partnership. Seago who had previously painted portraits of George VI and Queen Elizabeth now gave their son-in-law a lesson in brushwork, inspiring him to go on to become a skilled amateur landscapist. For his part, Seago produced sixty oil paintings on the expedition and, according to his biographer, gave them all to his host[20] (he had also regularly gifted the Queen Mother a couple of paintings a year).

The Norfolk artist's generosity illustrates how casual, unsolicited gift-giving can be turned into royal assets. Today, Seago's work regularly sell for £40,000-60,000 a canvas and a complete collection of Antarctic paintings with the added value of its royal cachet might easily bring in one hundred thousand pounds. Since it is so much at variance with his bluff public image, Philip's passion for art – including his private (and highly valuable) collection of paintings - has never received much attention. It is estimated that he owns over two thousand pieces of art among which were thought to be one hundred and fifty contemporary Scottish paintings.[21] His interest in Scottish art began soon after the coronation when to brighten up some of the dowdy walls of Holyroodhouse he began attending the Royal Scottish Academy's summer exhibition and buying eight or nine pieces a year.[22] The Edinburgh palace was soon transformed and its upstairs rooms are today home to over a hundred of his paintings.

Australian art also features prominently in his collection. On his Commonwealth tours he was able to pick up for a song a number of aboriginal works by Albert Namatjira as well as now valuable paintings by William Dobell and Sidney Nolan. Elsewhere, he also bought a Paul Nash – Cloud Flora Number One – worth in the region of £40-50,000. In pride of place in his first floor study on the north side of Buckingham Palace hang two other valuable paintings. A pair of handsome portraits of his parents - Princess Alice and Prince Andrea - painted in 1907 and 1913 when they were not yet out of their twenties by the Hungarian artist Philip de Laszlo. It is hard to value them precisely but a good Laszlo today fetches £90,000.

The study also contains an extensive library of thirteen thousand books which spill over into a second room. His tastes are eclectic – ranging from cookery to carriage driving, Shakespeare studies to Bob Dylan although there are relatively few works of fiction. The two biggest collections relate to wildlife – nine hundred books on birds and one thousand and two hundred titles on fish and animals.[23] Specialist book collections can fetch large fees at auction and as we noted earlier more than £200,000 was realised from the sale of the field sports books of Philip's uncle-in-law, Prince Henry, the Duke of Gloucester.

The combined book and art collection of the Duke of Edinburgh (along with his fine collection of original political and royal cartoons) must be worth several million pounds and when you add on his own personal possessions and gifts as well as some income from savings that might push the figure for his total wealth to something approaching £10 million, but to go as high as £28 million (as the Mail on Sunday's Royal Rich Report did in the original estimate without giving a precise breakdown of the assets) seems more than a little excessive.

The one category of wealth that might bump up the size of his estate would be the inclusion of wedding gifts. Their total worth could be as high as £50 million. But as we saw with Princess Margaret's probate sale it is not always clear where you draw the line between a public and a private gift – or indeed whether they are the property of the bride rather than the bride groom. At the time of writing, the grandly-titled Inventory Controller in the Gifts and Inventory Department at Clarence House had been unable to clarify the matter.

As someone well into his nineties and in declining health, the duke would undoubtedly have undertaken some detailed estate planning and been advised how to pass on his wealth to his family in the most tax efficient manner. If he pre-deceased the Queen, he could give her everything tax-free under the general spouse-spouse tax exemption. But if he survived the Queen, he could give everything tax-free to Charles, the new king, under the consort-sovereign tax exemption used so deftly by the Queen Mother.

Chapter Twenty
A Nation Mourns – 2022

"Its mystery is its life. We must not let in daylight upon magic"
Walter Bagehot on the undying appeal of the monarchy

This time, the BBC newsreader wore a black tie. After the media storm that erupted in March 2002 when Peter Sissons announced the Queen Mother's death wearing the wrong colour neckwear, Hugh Edwards was appropriately attired in April 2022 when he interrupted BBC 1's early evening programmes with a news flash.

"Within the last half hour we have received this statement from Buckingham Palace," intoned the veteran news anchor in a voice heavy with history.

"The Prince of Wales with the greatest sadness has asked for the following announcement to be made immediately: 'His beloved mother, Her Majesty Queen Elizabeth, died peacefully in her sleep this afternoon at Sandringham Palace. The Prince of Wales, the Duke of York, the Duke of Wessex and the Princess Royal were at her side.'"

After a long pause from the newsreader, the first bars of the national anthem rang out and the picture cut to a close up of the royal standard, the Queen's flag. All the BBC channels came together with the rolling news channel BBC News 24 and any comedy or light-entertainment programmes were suspended for the time being. Then, Hugh Edwards handed over to the BBC's royal correspondent, Nicholas Witchell for more detailed reports. The pre-recorded obituary material was played which had been kept in a locked box for more than a decade.

The drill had been laid out well before the death of the Queen Mother in 2002. It was similar to the formula that applied to announcing the death of all senior members of the royal family – or what in BBC jargon are called "Category A" royals. Even if the BBC newsroom received prior knowledge of a high profile royal death, that information would be embargoed until Buckingham Palace made a formal announcement. It was set in stone like the flint in the blocks of Windsor Castle.

If the BBC is ready for the Queen's sad demise then you can be sure that the palace is doubly prepared. There is reportedly a set of documents under lock and key in a special desk at Clarence House spelling out different scenarios for the death of the sovereign and the succession of the Prince of Wales.[1] What is common to them all is that the funeral (organized by the Duke of Norfolk, the hereditary Earl

Marshal, and employing the undertakers Leverton and Sons) would take place twelve days after the death. The best case scenario involving a smooth succession is one similar to that outlined above. In a mirror image to her father's death in 1952, the Queen dies suddenly at Sandringham. The nation's heart goes out to a family in grief and amidst a mood of widespread grief Prince Charles becomes a sympathetic figure and succeeds to the throne without a word of protest. All doubts about him not being up to the task – as whispered by many after the divorce from Diana - are quietly forgotten. He would already have received on-the-job training for the role after "the gradual glide" of the handover process whereby he had shared official duties with his mother. Their joint appearance on Sword Beach for the D-Day commemorations was the most visible illustration of this royal apprenticeship. At last, they were changing the guard at Buckingham Palace

The worst case scenario envisages a slow, lingering death and the alarming prospect of having to appoint a prince regent. "The Queen becomes ill and frail," explained one palace advisor in 2010. "The longer she lives, the more frustrated Charles becomes, the grumpier he gets, doing his 'Nobody's ever going to love me the way they did my Mama act.' The grumpier he gets, the more the public and the newspapers campaign for him to pass the mantle to William."[2]

The option of skipping a generation – once popular with some media commentators and critics of Charles – now appears redundant, overtaken by the fact that the handover process is up and running. There would be little logic in going to all the trouble of giving Charles on the job training and getting the public accustomed to seeing him as their head of state only for him to hand over the baton of sovereign to his son the moment the Queen passes away.

A more likely scenario to skipping a generation would be for Charles to be crowned king and then share some of his duties with his eldest son, just as his mother now shares her workload with him. Given that Charles is not as popular with some Commonwealth leaders as the Queen on account of their unease about his divorce and marriage to his mistress, there has occasionally been speculation that Prince William who made such a good impression on his tours of Canada in July 2011 and Australia and New Zealand in April 2014 might play the role of deputy head of the Commonwealth. In crude terms, the handsome young son could do some of the PR work that his elderly father is less good at, becoming the poster boy for New Windsor.

Under this scenario of Charles subletting some royal responsibilities, it was envisaged by one commentator in 2010 that he might also hand over Highgrove House to his son and use Sandringham (or possibly Balmoral) as his main country retreat.[3] The fate of the private residences is one of the thorniest issues raised by the succession process - as George VI found to his cost in 1936 when he had to buy out Edward VIII's title to the properties. It is widely believed that on her death the Queen will leave Balmoral and Sandringham to Prince Charles. If she left them to anyone other than her eldest son - for instance, Prince Andrew, Prince Edward or Princess Anne - they would be subject to inheritance tax at 40% like any other private bequest. Since their combined market value might be close to £100 million, any royal beneficiary would be left a crippling tax liability - and one so massive that they might have to consider selling parts of the property to pay the bill - as happened to some extent to the beneficiaries of the estates of the Duke of Gloucester and Princess Margaret (although in their cases they sold chattels, rather than land).

But if Prince Charles inherited Balmoral and Sandringham he would not have to pay a penny in tax. Under the controversial tax exemption deal agreed by John Major in 1992, any private transfers from sovereign to sovereign are tax free. The one possible road block to this smooth transfer was the general understanding that the exemption should not be used as a blanket tax waiver. But the palace could probably argue that Balmoral and Sandringham are part of the national heritage. Balmoral is more than a private residence as the Queen spends August and September there carrying out official constitutional duties and for several months of the year when Her Majesty is not in residence the castle ballroom, the gardens and the grounds are open to visitors. A similar policy of public access now operates in the grounds of Sandringham House.

No doubt Her Majesty would have received top-notch estate planning advice from the phalanx of financial consultants at her lawyers Farrers, or indeed from other experts in the field. It is easy to imagine the arguments they would rehearse to persuade her to leave the two private residences to Charles rather than her other two sons and daughter. "With respect, Ma'am, it's not a question of mitigating tax but of preserving part of one's national heritage. Would Her Majesty really want a situation where Prince Andrew is forced to sell his share of Balmoral to some overseas property developer – say, Donald Trump - who might turn the golf course and grounds into a luxury leisure centre for American multi-millionaires? How the new owners might promote the resort hardly bears contemplating – 'Live like a king and play like a prince at beautiful Balmoral.' God forbid."

It is no coincidence that the transfer of Balmoral and Sandringham from one sovereign to the next features so prominently in this story. The two royal residences dominate the royal finances because they are at one at the same time a valuable asset and a chronic liability. On the credit side of the ledger, they have since the mid nineteenth century when Queen Victoria and the future Edward VII first acquired them represented for the sovereign not only a place of private refuge but also a key private source of capital - and one that must be protected at all costs.

To avoid the fate of their aristocratic cousins whose landed estates have been decimated by death duties, the Windsors have fought to prevent their lands from being salami-sliced by the taxman. This is why the 1992 agreement on the tax exemption on sovereign to sovereign transfers was of such historic importance to them. It protected the royal estates from that most unwelcome of outcomes - a probate sale.

But on the debit side the two royal estates have eaten up vast amounts of money. Expenditure on Balmoral is running at over £3m a year and Sandringham haemorrhages money too with the constant pressure to update its old facilities. No wonder that the money-pinching Edward VIII wanted to sell off the Norfolk estate as soon as he became king. Without the bounty from the Duchy of Lancaster profits, it is difficult to see how the Queen could afford to run two exceedingly expensive country seats. So if one of the key questions that this book has sought to answer is how do the senior royals spend their money, then part of the response must lie in paying the overheads of their country houses. They are a luxury that only the mega rich - or those in receipt of generous tax and hereditary privileges - could afford. The more junior royals without any special tax benefits - notably, the Duke of Gloucester, the Duke of Kent and Prince Michael of Kent - have all had to transfer or dispose of their country houses and live within their means like their beleaguered aristocratic cousins.

It is likely that with the blanket benefit of the inheritance tax waiver the Queen would leave Charles more than just Balmoral and Sandringham. It is worth remembering that when the Queen Mother enjoyed the same exemption, she left her daughter practically her entire estate – including her valuable collection of twentieth century art and her jewellery box. So, one would expect Charles to receive at least some of her mother's fabulous jewels – including perhaps the emeralds that passed from Prince Francis to Lady Kilmorey to Queen Mary to the Queen to Diana and most probably back to the Queen. But if for any reason she doubted whether such private property qualified as items of national heritage, then provided she did it seven years before her death she could under the lifetime transfer rules gift the jewellery to her son (or any other family member) tax free. This is what Queen Mary may well have done after the war and over the years it has no doubt become as useful a vehicle of transferring royal wealth as the trust fund.

But even if death duties are successfully mitigated, family wealth may be decimated by another ancient enemy - marrying out. This was the unvoiced fear of the royal family when the Duke of Windsor married a double divorcée: if the marriage failed or the duke died, the duchess could run off with some of the family heirlooms. A similar concern applied to Princess Diana at the time of her divorce and why the settlement required her to hand back some of the family jewels. With the Windsors' long track record of keeping it all in the family, it is hardly surprising that one royal commentator suggested that the Queen's motto might read "To Have and To Hold."[4]

For similar reasons, the royal family must have been delighted when the Cameron government excluded the hereditary estates of the Duchies of Lancaster and Cornwall from the new funding settlement. But some critics saw this as a missed opportunity for a true root and branch reform of the royal finances. Since the stated aim of the changes was to simplify the fragmented sources of funding under a single arrangement, then it might have made sense to include the revenues from the two duchies in the same pot. This is what many backbench MPs have fought for since the Select Committee Report on the Civil List in 1971 and the issue was again raised in 2005 with the Public Accounts Committee inquiry into the two duchies. But, as we saw in previous chapters, the duchies are regarded by the palace (and some suspect a few sections of the Treasury too) as a no-go area. They are as tightly ring-fenced as the hi-tech security now surrounding Buckingham Palace.

It is worthwhile considering what a more comprehensive reform of the royal finances might look like in practice. If consolidating all revenue streams into a single pot was the overriding principle, then it would also have made sense to include (and perhaps maximise) the revenue from the Royal Collection. With its one million artefacts including seven thousand paintings and five hundred thousand engravings squirreled away in a variety of palaces (and their basements), this has long been an unexploited seam of income for the Royal Household. An obvious solution to the lack of palace space might be to turn one major residence, say Buckingham Palace, into a permanent museum displaying the royal treasures in much the same way as the Louvre was originally set up. At present "BP" has only limited opening to the public in the summer when the Queen is in Balmoral, a missed commercial opportunity that was recently criticised by the Public Accounts Committee. Given its prime, central London location, if open all year round it would certainly prove a big money-spinner with tourists who could be charged Louvre-style prices to enjoy the Royal Collection. That revenue could be used to pay for the upkeep of the palaces and other Royal Household expenditure. Privately, the royal family might well welcome vacating a property which according to one recent resident was like "living in the middle of a traffic roundabout" and which was openly detested by Princess Diana and Edward VIII.[5] Even George VI was in no hurry to move in after the abdication and neither was the Duke of Edinburgh after the coronation.

Reform of the Royal Collection could extend to producing a comprehensive catalogue of its treasures and a comprehensive on-line inventory available to the public. The difficulty of tracing the Queen Mother's bequest of a Monet painting which at first appeared to belong to the Royal Collection but turned out to be the private property of the Queen highlighted the problem of ambivalent ownership, raising the old suspicion that Royal Collection items have been mixed with private ones. A comprehensive inventory would establish once and for all who owns what and whether it is on public display or not.

In a similar spirit of transparency, the royal family could publish an inventory of their private jewellery collection to determine which items are private property and which are held in trust for the nation. This could allay the suspicion that in the distant past some jewels – particularly those received as gifts – have been flipped from one category to another. It is known that both Queen Victoria and Queen Mary made detailed inventories of crown and non-private jewels but very few people have been able to see these documents. The two jewellery experts who were granted limited access to the Royal Collection (Suzy Menkes and Leslie Field) were both left in the dark as to where to draw the line between public and private property.[6]

As part of this process of transparency, the palace might publish any guidelines they may have relating to the status of wedding gifts. In the wake of the Burrell trial and the subsequent Peat Report, a set of general guidelines on gifts was made widely available in March 2003, but it does not go into any detail about the thorny issue of wedding presents which - as we have seen - may prove extremely lucrative for bride and groom when the total number of gifts are valued in aggregate. Princess Margaret's children got their fingers burnt when they sold off what some thought "public" wedding gifts and it is noticeable that when Prince William got married, he requested that those wishing to give him and Kate a wedding present should make a donation to charity instead.

In a further step towards transparency, there could be a greater clarity in the rules governing the sealing of royal wills. Although the will of the sovereign is kept secret by statute, the rules governing the publication of the wills of other royals are simply based on a legal precedent set by Prince Francis in 1910. But as we saw with the case of the Duchess of Gloucester in reality the practice of sealing royal wills is totally arbitrary and may depend ultimately on the personal whim of the executor. If you have an open-minded royal like the current Duke of Gloucester you have an open will. This means that any member of the public can now inspect the will of the one-hundred-and-two-year-old Duchess of Gloucester - although they are not permitted to view the will of the one-hundred-and-one-year-old Queen Mother. By the same token, anyone can inspect the will of Princess Helena Victoria - although not the will of her sister Princess Marie Louise. Similarly, anyone can inspect the will of Prince Louis of Milford Haven but not the will of his son Prince Louis of Burma. And as for Princess Diana, the most famous deceased royal of them all - who lost her royal title and was then offered it back after her death - everyone in the world can view her will on the internet. The working group reviewing this anomaly as part of a wider revision of probate rules was expected by some optimists to publish its conclusions in the early 2010s but at the time of writing, all that has appeared is a set of draft rules which have been sent to the Ministry of Justice.

Some MPs and at least one QC suspect that sealed wills are used to disguise the extent of royal wealth. Norman Baker MP as a backbencher often advanced this charge, arguing that if the parliament knew the scale of the wealth of the Windsors, it would be reluctant to grant them a generous financial settlement. As it turns out, parliament *has* recently granted them a generous settlement and now that they have to some degree safeguarded the publicly-controlled side of their income and wealth, one would hope that there is less reason for them to be so secretive about their testamentary affairs.

It was clear from the trials and tribulations surrounding the Duke of Gloucester's estate that one of the most sensitive aspects of the succession process is the transfer of landed property. A root and branch reform of the royal finances might clarify this. If under the new regime, the future sovereign were asked to vacate Buckingham Palace for the Royal Collection, then this could set in motion a long-overdue chain reaction in property transactions. Charles could then move to, for instance, Windsor Castle and use Highgrove or Sandringham as his private country residence. But a comprehensive reform of the royal finances might also encompass bringing Sandringham and Balmoral under some degree of public control. If the royal family claim that they cannot afford to keep the two private residences (which are also used for official duties) without a tax exemption from the public purse, then would it not be simpler to give the properties to the National Trust or some other public body? This is what customarily happens to other great landed families when they lack the means to pay death duties and this is indeed what Edward VII was obliged to do when he agreed to give Osborne House, the private residence of Queen Victoria, to the nation. If Charles or William wanted to continue to use Balmoral, there is no reason why they could not retain a smaller house like Birkhall on the estate or simply rent the property as Charles has done with the Queen Mother's Castle of Mey, which incidentally is another royal residence that was transferred out of private ownership.

This property down-sizing might signal an important step towards a leaner, slimmed-down monarchy. If there are too many royal palaces, then the same could be said of the royals themselves. Many now question why such a large and costly royal family is necessary when the hereditary principle in its crudest form requires no more than "an heir and a spare" – or perhaps for safety's sake, a few more extras. An accusing finger has sometimes been pointed at the current sixth in line of succession, Princess Beatrice, who was accorded extremely expensive security when she went on a beach holiday to Thailand. As we have seen, some estimates of the cost of protecting all members of the royal family run as high as £100m a year – more than three times the official cost of the Royal Household. Considerable savings to the security bill could be made by having a smaller royal family along Scandinavian lines. This could well work to the financial advantage of many junior royals like the Kents and Gloucesters whose elevated status as HRHs limits their range of paid employment. In practice, the closer one gets to the throne, the harder it is to do commercial work. When Prince William left his job as a RAF rescue helicopter pilot, there was little question of him pursuing a professional career elsewhere and he was obliged to go back to college for a management course in preparation for running the Duchy of Cornwall's landed estate. Some wondered at the time whether he would have been better off remaining in the armed services where at least he had a well-defined job to do. Indeed, in August 2014 it was announced that he had decided to join the East Anglian Air Ambulance as a pilot.

When Prince Edward ventured into the television business through his company Ardent Productions, he was pilloried in the press for exploiting his family name and only making films about the Windsors. In the end his firm floundered. Prince Michael of Kent has encountered similar publicity problems with his company Cantium Services. Prince Richard had to give up a promising architectural career when he became Duke of Gloucester and now faces public censure when he tries to run his country estate in a commercial manner. His mother may have had a point when she wrote that you had to choose between leading a royal life and pursuing a professional career.

Having a leaner monarchy might also require the media to cut junior royals more slack and allow them to fail at business without intrusive scrutiny – or indeed to succeed. Who knows the new House of Windsor might even add to their wealth through old-fashioned private enterprise rather than tax privileges from the state.

⚜   ⚜   ⚜

Fewer royals, fewer palaces, fewer tax privileges and greater transparency over wealth, wills and gifts - how likely is it that any future sovereign would agree to such a radical break with the past?

For all his image as an old fogey, some palace insiders maintain that Charles as king would willingly embrace change. After all, he has spent much of his time as Prince of Wales being a fountain of ideas, chairing debates on environmental issues and bombarding government ministers with letters on new policy directions. According to this school of thought, once on the throne he would want to move with the times and if that meant reform beyond the existing Sovereign Grant, then he might be willing to negotiate a long term financial settlement.[7]

A move from Buckingham Palace to Windsor Castle has in the past been seriously considered. However, given Charles' sentimental attachment to Balmoral, it is difficult to imagine him agreeing to dispose of his mother's Highland estate so that for twelve months of the year it would be trampled over by tourists. The same might be true of Sandringham on which, some say, he would love to stamp his own personality with a major refit. Even if his desire to move with the times is sincere, it might be difficult for a sovereign in his seventies to change a habit of a lifetime and live less lavishly.

Realistically one might have to wait a generation for a genuine new broom. Providing he is also not too old when he succeeds to the throne, William would be more likely to downsize the royal household than his father. Already the signs are encouraging – his wedding gifts were donated to charity, his first married home was an unostentatious residence in Anglesey and the size of his household staff in his new flat at Kensington Palace has been kept relatively modest, even though the cost of the palace refurbishment has far exceeded the estimated budget and brought some rare criticism. When he went to Canada on his first foreign trip as a married man and then to Australia on his first overseas visit as a father, his entourage was considerably smaller than is customary on such tours. As the son of Princess Diana, he knows only too well what happens when the media circus gets too large and the royals lose control of the reins. After her death he saw how her executors had to rewrite her will to protect her intellectual property rights after an explosion of merchandise bearing her famous face and now he, Kate and Harry have wisely set up their own companies to safeguard their brand name.

The death of Diana also showed how quickly the public mood can change. In the space of a few days the popularity of the royal family plummeted as a hitherto revered monarch was suddenly perceived as cold and uncaring. So, even if today the Queen enjoys very high approval ratings and her subjects seem unperturbed by the special treatment granted to the royal finances, it might only take one sudden event – a financial scandal at a time of nationwide belt-tightening (as happened with the Spanish royal family in 2014) or the death of a less popular royal and the disclosure of the true size of their estate - for the consensus to change.

As one of the royal family's savers rather than spenders – and like her sister a great planner rather than an improviser when it comes to succession matters - the Queen may leave a legacy of financial prudence and probity along with her estimated £300 million estate, but her successors risk diluting the worth of the Windsor brand unless they move with the times and bring their finances into the twenty-first century. As we enter into a more transparent digital age and a younger generation takes up the royal reins, the hour may be right – to rework Walter Bagehot's famous phrase - to let in daylight upon their money.

Acknowledgements

Anyone dipping a toe into the little-navigated waters of the royal finances owes a huge debt to that master mariner Phillip Hall who first started the long voyage of discovery with his pioneering work "Royal Fortune: Tax, Money and the Monarchy" (Bloomsbury, 1992). He was also a principal contributor to the most comprehensive valuation of royal wealth - The Mail on Sunday's "The Royal Rich Report." Both those works inform this one, even though my emphasis and conclusions are very different.

When it comes to royal jewellery, two other ground-breaking studies - Suzy Menkes's "The Royal Jewels" and Leslie Field's "The Queen's Jewels" - provided through their unprecedented access to the Royal Collection an invaluable source for tracing the provenance of the Windsors' jewellery box.

I am also indebted to several recent royal biographers who were granted access to the Royal Archives: the most recent Jane Ridley for her magisterial portrait of Edward VII ("Bertie" 2013) which followed

Philip Eade's study of the Duke of Edinburgh ("Young Prince Philip" 2011), William Shawcross's authorized biography of the Queen Mother ("Queen Elizabeth" 2009) and Jonathan Dimbleby's biography of Prince Charles ("The Prince of Wales" 1994).

Three other prolific royal chroniclers – Philip Ziegler ("King Edward VIII" and "Mountbatten"), Sarah Bradford ("Diana," "Elizabeth" and "George VI") and Hugo Vickers ("Elizabeth, the Queen Mother" and "Behind Closed Doors – the tragic, untold story of the Duchess of Windsor") provided a treasure trove of financial and biographical information.

I also owe a large debt to the work of Michael Bloch, Gyles Brandreth, Tina Brown, Paul Burrell, Alastair Campbell, David Cannadine, Caroline Blackwood, John Dean, Anne de Courcy, Noble Frankland, Robert Hardman, Nicholas Haslam, William Hamilton, Tim Heald, Simon Heffer, Brian Hoey, Anthony Holden, Robert Lacey, Andrew Marr, Chris Mullin, Gavan Naden, Max Riddington, Andrew Roberts, Geoffrey Robertson, Peter Russell, Anne Sebba, Jon Temple and Christopher Warwick

I wish to thank the following copyright holders – HarperCollins (Reprinted by permission of Harper Collins Publishers Limited Copyright Philip Ziegler, "Edward Heath", 2010), Sheil Land (Robert Rhodes James "Chips – The Diaries of Sir Henry Channon" Weidenfeld & Nicolson 1967 'granted by permission of Sheil Land Associates Ltd'), Random

House ("Behind Closed Doors" by Hugo Vickers published by Hutchison Reprinted by permission of the Random House Group Ltd) and John Murray Press, an imprint of Hodder and Stoughton Ltd, ("Inside Asquith's Cabinet" by Sir Charles Hobhouse [ed. Edward David] © reproduced by permission of the publisher John Murray Press). I am also grateful to the Oxford University Press and Hull University Press/Library of the University of Hull for granting me permission to reprint extracts from Robert Bahlman (ed) "The Diaries of Sir Edward Hamilton."

Strenuous efforts have been made to trace the copyright holders to quote from their books and diaries. I apologise to any copyright holders I have been unable to reach and I promise to rectify the situation in future editions.

I would like to thank my indefatigable agent Andrew Lownie who helped shape the scope and focus of this book. Without his work as literary executor, "Royal Legacy" would never have been granted probate. I am also indebted to David Haviland at Thistle Publishing for his expert guidance in preparing the manuscript for publication.

I am also grateful to the staff of the Rothschild Archive and the National Archives for their assistance and advice. I would like to extend one final word of thanks to the hard-working and highly professional staff of the British Library - a national institution which is a living testament to the value of open access of information to the general public.

Select Bibliography

Aaronovitch, David *Voodoo Histories* Jonathan Cape, 2009

Princess Alice, Duchess of Gloucester *The Memoirs of Princess Alice* Collins, 1983

_____ *Memories of Ninety Years* Anova Books, 1991

Allfrey, Anthony *Edward VII and his Jewish Court* Weidenfeld & Nicolson, 1991

Bahlman, Dudley (ed) *The Diary of Sir Edward Hamilton* Clarendon Press, 1972

Blackwood, Caroline *The Last of the Duchess* Picador, 1996

Blair, Tony *A Journey* Hutchinson, 2010

Bloch, Michael (ed) *Wallis and Edward – Letters 1931-1937* Summit Book, 1986

Bloch, Michael *The Secret File of the Duke of Windsor* Bantam Press, 1988

_____ *The Duchess of Windsor* Weidenfeld & Nicolson, 1996

Boyd Carpenter, John *Way of Life* Sidgwick & Jackson, 1980

Bradford, Sarah *Diana* Viking, 2006
_____ *Elizabeth* William Heinemann, 1996
_____ *George VI* Weidenfeld & Nicolson, 1989
Brandreth, Gyles *Philip and Elizabeth* Century, 2004
Bryan, J & Murphy, Charles *The Windsor Story* William Morrow, 1979
Brown, Tina *Diana Chronicles* Century, 2007
Burgess, Colin *Behind Palace Doors* John Blake, 2006
Burrell, Paul *A Royal Duty* Thorndike, 2004
_____ *The Way We Were* HarperCollins, 2006
Campbell, Alastair *The Alastair Campbell Diaries Vol III* Hutchison, 2011
Cannadine, David *The Decline and Fall of the British Aristocracy* Penguin, 2005
Courtney, Nicholas *The Queen's Stamps* Methuen, 2004
Crawford, Marion *The Little Princesses* St Martin's Press, 2002
Crossman, Richard *The Crossman Diaries Vol III* Hamish Hamilton, 1977
Dean, John *HRH Prince Philip, Duke of Edinburgh* Robert Hale, 1954
De Courcy, Anne *Snowdon* Orion, 2009
Dimbleby, Jonathan *The Prince of Wales* Warner Books, 1994
Eade, Philip *Young Prince Philip* HarperCollins, 2011
Fabian Commission *Report of the Future of the Monarchy* Crowes, 2003
Field, Leslie *The Queen's Jewels* Guild, 1987
Frankland, Noble *Prince Henry, Duke of Gloucester* Weidenfeld & Nicolson, 1980

Goodman, Jean *Seago – A Wider Canvas* Erskine Press, 2002

Hall, Phillip *Royal Fortune* Bloomsbury, 1992

Hamilton, William *My Queen and I* Quartet Books, 1975

Hardman, Robert *Our Queen* Hutchinson, 2011

Haslam, Nicholas *Redeeming Features* Jonathan Cape, 2009

Heald, Tim *Princess Margaret* Orion, 2008

_____ *The Duke, A Portrait of a Prince* Hodder & Stoughton, 1991

Heffer, Simon *Power and Place* Weidenfeld & Nicolson, 1998

Hobhouse, Sir Charles (ed. Edward David) *Inside Asquith's Cabinet* John Murray (an imprint of Hodder and Stoughton) 1977

Hoey, Brian *At Home with the Queen* HarperCollins, 2002

_____ *Mountbatten* Sidgwick & Jackson, 1994

Holden, Anthony *Charles - A Biography* Bantam Press, 1998

Jephson, Patrick *Shadows of a Princess* HarperCollins, 2001

King, Stella *Princess Marina* Cassel, 1969

Knatchbull Timothy *From a Deep Blue Sky* Random House, 2009

Lacey, Robert *Royal* Little Brown, 2002

_____ *Majesty* Hutchison, 1978

Lees-Milne, James *Ancestral Voices* Faber & Faber, 1984

Magnus, Philip *Edward VII* Penguin, 1964

Princess Marie Louise *My Memories of Six Reigns* Evans Brothers, 1979

Mail on Sunday Royal *Royal Rich Report* Associated Newspapers, 2001

Marr, Andrew *The Diamond Queen* Macmillan, 2011

Menkes, Suzy *The Royal Jewels* Granada, 1985

Morgan, Janet *Edwina Mountbatten* Fontana, 1992

Mullin, Chris *A Walk on Part* Profile, 2012

_____ *Decline and Fall* Profile 2011

Naden, Gavan & Riddington, Max *Frances: the remarkable story of Princess Diana's mother* Michael O'Mara, 2003

Nicolson, Harold *George V* Constable, 1952

Nicolson, Nigel (ed) *Diaries and Letters 1907-1964 Harold Nicolson* Weidenfeld &Nicolson, 2004

Paxman, Jeremy *On Royalty* Viking, 2006

Payn, Graham and Morley, Sheridan (ed) *The Noel Coward Diaries* Weidenfeld & Nicolson,1982

Pimlott, Ben *The Queen* HarperCollins, 1996

Pope-Hennessy, James *Queen Mary* George Allen & Unwin, 1959

Rappoport, Helen *Queen Victoria* ABC-Clio, 2003

Rhodes, Margaret *The Final Curtsey* Birlinn, 2011

Rhodes James, Robert *Chips – The Diaries of Sir Henry Channon* Weidenfeld & Nicolson,1967

Ridley, Jane *Bertie – The Life of Edward VII* Vintage, 2013

Roberts, Andrew *Eminent Churchillians* Phoenix, 1994

Roberts, Hugh *The Queen's Diamonds* Royal Collection Publications, 2012

Robertson, Geoffrey *The Justice Game* Chatto & Windus, 1998

Russell, Peter *Butler Royal* Hutchison, 1982

Sebba, Anne *That Woman* Weidenfeld & Nicolson, 2011

Shawcross, William *Queen Elizabeth* Macmillan, 2009

Temple, Jon *Living off the State* Progressbooks, 2008

Van der Kiste, John *Queen Victoria's Children* History Press, 2009

Vickers, Hugo (ed) *The Unexpurgated Beaton* Weidenfeld & Nicolson, 2002

Vickers, Hugo, *Behind Closed Doors* Hutchison, 2011

_____ *Elizabeth, the Queen Mother* Random House, 2006

Vidal, Gore *Point to Point Navigation* Little Brown, 2006

Warwick, Christopher *George and Marina* Weidenfeld & Nicolson, 1988

_____ *Princess Margaret* Andre Deutsch, 2002

Watson, Sophia *Marina* Weidenfeld & Nicolson, 1994

Wheeler Bennett, John *King George V* Macmillan, 1956

Wilson, A.N. *Victoria: A Life* Atlantic Books, 2014

Ziegler, Philip (ed) *From Shore to Shore - Diaries of Lord Mountbatten* Collins, 1989

Ziegler, Philip *Edward Heath* HarperCollins, 2010

_____ *King Edward VIII* HarperCollins, 1990

_____ *Mountbatten* HarperCollins, 1988

Archival Sources

NATIONAL ARCHIVES
   Treasury papers of 1901 Civil List (T326)
   Treasury papers on the 1911 Civil List (T168)
   Treasury papers on the Civil List 1970-71 (T326)

PUBLIC RECORD OFFICE OF NORTHERN IRELAND
   Private papers of Earl of Kilmorey

MOUNTBATTEN ARCHIVE
   Private papers of Lord Mountbatten

ROTHSCHILD ARCHIVE
   Private papers of Leopold de Rothschild

PRINCIPAL REGISTRY OF THE FAMILY DIVISION
   Will of HRH Princess Alice, Duchess of Gloucester
   Will of HH Princess Helena Victoria
   Will of HH Prince Louis of Milford Haven
   Will of Diana, Princess of Wales
   Will of Edwina, Countess Mountbatten of Burma

PARLIAMENTARY REPORTS etc

Report of the Select Committee on the Civil List, 1971

Report of the Public Accounts Committee on the Duchy of Cornwall, 2013

Report of the Public Accounts Committee on the Duchies of Cornwall and Lancaster, 2006

Sovereign Grant Bill, House of Commons Research Paper, July 2011

Memorandum of Understanding on Royal Taxation 1993

Memorandum of Understanding on Royal Taxation 2013

Report by Sir Michael Peat and Edmund Lawson QC to HRH The Prince of Wales [on the collapse of the Paul Burrell trial] 2003

Notes

PROLOGUE

1. *The Mail on Sunday* 19 January 2014
2. *The Times* 20 January 2014
3. *The Sunday Times* 19 January 2014
4. Campbell, Alastair *The Alastair Campbell Diaries Vol III* Hutchison, 2011, entry for 22 October 1999
5. *The Guardian* 17 February 2014
6. Hardman, Robert *Our Queen* Hutchinson, 2011 p.110
7. *Press Trust of India* 19 January 2014
8. *The Daily Mail* 1 February 2014
9. *The Daily Mail* 20 January 2014

CHAPTER ONE
THE QUEEN'S TRUE WORTH - 2014

1. Bradford, Sarah *Elizabeth* William Heinemann, 1996 p.33
2. Crawford, Marion *The Little Princesses* Saint Martin's Press, 2002 p.26
3. Bradford, p.39

[4] Pimlott, Ben *The Queen* HarperCollins, 1996, p.423
[5] Lacey, Robert *Majesty* Hutchison, 1978, p.328
[6] *The Daily Telegraph* 10 June 1971
[7] Nicolson, Harold *George V* Constable, 1952, p.367
[8] Mail on Sunday, *Royal Rich Report* Associated Newspapers, 2001, p.14
[9] Courtney, Nicholas *The Queen's Stamps* Methuen, 2004, p.308
[10] *Royal Rich Report* pp.11-17
[11] *The Guardian* 30 May 2002
[12] *The Sunday Times* 4 December 2011
[13] *The Sunday Times Rich List 2011*
[14] Blair, Tony *A Journey* Hutchinson, 2010, p.149
[15] *Royal Rich Report* p.17
[16] Hall, Phillip *Royal Fortune* Bloomsbury, 1992, p.179
[17] ibid, p.151
[18] Lacey, Robert *Royal* Little Brown, 2002, p.392
[19] *The Daily Telegraph* 25 July 2004
[20] Temple, Jon *Living off the State* Progressbooks, 2008, p.30
[21] Balmoral Castle official website
[22] Blair, pp.148-9
[23] Hall, p.164

CHAPTER TWO
EDWARD THE CARESSER – 1901-1910
[1] *The Daily Telegraph* 10 June, 1971
[2] Campbell, Alastair *The Alastair Campbell Diaries Vol III* entry for 16 March 2001 Hutchison, 2011

[3] Magnus, Philip *Edward VII* Penguin, 1964, p.246
[4] Allfrey, Anthony *Edward VII and his Jewish Court* Weidenfeld & Nicolson, 1991, p.24
[5] Ridley, Jane *Bertie – The Life of Edward VII* Vintage, *2013*, p.317
[6] Bahlman, Dudley (ed) *The Diary of Sir Edward Hamilton* 1972 entry for 12 April 1896, p.324 [by permission of Oxford University Press]
[7] ibid, entry for 21 December 1902, p.428
[8] The National Archives NA- T168/7 Hamilton letter dated 11 June 1904, p.451
[9] ibid, Hamilton 29 April 1904
[10] NA T168/71
[11] Ridley, p. 335
[12] Cannadine, David *The Decline and Fall of the British Aristocracy* Penguin, 2005 p.349
[13] Bahlman, diary entry of Hamilton 7 November 1902 p.427 [by permission of OUP]
[14] Magnus, Philip *Edward VII* Penguin, 1964, p.357
[15] Heffer, Simon *Power and Place* Weidenfeld & Nicolson, 1998, p.67
[16] Bahlman, Hamilton diaries 7 May 1901, p.406 [by permission of OUP]
[17] ibid. entry for 1 June 1904, p.452
[18] Ridley, p.335
[19] Allfrey, Anthony *Edward VII and his Jewish Court* Weidenfeld & Nicolson, 1991, p.247
[20] Lacey, Robert *Royal* Little Brown, 2002, p.236
[21] Hall, Phillip *Royal Fortune* Bloomsbury, 1992 p.12
[22] NA T160/631

[23] Hamilton Diaries entry for 1 July1889 [by permission of OUP]
[24] NA T168/52
[25] Dimbleby, Jonathan *The Prince of Wales* Warner Books, 1994, p.293
[26] NA T171/338
[27] In his recent biography *Victoria: A Life*, Atlantic Books, 2014, p.341 A.N. Wilson argues that the bulk of her private wealth derived from the reorganised revenues of the Duchy of Lancaster
[28] NA T326 1327
[29] Magnus p.68
[30] Hobhouse, Sir Charles *Inside Asquith's Cabinet* John Murray, 1977, p.59
[31] Hamilton diary entry for 2 March 1894 [by permission of OUP]
[32] Daunton, Martin (ed) Charity, *Welfare and Self-Interest in Britain*, UCL Press, p.138
[33] Hobhouse diary entry for 30 June 1910, p.59
[34] Rappoport, Helen *Queen Victoria* ABC-Clio, 2003, pp.142-3
[35] Van der Kiste, John *Queen Victoria's Children* History Press, 2009, p.173
[36] Pope-Hennessy, James *Queen Mary* George Allen & Unwin, 1959, p.540

CHAPTER THREE
MARY'S BAD BROTHER – 1910-1922
[1] Heffer, Simon *Power and Place* Weidenfeld & Nicolson, 1998, p.67

[2] Menkes, Suzy *The Royal Jewels* Granada, 1985, p.69 (the story of the Cambridge jewels is drawn largely from this account)
[3] Vickers, Hugo *Elizabeth, the Queen Mother* Random House, 2006, p.70
[4] Eade, Philip *Young Prince Philip* HarperCollins, 2011, p.22
[5] Rhodes James, Robert *Chips – The Diaries of Sir Henry Channon* Weidenfeld & Nicolson, 1967, p.241 [granted by permission of Sheil Land Associates Ltd]
[6] *Evening News* 23 October 1978
[7] ibid.
[8] Hoey, Brian *Mountbatten* Sidgwick & Jackson, 1994 p.36

CHAPTER FOUR
THE PRINCES AT WAR – 1936-1945
[1] Ziegler, Philip *King Edward VIII* HarperCollins, 1990, p.240
[2] Shawcross, William *Queen Elizabeth* Macmillan, 2009, p.308
[3] Ziegler *op cit* p.247
[4] Hall, Phillip *Royal Fortune* Bloomsbury, 1992, p.44-5
[5] Ziegler p.247
[6] Shawcross p.358
[7] Ziegler p.259
[8] NA T171/338
[9] NA T171/338
[10] Shawcross p.368

[11] Victor Cazelet in Rhode James, Robert *Victor Cazelet Hamish* Hamilton, 1976, p.181
[12] Sebba, Anne *That Woman* Weidenfeld & Nicolson, 2011, p.169
[13] Ziegler p.326
[14] ibid p.328
[15] Bloch, Michael, *The Secret File of the Duke of Windsor* Bantam Press, 1988, p.67
[16] Bryan, J & Murphy, Charles *The Windsor Story* William Morrow, 1979, p.298
[17] Bradford, Sarah *Elizabeth* William Heinemann, 1996, p.70
[18] Bloch p.47
[19] Ziegler p.327
[20] Bryan and Murphy, pp.333-4
[21] Shawcross p.380
[22] Marr, Andrew *The Diamond Queen* Macmillan, 2011, pp.49-50
[23] Shawcross p.551
[24] Ziegler p.484
[25] Freda Dudley Ward in Vickers, Hugo, *Behind Closed Doors* Hutchison, 2011, p.283
[26] Rhodes James, Robert *Chips – The Diaries of Sir Henry Channon* Weidenfeld & Nicolson, 1967, pp.43-4 [granted by permission of Sheil Land Associates Ltd]
[27] Watson, Sophia *Marina* Weidenfeld & Nicolson, 1994, p.120
[28] Vickers, Hugo *Elizabeth, the Queen Mother* Random House, 2006, p.230

[29] Rhodes James p.159 [granted by permission of Sheil Land Associates Ltd]
[30] ibid p.37
[31] ibid p.329
[32] Warwick, Christopher *George and Marina* Weidenfeld & Nicolson, 1988, p.72
[33] Mail on Sunday *Royal Rich Report* Associated Newspapers, 2001, p.85
[34] ibid p.85
[35] Rhodes James, op cit, p.396 [granted by permission of Sheil Land Associates Ltd]

CHAPTER FIVE
THE PRINCESSES OF NOTHING – 1948-1952

[1] Pope-Hennessy, James *Queen Mary* George Allen & Unwin, 1959, p.252
[2] ibid, p.266 + p.216
[3] Watson, Sophia *Marina* Weidenfeld & Nicolson, 1994, p.68
[4] Princess Marie Louise *My Memories of Six Reigns* Evans Brothers, 1979, p.36
[5] Hicks, Pamela *Daughters of Empire* Phoenix, 2013, p.161
[6] Rappoport, Helen *Queen Victoria* ABC-Clio, 2003, p.187
[7] Princess Marie Louise p.37
[8] Rhodes James, Robert *Chips – The Diaries of Sir Henry Channon* Weidenfeld & Nicolson p.422
[9] Bradford, Sarah *Elizabeth* William Heinemann, 1996, p.96

10 Princess Marie Louise p.269
11 Field, Leslie *The Queen's Jewels* Guild, 1987 p.137

CHAPTER SIX
GEORGE AND MARY'S LEGACY – 1952-1953
1   Bradford, Sarah *George VI* Weidenfeld & Nicolson, 1989, p.183
2   Heald, Tim *Princess Margaret* Orion, 2008, p.88
3   Bradford, Sarah *Elizabeth* William Heinemann, 1996, p.162
4   *Daily Telegraph* 12 May 2002
5   Bradford, Sarah *Elizabeth* William Heinemann, 1996, p.482
6   Hardman, Robert *Our Queen* Hutchinson, 2011, p.86
7   Bradford, Sarah *George VI* Weidenfeld & Nicolson, 1989, p.399
8   Field, Leslie *The Queen's Jewels* Guild, 1987, p.104
9   Pope-Hennessy, James *Queen Mary* George Allen & Unwin, 1959, p.619
10 ibid, p. 620
11 Ziegler, Philip *King Edward VIII* HarperCollins, 1990, p.537
12 Pope Hennessy, p.621
13 Rhodes James, Robert *Chips – The Diaries of Sir Henry Channon* Weidenfeld & Nicolson, 1967 p.472-3 [granted by permission of Sheil Land Associates Ltd]
14 Princess Marie Louise *My Memories of Six Reigns* Evans Brothers, 1979, p.306

[15] Field p.16
[16] ibid, pp.72-4
[17] Menkes, Suzy *The Royal Jewels* Granada, 1985, p.52
[18] ibid, p53
[19] Pope Hennessy, p.525
[20] NA T171/331
[21] NA T171 329
[22] Courtney, Nicholas *The Queen's Stamps* Methuen, 2004, p.161
[23] ibid, p.151
[24] Menkes p.76
[25] Dimbleby, Jonathan *The Prince of Wales* Warner Books, 1994, p.17
[26] Pope Hennessy, p.525
[27] Field, p.16
[28] Roberts, Hugh *The Queen's Diamonds* Royal Collection Publications, 2012 see Bibliography, Unpublished Sources
[29] ibid, p.93
[30] Bradford, Sarah *Elizabeth* William Heinemann, 1996, p.183. Roberts, *op cit* p.113, confirms that Queen Mary left the majority of her jewellery to the Queen, with a few items also bequeathed to the Queen Mother
[31] Mail on Sunday *Royal Rich Report* Associated Newspapers, 2001, pp.11-17
[32] Field, p.143
[33] Christie's auction of Prince Henry's property 26/27 January 2006

34 Burrell, Paul *A Royal Duty* Thorndike, 2004, p.582

CHAPTER SEVEN
THE DUCHESS AND THE COUNTESS – 1960-1968
1 Hoey, Brian *Mountbatten* Sidgwick & Jackson, 1994, p.104
2 Peter Russell *Butler Royal* Hutchison, 1982, p.70
3 ibid, p.80
4 Watson, Sophia *Marina* Weidenfeld & Nicolson, 1994, p.201
5 Russell p.32
6 Watson p.213
7 Payn, Graham and Morley, Sheridan (ed) *The Noel Coward Diaries* Weidenfeld & Nicolson, 1982, p.667
8 King, Stella *Princess Marina* Cassel, 1969, p.218
9 Watson p.237
10 Russell p.50
11 Menkes, Suzy *The Royal Jewels* Granada, 1985 p.126
12 Field, Leslie *The Queen's Jewels* Guild, 1987 p.37 + p.139
13 Mail on Sunday *Royal Rich Report* Associated Newspapers, 2001, p.85
14 Quotation from *The Sunday Times* quoted in *The Mail on Sunday* 5 January 2014
15 *Mail on Sunday* 5 January 2014
16 Vickers, Hugo *Elizabeth, the Queen Mother* Random House, 2006, p.394/396

[17] Ziegler, Philip *Mountbatten* HarperCollins, 1988 p.571
[18] ibid, p.67
[19] Hoey, Brian *Mountbatten* Sidgwick & Jackson, 1994, p.85
[20] ibid, p.2. Information from this section based on Hoey, op cit
[21] Marr, Andrew *The Diamond Queen* Macmillan, 2011, p.76
[22] Hoey, p.102
[23] Knatchbull, Timothy *From a Deep Blue Sky* Random House, 2009, p.167
[24] ibid, p.246
[25] ibid, p.200

CHAPTER EIGHT
THE BURIAL OF BAD NEWS – 1969-1971
[1] The National Archives NA T326/1325
[2] Ziegler, Philip *Edward Heath* HarperCollins, 2010, p.25
[3] ibid, p.319
[4] ibid, p.319
[5] Pimlott, Ben *The Queen* HarperCollins, 1996, p.399
[6] Ziegler, p.320
[7] NA T326/1325
[8] Pimlott, p.402
[9] NA T326/1312 [author's italics]
[10] Lacey, Robert *Royal* Little Brown, 2002, p.234

[11] Crossman, Richard *The Crossman Diaries Vol III* Hamish Hamilton, 1977, p.723
[12] ibid, p.724
[13] NA T326/1321
[14] *Daily Telegraph* 31 May 2002
[15] NA T326/1321
[16] NA T326/1321
[17] Peter Hennessy *The Secret World of Whitehall* BBC-4 Television 30 March 2011
[18] NA T326/1321 [author's italics]
[19] NA T326/1328
[20] NA T326/1328
[21] NA T326/1330
[22] NA T326/1329
[23] NA T326/1329
[24] Treasury note dated 6 May 1971 NA T326/1312
[25] Letter to LJ Taylor 1 September 1970 NA T326/1310
[26] Letter from Barber to Whitelaw 20 September 1971 NA T326/1329
[27] Public Accounts Committee HC475
[28] Paper headed Duchy of Cornwall and the Prince of Wales T326/1312
[29] NA T326/1325
[30] Oral evidence of E.R. Wheeler to the Select Committee on the Civil List 1971 on 21 July, minute 531, 1971 *Parliamentary Papers* 1970-71 Vol 24
[31] NA T326/1327

[32] NA T326/1328
[33] NA T326/1329
[34] NA T326/1316
[35] NA T326/1325 Treasury note of 11 June 1971 meeting with Cobbold et al
[36] NA T326/1326 memo 25 June 1971 from Michael Adeane to Russell Wills
[37] Oral evidence of Adeane to Select Committee on the Civil List 1971 on 29 June 1971, minute 227 *Parliamentary Papers 1971-72* Vol 24
[38] NA T326/13 memo dated 22 October 1971
[39] Hansard, debate House of Commons 14 December 1971
[40] NA T326/1329 dated 20 September 1971 Barber-PM marked "confidential"
[41] NA T326/1330 dated 12 October 1971
[42] NA T326/1330
[43] Hamilton, William *My Queen and I* Quartet Books, 1975, p.44
[44] Evidence of Lord Cobbold on 27 July 1971, minute 560 of *Parliamentary Papers 1970-*71 vol 24
[45] Select Committee Report on the Civil List 1971 p.xi
[46] NA T326/1328
[47] NA T326/1322
[48] Hamilton, p.65
[49] *Financial Times* 3 December 1971
[50] Hamilton, p.43
[51] NA T326/1628

CHAPTER NINE
THE WINDSORS AND THEIR WEALTH – 1972-1986

[1] Blackwood, Caroline *The Last of the Duchess* Picador, 1996, p.7

[2] Ziegler, Philip, *Mountbatten* HarperCollins, 1988, p.680 [originally spoken in the 1972 television broadcast]

[3] ibid, p.680

[4] Vickers, Hugo *Behind Closed Doors*, Hutchinson, 2011, p.32 [Reprinted by permission of The Random House Group Ltd]

[5] Vickers, Hugo *Behind Closed Doors*, Hutchinson, 2011 p.63

[6] ibid, p.98

[7] Cannadine, David *The Decline and Fall of the British Aristocracy* Penguin, 2005 p.354

[8] Bryan, J & Murphy, Charles *The Windsor Story* William Morrow, 1979, p.402

[9] Ziegler, Philip, *King Edward VIII* HarperCollins, 1990, p.506

[10] Cannadine, p.644

[11] Ziegler, Philip, *King Edward VIII* HarperCollins, 1990, p.516

[12] Cannadine, p.640

[13] ibid, pp.642-644

[14] Bryan, J & Murphy, Charles *The Windsor Story* William Morrow, 1979, p.572

[15] Vickers, Hugo, *Behind Closed Doors* Hutchison, 2011, p.356

[16] Bloch, Michael, *The Secret File of the Duke of Windsor* Bantam Press, 1988, p.301
[17] Vickers Hugo, *Behind Closed Doors* Hutchison, 2011, p.46
[18] ibid, p.58
[19] Blackwood, p.6
[20] Bryan & Murphy, p.595
[21] Sebba, Anne *That Woman* Weidenfeld & Nicolson, 2001, p101
[22] Rhodes James, Robert *Chips – the Diaries of Sir Henry Channon* Weidenfeld & Nicolson, 1967, p.43 [granted by permission of Sheil Land Associates Ltd]
[23] Sebba p.103
[24] ibid, p.104
[25] Vickers p.159
[26] Bloch, Michael *The Duchess of Windsor* Weidenfeld & Nicolson, 1996, p.281
[27] Roberts, Andrew *Eminent Churchillians* Phoenix, 1994, p.282
[28] Sebba, p.242
[29] Vickers, p.346
[30] Vickers, Hugo (ed) *The Unexpurgated Beaton* Weidenfeld & Nicolson, 2002, p.105
[31] Vickers Hugo, *Behind Closed Doors* Hutchison, 2011, p.25
[32] Blackwood, p.23
[33] Vickers Hugo, *Behind Closed Doors* Hutchison, 2011, p.58

[34] Bloch, p.222
[35] Vickers, p.116
[36] Vickers, p.124
[37] Bloch, p.222
[38] Blackwood, p.226
[39] Vickers, p.39
[40] Bradford, Sarah, *Elizabeth* William Heinemann, 1996, p.416
[41] Ziegler, p. xi
[42] Bloch, Michael (ed) *Wallis and Edward – Letters 1931-1937* Summit Book, 1986, p.8
[43] Blackwood, p.138

CHAPTER TEN
DIANA'S ESTATE OF WAR – 1996-1998
[1] *The Lawyer* 12 August 1998
[2] *The Lawyer* 12 August 1998
[3] Brown, Tina *Diana Chronicles* Century, 2007, p.423
[4] *The Sunday Times* 7 October 1997
[5] *The Times* 27 February 1998
[6] *The Times* 24 November 1997
[7] Burrell, Paul *A Royal Duty* Thorndike, 2004, p.308
[8] Naden, Gavan & Riddington, Max *Frances: the remarkable story of Princess Diana's mother* Michael O'Mara, 2003, pp.222-3
[9] *The Daily Telegraph* 24 October 2002
[10] Brown, p.372
[11] *The Daily Telegraph* 7 November 2002

[12] *The Daily Telegraph* 25 October 2002
[13] *The Daily Telegraph* 24 October 2002
[14] *The Daily Telegraph* 3 November 2002
[15] *The Tatler* February 2003
[16] *The Times* 8 February 2003
[17] Naden & Riddington p.230
[18] *The Guardian* 25 October 2002
[19] Burrell p.383
[20] *The Daily Telegraph* 24 October 2002
[21] *The Daily Telegraph* 3 November 2002
[22] *Report by Sir Michael Peat and Edmund Lawson QC to HRH The Prince of Wales,* 2003, Summary - conclusion 2.125
[23] *The Daily Telegraph* 7 October 2002
[24] Burrell p.391
[25] Naden & Riddington p.221
[26] *The Daily Telegraph* 7 November 2002
[27] Peat Report para 2.67
[28] ibid, para 2.67
[29] Burrell p.327
[30] ibid, p. 308
[31] ibid, p.266
[32] *The Independent* 9 March 1998
[33] *Metropolis* 20 March 1998
[34] *The Times* 23 October 1998

CHAPTER ELEVEN
MARGARET, MUSTIQUE AND MONEY - 2002
[1] Vidal, Gore *Point to Point Navigation* Little Brown, 2006, p.212

[2] Shawcross, William *Queen Elizabeth* Macmillan, 2009, p.899
[3] ibid p.899
[4] *The Daily Telegraph* 20 September 2009
[5] Heald, Tim *Princess Margaret* Orion, 2008, p.291
[6] *The Daily Mail* 26 June 2002
[7] Mail on Sunday (Phillip Hall et al) *Royal Rich Report* Associated Newspapers, 2001, p.74
[8] Christie's press releases 13/14 June 2006
[9] Christie's press releases 13/14 June 2006
[10] *Royal Rich Report* pp.74-77
[11] Lacey, Robert *Royal* Little Brown, 2002, p.194
[12] *Royal Rich Report* p.76
[13] Heald p.122
[14] Warwick, Christopher *Princess Margaret* Weidenfeld & Nicolson, 1983 p 121 [in correspondence with the author, Warwick disputed whether Jocelyn Stevens' remark could apply to anything other than planning "while on holiday", although in an updated edition of his biography (*Princess Margaret – A Life of Contrasts*, 2002) he wrote that Princess Margaret was always a great planner and gave considerable thought to plans for her funeral]
[15] Vidal, Gore *Point to Point Navigation* Little Brown, 2006, p.212
[16] Heald, p.17
[17] *Royal Rich Report* p.77
[18] Field, Leslie *The Queen's Jewels* Guild, 1987, p.158

CHAPTER TWELVE
FROM QUEEN MOTHER TO DAUGHTER - 2002

[1] Vickers, Hugo *Elizabeth, the Queen Mother* Random House, 2006, p.499
[2] Burgess, Colin *Behind Palace Doors* John Blake, 2006, p.268
[3] Hardman, Robert *Our Queen* Hutchinson, 2011, p.88
[4] Lacey, Robert *Royal* Little Brown, 2002, p.326
[5] Marr, Andrew *The Diamond Queen* Macmillan, 2011, p.286
[6] Shawcross, William *Queen Elizabeth* Macmillan, 2009, p.894
[7] Dimbleby, Jonathan *The Prince of Wales* Warner Books, 1994, p.618
[8] Bradford, Sarah, *Elizabeth* William Heinemann, 1996, p.482
[9] *Memorandum of Understanding on Royal Taxation* 1993
[10] Dimbleby p.536
[11] Fabian Commission, *Report on the Future of the Monarchy* Crowes, 2003, pp.129-130
[12] *Royal Rich Report* p.46
[13] Shawcross p.545
[14] ibid p.554
[15] Nicolson, Nigel (ed) *Diaries and Letters 1907-1964 Harold Nicolson* Weidenfeld & Nicolson, 2004, p.186
[16] Lees-Milne, James *Ancestral Voices* Faber & Faber, 1984, p.122

17 Shawcross p.554
18 *The Guardian* 27 March 2007
19 Hugh Roberts *op cit* has established that Queen Elizabeth gifted one item of the Greville bequest, the Greville Ivy Leaf Clips, to Princess Elizabeth on her 21st birthday in 1947
20 Shawcross p.790
21 ibid, p.708
22 Vickers p.459
23 Haslam, Nicholas *Redeeming Features* Jonathan Cape, 2009, p.290 [Reprinted by permission of the Random House Group Ltd and Aitken Alexander Associates]
24 *The Guardian* 30 May 2002
25 Shawcross p.707
26 ibid, p.907
27 *The Times* 21 May 2002
28 Shawcross p.688
29 ibid, p.412
30 ibid, p.270
31 ibid, p.583
32 Email letter to author from Lucy Whitaker, Senior Curator of Paintings, Royal Collection Trust, 16 July 2014
33 Temple, Jon *Living off the State* Progressbooks, 2008 p.176
34 Mullin, Chris *Decline and Fall* Profile 2011 pp.55-6
35 Email letter to author from Lucy Whitaker, op cit

CHAPTER THIRTEEN
A ROYAL CAR BOOT SALE - 2006

[1] *The Daily Telegraph* 12 June 2006
[2] De Courcy, Anne *Snowdon* Orion, 2009, p.366
[3] *The Sunday Telegraph* 18 June 2006
[4] Heald, Tim *Princess Margaret* Orion, 2008 p.299
[5] Christie's press release 13 June 2006
[6] *The Daily Express* 23 June 2006
[7] Christie's press release 13 June 2006
[8] Heald p.301
[9] *The Sunday Telegraph* 14 January 2007
[10] *Royal Rich Report* p.66
[11] ibid, p.99
[12] *The Independent* 18 June 2006
[13] Christie's press release 14 June 2006

CHAPTER FOURTEEN
THE PRINCESS'S "LOVE" CHILD – 2006-2008

[1] *Brown v Executors of the Estate of HM Queen Elizabeth the Queen Mother and others* (2007) EWHC 1607 (Fam) para 25
[2] *The Daily Mail* 5 March 2005
[3] Ridley, Jane *Bertie – The Life of Edward VII* Vintage, 2013 p.147
[4] *Brown v Executors of the Estate of HM Queen Elizabeth the Queen Mother and others* [2007] EWHC 1607 (Fam) – this section based on the above ruling and evidence

[5] Robertson, Geoffrey *The Justice Game* Chatto & Windus, 1998, p.348
[6] *The Daily Telegraph* 28 June 2007
[7] Heald, Tim *Princess Margaret* Orion, 2008 pp.265-6
[8] *The Guardian* 28 March 2007
[9] [2007] EWHC 1607 *op cit* conclusion para 69
[10] [2008] EWCA Civ 56 8. *Brown v Executors of the Estate of Her Majesty Queen Elizabeth the Queen Mother and others* – this section based on the above ruling
[11] *The Mail on Sunday* 20 October 2008
[12] *The Daily Telegraph* 9 February 2008
[13] *The Express on Sunday* 17 January 2008
[14] *The Guardian* 11 January 2008

CHAPTER FIFTEEN
THE STORMING OF THE PALACE - 2008

[1] *The Guardian* 9 February 2008 (quoted from a 2006 speech in the House of Commons)
[2] ITN 8 February 2008
[3] *Hansard* 8 February 2008
[4] Aaronovitch, David *Voodoo Histories* Jonathan Cape 2009, p.259
[5] ibid, p.259
[6] quoted in *The New Statesman* 7 August 2000
[7] *Hansard* 12 January 2009
[8] ibid, 12 January 2009
[9] *Hansard* 22 January 2009

[10] *The Times* 24 January 2009
[11] *The Express on Sunday* 1 February 2009
[12] FTT Info Rights Case No. EA/2010/0119 (para 26)
[13] *The Guardian* 21 December 2013

CHAPTER SIXTEEN
THE BEST LAID PLANS OF ALICE AND MEN – 2008-2009

[1] Princess Alice, Duchess of Gloucester *The Memoirs of Princess Alice* Collins, 1983 p.33
[2] Hardman, Robert *Our Queen* Hutchinson, 2011, p.85
[3] Russell, Peter *Butler Royal* Hutchison, 1982, p.76
[4] Princess Alice p.107
[5] ibid, p.109
[6] Frankland, Noble *Prince Henry, Duke of Gloucester* Weidenfeld & Nicolson, 1980, p.123
[7] Princess Alice p.174
[8] Princess Alice p.174
[9] Princess Alice, Duchess of Gloucester, *Memories of Ninety Years* Anova Books, 1991, p.173
[10] Frankland, p 250
[11] Field, Leslie *The Queen's Jewels* Guild, 1987, p.62 + p. 81
[12] Frankland p.283
[13] Princess Alice, Duchess of Gloucester, *Memories of Ninety Years* Anova Books, 1991,p.92
[14] *Royal Rich Report* p.80

[15] Princess Alice, Duchess of Gloucester *The Memoirs of Princess Alice* Collins, pp.193-4
[16] Vickers, Hugo, *Behind Closed Doors* Hutchison, 2011, p.61
[17] Cannadine, David *The Decline and Fall of the British Aristocracy* Penguin, 2005, pp.260-2
[18] Telephone conversation between the author and David Pogson (Buckingham Palace Communications Office) 7 August 2014
[19] Princess Alice, Duchess of Gloucester *Memories of Ninety Years* Anova Books, 1991 p.201
[20] *Royal Rich Report* p.80
[21] *The Guardian* 1 November 2004
[22] *The Sunday Times* 29 January 2006
[23] *The Sunday Times* 29 January 2006
[24] Russell p.165
[25] ibid p.172
[26] *The Daily Mail* 5 November 2005
[27] Princess Alice, Duchess of Gloucester *Memories of Ninety Years* Anova Books, 1991 p.156
[28] *Royal Rich Report* p.80
[29] Princess Alice, Duchess of Gloucester *The Memoirs of Princess Alice* Collins, p.250
[30] ibid, p.193
[31] *The Sunday Times* 29 January 2006
[32] *The Daily Mail* 30 August 2004
[33] Princess Alice, Duchess of Gloucester *The Memoirs of Princess Alice* Collins, p.105
[34] *The Daily Telegraph* 3 January 2014

CHAPTER SEVENTEEN
CHARLES'S CASH COW - 2010-2014

[1] *The Sunday Times* 12 December 2010
[2] *The Daily Telegraph* 13 April 2014
[3] Mullin, Chris *Decline and Fall* Profile 2011, p.208
[4] Holden, Anthony *Charles - A Biography* Bantam Press, 1998 p.334
[5] Hoey, Brian *At Home with the Queen* HarperCollins, 2002, p.68
[6] *The Daily Mail* 14 March 2014
[7] *The Sunday Times* 12 December 2010
[8] Paxman, Jeremy *On Royalty* Viking, 2006, p.275
[9] *Time Magazine* 24 October 2013
[10] Dimbleby, p.294
[11] *Public Accounts Committee Report on the Duchy of Cornwall 2013* oral evidence questions 169-70 HC 475
[12] *Duchy of Cornwall Annual Financial Statement* 26 June 2014
[13] Dimbleby, pp. 563-4
[14] Holden, Anthony *Charles - A Biography* Bantam Press, 1998, p.225
[15] See *Public Accounts Committee Report on the Accounts of the Duchies of Cornwall and Lancaster 2005*, HC 313
[16] *The Independent* 14 June 2013
[17] *Public Accounts Committee Report on the Duchy of Cornwall 2013* oral evidence question 41
[18] *Dispatches* Channel Four 1 July 2013

[19] *Public Accounts Committee Report on the Duchy of Cornwall 2013* oral evidence question 54
[20] ibid, recommendation no 5 p.6
[21] ibid, oral evidence question 223
[22] ibid, question 103
[23] ibid, question 176
[24] Email to author from Patrick Harrison, Press Secretary and Special Advisor, Clarence House, 9 July 2014
[25] *Public Accounts Committee Report on the Duchy of Cornwall 2013* oral evidence question 102

CHAPTER EIGHTEEN
SOVEREIGN GRANT OR SOVEREIGN GREED? – 2011-2013

[1] *Hansard* 14 July 2011 (all subsequent quotations taken from this Sovereign Grant debate unless stated)
[2] Marr, Andrew *The Diamond Queen* Macmillan, 2011, p.295
[3] *The Financial Times* 1 July 2011
[4] ibid, 2 July 2011
[5] *Hansard* 30 June 2011
[6] *The Mail on Sunday* 10 July 2011
[7] *National Audit Office Report on the Sovereign Grant* HC 722 2013, p.15
[8] *Public Accounts Committee Report on the Sovereign Grant 2014*, HC 665, 2014 oral evidence question 7
[9] ibid, oral evidence

CHAPTER NINETEEN
THE DUKE'S FAREWELL - 2014

[1] *Independent on Sunday* 13 December 1992, Fiammetta Rocco "A Strange Life – Profile of Prince Philip"

[2] *The Sunday Times* 10 December 2013

[3] *The Express on Sunday* 11 November 2007

[4] Ziegler, Philip *Mountbatten,* HarperCollins, 1988 p.101

[5] *Royal Rich Report* p.55

[6] Brandreth, Gyles *Philip and Elizabeth* Century, 2004, p.159

[7] Eade, Philip *Young Prince Philip* HarperCollins, 2011, p.117

[8] Brandreth, p.83

[9] ibid, p.83

[10] ibid, p.206

[11] Eade, p.177

[12] ibid, p.190

[13] Dean, John *HRH Prince Philip, Duke of Edinburgh,* Robert Hale, 1954, pp. 35-6

[14] Heald, Tim *The Duke, A Portrait of a Prince* Hodder & Stoughton, 1991, p.118

[15] op cit. *Independent on Sunday,* Fiammetta Rocca

[16] Brandreth, p.181

[17] Hall, Phillip *Royal Fortune* Bloomsbury, 1992, p.134

[18] Brandreth, p.276

[19] *Royal Rich Report,* p.55

[20] Goodman, Jean *Seago – A Wider Canvas* Erskine Press, 2002, p.236
[21] Hardman, Robert *Our Queen* Hutchinson, 2011, p.290
[22] ibid, p.290
[23] ibid, p.291

CHAPTER TWENTY
A NATION MOURNS - 2022

[1] *The Sunday Times* 12 December 2010
[2] ibid, 12 December 2010
[3] ibid, 12 December 2010
[4] Lacey, Robert *Royal* Little Brown, 2002, p.237
[5] *The Sunday Times* 12 December 2010
[6] Hugh Roberts who also had access to the royal jewellery collection for his work *The Queen's Diamonds* makes a further distinction between the Queen's "personal jewellery" and the "heirlooms of the Crown" although when he examines individual pieces of jewellery he does not specify which category they fall into.
[7] *The Sunday Times* 12 December 2010

Printed in Great Britain
by Amazon.co.uk, Ltd.,
Marston Gate.